MASTERING
SKATEBOARDING

Per Welinder
Peter Whitley

Photography by Bryce Kanights

HUMAN KINETICS

Library of Congress Cataloging-in-Publication Data

Welinder, Per.
 Mastering skateboarding / Per Welinder, Peter Whitley; photography by
Bryce Kanights.
    p. cm.
 Includes index.
 ISBN-13: 978-0-7360-9599-0 (soft cover)
 ISBN-10: 0-7360-9599-3 (soft cover)
 1. Skateboarding. I. Whitley, Peter. II. Title.
 GV859.8.W45 2012
 796.22--dc23

                                        2011029051

ISBN-10: 0-7360-9599-3 (print)
ISBN-13: 978-0-7360-9599-0 (print)

The web addresses cited in this text were current as of September 2011, unless otherwise noted.

Acquisitions Editor: Justin Klug; **Developmental Editor:** Carla Zych; **Assistant Editors:** Claire Marty and Elizabeth Evans; **Copyeditor:** Patricia MacDonald; **Indexer:** Nan N. Badgett; **Graphic Designer:** Bob Reuther; **Graphic Artist:** Tara Welsch; **Cover Designer:** Keith Blomberg; **Photographer (cover):** Bryce Kanights; **Photographer (interior):** Bryce Kanights, unless otherwise noted; photos on pages 5, 106, 107, 109, and 161 provided by Peter Whitley; photos on pages 37, 98-99, 182, and 236 courtesy of Patrick Nagy; photos on pages 211 and 213 courtesy of Maxwell Dubler; **Visual Production Assistant:** Joyce Brumfield; **Photo Production Manager:** Jason Allen; **Art Manager:** Kelly Hendren; **Associate Art Manager:** Alan L. Wilborn; **Illustrations:** © Human Kinetics; **Printer:** Versa Press

Human Kinetics books are available at special discounts for bulk purchase. Special editions or book excerpts can also be created to specification. For details, contact the Special Sales Manager at Human Kinetics.

Printed in the United States of America   10 9 8 7 6 5 4 3 2 1

The paper in this book is certified under a sustainable forestry program.

Human Kinetics
Website: www.HumanKinetics.com

United States: Human Kinetics
P.O. Box 5076
Champaign, IL 61825-5076
800-747-4457
e-mail: humank@hkusa.com

Canada: Human Kinetics
475 Devonshire Road Unit 100
Windsor, ON N8Y 2L5
800-465-7301 (in Canada only)
e-mail: info@hkcanada.com

Europe: Human Kinetics
107 Bradford Road
Stanningley
Leeds LS28 6AT, United Kingdom
+44 (0) 113 255 5665
e-mail: hk@hkeurope.com

Australia: Human Kinetics
57A Price Avenue
Lower Mitcham, South Australia 5062
08 8372 0999
e-mail: info@hkaustralia.com

New Zealand: Human Kinetics
P.O. Box 80
Torrens Park, South Australia 5062
0800 222 062
e-mail: info@hknewzealand.com

E5197

To every one of you who is looking for inspiration and fun from skateboarding.

—**Per Welinder**

This book is dedicated to my wife, Jennie, and boys, Levi and Jacob, for their patience while I endured hundreds of hours skating and hanging out on the computer.

—**Peter Whitley**

CONTENTS

Preface **vi** ● Acknowledgments **viii** ● Trick Finder **ix**

PART I	Skateboarding Essentials	1

CHAPTER 1
Equipment and Safety 3

CHAPTER 2
Building and Maintaining a Board. 13

CHAPTER 3
Balance and Control 29

PART II	Techniques and Tricks	43

CHAPTER 4
Basic Maneuvers 45

CHAPTER 5
Ollies and Shuvits. 61

CHAPTER 6
Lip Tricks. **105**

CHAPTER 7
Grinds and Slides **159**

CHAPTER 8
Vert, Downhill, and Slalom **185**

PART III   The Skateboarding Life   217

CHAPTER 9
Challenging Your Environment. **219**

CHAPTER 10
Skating Competitively **243**

Index **251** • About the Authors **259**

I started out skateboarding by renting a board from a kid in my neighborhood. He charged about $1.00 a day. This made a pretty good case to convince my mother to buy one for me. I got my first skateboard in 1977: a black plastic Newporter. It had no grip, so I glued sandpaper to the top. The wheels were translucent yellow with loose ball bearings.

The first trick I learned was riding slalom through cones, if you can call that a trick. After that I learned nose wheelies.

I grew up in Sweden and skated with Hazze Lindgren, Fabian Mansson, Fabian Bjornstjerna, Bjorn Konig, and others. Some of my most vivid memories from being a skateboarder in Sweden in the late '70s are from the cold winter days where everything in Stockholm was covered with snow. At the end of the day we would take the train into Stockholm to one of the quieter subway stations. It was deep underground and offered perfectly smooth concrete. The train would come every 20 minutes, so we would have enough time to skate uninterrupted and then take a break as our skate spot erupted into activity. It was so cold—below freezing—we had to skate in warm jackets, beanies, and mittens.

After years of skating subway stations and outside during the few summer months when it was warm and dry enough to skate, I saved up enough money to travel across the world to California. This was a dream come true—the chance to skate with the best professional skaters in the world.

At first Steve Rocco and his family took good care of me. Stacy Peralta was always there with helpful advice, encouraging words, and a sponsorship offer that eventually led to my spot on the Powell-Peralta team, the Bones Brigade. New opportunities started rolling in and allowed me to earn a living while still skating all day, every day. To this day I am grateful for the generous support of these skateboarding legends. They opened my eyes to something that is important to me: helping and encouraging others in pursuit of their dreams.

Today I do that by running a company called Blitz. Blitz is a brand incubator that helps start-up skateboard and apparel companies grow. We have helped manufacture and distribute some of the best-known skateboard brands in the world. These products are sold in more than 70 countries all around the world. Located in Huntington Beach, California—the very epicenter of skateboarding—Blitz has a staff of 20 people who are passionate about building brands that have something special to offer skateboarders. I spend my days figuring out ways that skateboarding can keep getting better and more exciting.

My purpose in writing this book is to reach out to skaters and offer advice and encouragement.

—Per Welinder

wasn't sure what to do with my first skateboard. It was plastic, it had a tiny little pointed tail, the trucks didn't turn, and every now and then the bearings would fly out of the wheels and down the street on their own. That skateboard was popular in the neighborhood, and we would pass it around while challenging each other to try new things. It didn't take long for the other kids in the neighborhood to ask their parents for skateboards, and after a while they were all over the place. This was around 1974. Good days.

Eventually I started getting real skateboards in my life. The first ones were enormous, basically flat, and covered with plastic devices—nose guards, rails, tail plates, lappers, and copers. It seemed as if they were almost as heavy as our BMX bikes. Tricks were hard to learn, but skateboarding was fun and that was important to us. Our "local" skatepark was 5 miles (8 km) away. We would make the trek every weekend day through the 100-plus (38-plus C) degree heat of Las Vegas summers, skate all day, and make the slow haul back to our neighborhood, tired, dehydrated, broke, and chattering about all the tricks we did, tried, and saw.

Skateboarding is as important to me today as it was when I was a little kid. I've never believed that I was a very talented skateboarder. I lack those characteristics that all great skateboarders possess—I'm afraid of falling, I hate pain, and I don't tend to challenge myself physically—but skating fits with me. I love the feeling of moving without having to walk, of carving just by dipping a shoulder, of rolling over the hips and pockets of a bowl, and of moving smoothly over weird terrain. Skateboarding resonates with the kind of person I am: creative, curious, and interested in new ideas.

As the former director of Skaters for Public Skateparks (www.skatepark.org) and in my current position as program director for the Tony Hawk foundation, I have had the opportunity to help communities build excellent skateparks. Behind every skatepark in the world is a group of passionate skaters who put years of work into advocacy, fund-raising, and planning. These people are my heroes. They do this because they need a place to skate but also because, like you and me, they love skateboarding.

When Per contacted me about the opportunity to work with him on this book, I immediately said yes. I grew up carefully dissecting Per's tricks and tried, usually unsuccessfully, to match them somehow to my own skills. Growing up with my nose in *Skateboarder* and *Action Now* magazines, I thought Per and skaters of his caliber were impossibly talented and fearless, and I admired their bottomless determination. As I grew older, I began to see these qualities in *all* skaters . . . skaters like you.

I'm stoked to be able to contribute to this book, but I'm *more* stoked that you are reading it. I'm sure you'll find some fun things to think about and try the next time you step on your board.

—**Peter Whitley**

ACKNOWLEDGMENTS

I am very thankful for and appreciative of the work of all the talented people involved in making this book a reality. In particular I would like to thank Maryann Karinch, our agent, who provided the original spark. I also want to express a special thank you to Peter Whitley, my co-author and illustrator, and to Bryce Kanights, our senior photographer, for their relentless hard work and level of professionalism. And last but not least, thanks to my parents, Nils and Gunnel, and to my wonderful wife, Elaine, and our sons, Lukas and Benjamin, for their energy and love.

—**Per Welinder**

This book would not have been possible without the brave and legendary skateboarding innovators. Without the people who tried to do something that didn't seem possible, skateboarding would not be what it is today. This book is also in debt to the bottomless patience of the Human Kinetics editors who calmly endured the irritable tirades of an uncompromising skater. The spirit of DIY skateboarding and skatepark enthusiasts permeate the pages of *Mastering Skateboarding*. The passion and wisdom of these fearless bridge pirates and city hall raiders provided inspiration. Keep up the good fight!

—**Peter Whitley**

TRICK FINDER

Basic tricks

Code	Page	Trick	Description
B	35	Push	Moving forward by kicking the ground with the rear foot
B	36	Switch	Traveling forward with the rear foot in front
B	47	Slowing and breaking	Four-wheel lateral slides
B	48	Kickturn	Redirecting the board by lifting the nose
B	49	Tic tac	Sequence of back and forth kickturns
B	50	Up the curb	Riding over a curb without lifting the feet
B	52	Manual	Wheelie
B	53	Spacewalk	Sequence of tic tacs in a manual
B	55	Nose manual	Wheelie on the front wheels
B	56	180	180-degree kickturn
B	57	360	360-degree kickturn; full circular rotation on the rear wheels
B	58	No comply	Scoop and lift the board with the rear foot

Ollie and shuvit tricks

Code	Page	Trick	Description
OS	64	Ollie	Basic pop on flat ground without touching the board or the ground
OS	66	Frontside 180 ollie	Ollie while skater and board rotate 180 degrees frontside
OS	68	Backside 180 ollie	Ollie while skater and board rotate 180 degrees backside
OS	69	Switch Ollie	Ollie starting from a switch stance
OS	70	Shifty	Ollie with the board rotating laterally while airborn
OS	72	Ollie north	Ollie while kicking the lead foot out over the nose
OS	74	Nollie	Ollie off the nose of the board from a regular stance.
OS	76	Kickflip	Ollie while kicking the board so that it rotates along its axis in a heelside direction
OS	80	Heelflip	Ollie while kicking the board so that it rotates along its axis in a toeside direction
OS	82	M-80	Flip the board for a kickflip and revert right after landing
OS	84	Pressure flip	Backside 180 ollie with half a heelflip
OS	86	Frontside pop shuvit	Kicking the tail end of the board 180 degrees frontside
OS	88	Backside pop shuvit	Kicking the tail end of the board 180 degrees backside
OS	90	Backside 360 shuvit	Kicking the tail end of the board 360 degrees; sometimes done off the nose of the board
OS	92	Bigspin	Kicking the tail end of the board 360 degrees with the skater rotating 180 degrees
OS	94	Varial kickflip	Backside 180 pop shuvit with a toe flick
OS	96	Boneless	Footplant with lead foot and grab board with the rear hand on the toeside
OS	98	No comply 180	Scoop and lift the board with the rear foot while board and skater rotate 180 degrees.
OS	100	Hardflip	Frontside 180 pop shuvit with a kickflip
OS	102	Inward heelflip	Backside 180 pop shuvit with a heelflip

Tranny tricks

Code	Page	Trick	Description
T	112	Pump	Using mass and pressure to gain speed over terrain elevation changes
T	114	Drop in	Entering tranny from a tail stall
T	116	Roll in	Entering tranny from the deck by rolling over the coping with a slight manual
T	118	Ollie in	Entering tranny from the deck by ollieing over the coping
T	120	Backside kickturn	Redirecting the board 180 degrees backside
T	122	Frontside kickturn	Redirecting the board 180 degrees frontside
T	124	Tail stall	Pausing on the coping with the tail on the deck and the rear wheels in the ramp
T	125	Revert	Redirecting the board 180 degrees by sliding the wheels
T	126	Nose stall	Pausing on the coping with the nose on the deck and the front wheels in the ramp
T	128	Rock to fakie	Tapping the nose end of the board onto the deck, then tapping back in fakie
T	129	Fakie rock	Tapping the tail end of the board onto the deck then tapping back in regular
T	130	Backside rock and roll	Rock to fakie but with a backside 180 kickturn just before tapping back in fakie
T	132	Frontside rock and roll	Rock to fakie but with a frontside 180 kickturn just before tapping back in fakie
T	134	Fakie ollie	Switch ollie on tranny then rolling out regular
T	136	Fakie ollie / Ollie to fakie	Regular ollie on tranny then rolling out fakie
T	136	Frontside ollie	Frontside ollie on transition
T	142	5-0 stall	A 5-0 stall with the front trucks hovering above the coping
T	144	Pivot	A quick 5-0 stall then reversing back into the ramp
T	146	Disaster	180 ollie onto the coping so that the tail end of the board and rear wheels are on the deck
T	148	Frontside 50-50 stall	90-degree frontside kickturn onto the coping
T	150	Blunt (to fakie)	Tail stall with the rear wheels on the deck and the tail on the tranny, then popping off and coming back in fakie
T	152	Fastplant and beanplant	Footplant with rear (fastplant) or lead (beanplant) foot and grab board with lead hand
T	154	5-0 stall	A 5-0 stall with the front trucks hovering above the coping
T	155	Sweeper	Footplant the rear foot with a frontside sweep
T	156	Russian boneless	Footplant with lead foot and jump over the board as it rotates with lead foot

Grind and slide tricks

Code	Page	Trick	Description
GS	138	Backside 50-50 stall	90-degree backside kickturn onto the coping
GS	162	Backside 5-0 grind	Grind on the tail with the skater's back to the ledge
GS	164	Frontside 5-0 grind	Grind on the coping with the skater's front along the ledge
GS	166	Backside 50-50 grind	Both trucks grind on the ledge/rail approaching on the skater's frontside
GS	168	Frontside 50-50	Both trucks grind on the coping with the skater's back to the rail
GS	170	Backside 50-50	Both trucks grind on the ledge approaching on the skater's backside
GS	172	Feeble grind	5-0 grind with the front wheels leaning/hanging diagonally on the rail
GS	174	Smith grind	Frontside 5-0 grind with the front wheels angled away from the ledge/rail
GS	176	Crooked grind	Nose grind with the tail end of the board angled away from the railing
GS	178	Bluntslide	Tail slide with the tail on the top and the nose sticking out over the coping
GS	181	Boardslide	Crossbar/frontside slide 90 or 180 with the tail of the wheels cross over the railing

Vert tricks

Code	Page	Trick	Description
V	189	Knee slide	Drop heavily onto the kneepads and slide along the concrete to come to a stop
V	190	Pumping	Using mass and pressure to gain speed through corners and pockets
V	191	Kickturns	Redirecting the board by lifting the nose on vert
V	192	Drop in to vert	Entering vert from a tail stall
V	193	Ollie on vert	Entering vert from the deck by ollieing over the coping
V	196	Indy air	Backside air while grabbing the board with the rear hand between the feet
V	197	Lien air	Frontside air while grabbing the back of the nose with the lead hand
V	198	Body jar	Dropping in from being airborn with a quick tail stall or tail tap
V	199	Method air	Backside air with the bottom of the board facing up
V	200	Mute air	Backside air while grabbing the front of the nose with the lead hand
V	201	Japan air	Backside air while grabbing the front of the nose with the lead hand and pulling the board back
V	202	Slob air	Frontside air while grabbing the toeside of the board with the front hand
V	203	Stalefish	Air while grabbing the heelside of the board behind the legs
V	204	Judo air	Nosegrab air with the front foot kicked out
V	205	Madonna	Frontside judo to a body jar
V	206	Benihana	Tailgrab air with the rear leg out behind the board
V	207	Airwalk	Nosegrab air while legs scissor kick
V	208	Inverts	One-handed handplants on the coping while holding the board with the other

PART I

Skateboarding Essentials

So you want to learn more about skateboarding? That's great news. Every skateboarder you see on the streets, at the skatepark, or you happen to know has been exactly where you are today. No one starts out with awesome skills and a complete understanding of every trick. You're in good company!

To many beginners, skateboarding seems mysterious and confusing. It is peppered with slang words, atypical fashion, profound creativity, and a tribe-like community that seems to shun outsiders. But once you start getting involved, you quickly find that skateboarders are friendly and supportive to their fellow skaters and that there exists an air of mutual support and encouragement. This sense of community is one reason so many people find that skateboarding speaks to them on a personal level. You may be one of these people. We sure hope so!

CHAPTER 1

EQUIPMENT
AND SAFETY

Getting into skateboarding can be a pivotal event in someone's life. Skating speaks to many people in a personal and deeply enriching way. It is like few other sports or physical activities because it merges creativity, physicality, bravery, and tenacity with the found environment. It is not played on a defined field, and when it is done well it is as much about style and what the trick is done on as it is about the specific stunt being performed. Skateboarding is so personal for most skaters that it is much more than something to do when they're bored. For many people, skating becomes a fundamental part of what they do and who they are. For most skaters it is a lifestyle, a source of recreation, an athletic regimen, and a social event.

The unique mix of skateboarding's qualities is attracting people to the activity in record numbers. It is both individualistic and social. It is inexpensive to do but can become expensive for those who go on to travel to different skateparks and buy high-end equipment. Although the pace of learning new tricks is self-driven, the sport can also be competitive. Skating is free form and all about personal expression, but there is also an order of skills and techniques that must be mastered in order to progress to the more difficult variations. Although skateboarding is steeped in counterculture folklore, skaters themselves are incredibly diverse, and you can find people from all walks of life at any typical skatepark. Skateboarding may not speak to everybody, but those who respond strongly to the sport consider it an essential part of their lives and their identities. Because skateboarding is personal, it mirrors the diversity of our society. Different people skate for different reasons and bring their own unique viewpoints and styles to the mix. If some aspect of skateboarding doesn't appeal to you, there's a good chance you can discover other ways to skate that you are comfortable with.

People who begin skateboarding when they are young tend to stick with it. Their involvement is reinforced by the friendships formed with other skaters. With a skateboard, no additional expense is required, and any small patch of smooth concrete can be used to perform hundreds of different tricks. When a skater's skills are developed enough to enjoy public skateparks, thousands of hours can be devoted to mastering tricks on a particular structure or form. Those skills can be taken to new places and often need to be adjusted to the nuances of the new place. For this reason, skating presents eternal opportunities for improvement in myriad ways. Few people skate "bored." Furthermore, with hundreds of new skateparks being built every year, more people than ever before are being exposed to the creative athleticism of skateboarding and become interested in trying it out themselves. People new to skateboarding suddenly realize what skaters have known all along: Skating is fun whether it's just pushing around on flat or doing huge tricks on vert.

Whole communities are starting to see the benefits of supporting this activity. A growing number of school districts are including skateboarding as part of their physical education curriculum, and some are even organizing interscholastic skateboarding leagues. Parks departments are finally seeing skateparks as a low-cost, high-return addition to their park districts. Skaters are less commonly characterized as delinquents and troublemakers and instead are seen as ordinary people who are doing what they love to do. It's a great time to be a skateboarder!

SKATE CULTURE

Some people still think of skateboarding in a negative light. As a skater you will encounter and eventually learn to tolerate these stereotypes and misconceptions. Some skaters even take pride in working against these ideas by being the opposite of what we see in the magazines and videos. Your "typical" skater might be a straight-A student. Another might be into fantasy literature and know everything about *The Lord of the Rings*. Maybe one of the skaters down at the skatepark is also into hot rods and is working on some car project in her garage. Skateboarders are a diverse bunch, and some have only one thing in common: They love to skate. Older skaters encounter surprised spectators and get comments such as "Aren't you a little old to be doing that?" These same spectators would not be surprised to see an older skater riding a bicycle. There are still some crazy ideas floating around out there about what type of person rides a skateboard, and many skaters find it amusing to defy those preconceptions by being the exact opposite.

Riding a skateboard instantly qualifies you to be a member of a special group. As simple as that may sound, there is actually a powerful camaraderie among skaters. Anywhere skaters travel, they will enjoy the benefits of skateboarding culture, whether it's a nearby town or another country. A skater can easily strike up a conversation with another skater and bond over a common interest. They can talk about things that only skaters truly understand, and this is usually enough to generate an easy friendship, even if just for a day.

Camaraderie is the glue that holds skate culture together. Intolerance, hostility, carelessness, and bad attitudes simply don't fit with the easygoing vibe that most skaters value. New skaters soon realize they need to follow

three fundamental rules if they want to spend time among other experienced skaters without feeling out of place:

1. **No whining, excuses, or bragging.** Some people try to fit in with big talk about skating. It just doesn't work. Whether it's a skatepark or a popular skate spot, people show up to skate. Nobody wants to hear someone going on about the tricks they used to be able to do or why they can't do them anymore. Instead, do the tricks you know or try the tricks you want to learn. Ask for advice if you are having a hard time and relax. Talk about tricks if you must, but don't waste an opportunity to skate by regaling everyone with stories about your accomplishments. The only thing worse than talking about the tricks you can do is talking about the tricks your friend, who happens to not be there, can do.

2. **Have fun no matter what your skill level.** Fun is contagious. When you are happy to be at the park or spot, people will enjoy skating with you. On the other hand, if you are constantly frustrated because you're not landing a trick, people are going to roll their eyes behind your back—not at your inability to land the trick but at your dramatic reaction to your failure. All skaters have tricks they can't do, whether it's an ollie or an eggplant. Your character as a skater is largely determined by how you handle your own failed attempts. At every session there seems to be that one person who can't land a trick and takes out his frustration by throwing his board around. Don't be that guy. Getting bent out of shape because you didn't land a challenging trick is a great way of bumming everyone out. If you want to be a part of your local skate scene, be the type of person people want to skate with: easygoing, positive, and stoked to be there.

3. **Protect yourself and those around you.** Engaging in dangerous behavior or being inconsiderate of those around you will tick people off and maybe even get you into trouble. Shooting your board, throwing your trash around, breaking glass, making a big stink when something isn't going your way, and bullying other people are all great ways to find yourself with nobody to skate with. Be cool, friendly, and considerate and treat your fellow skaters and their friends with respect. In return, they'll respect you and want you there.

When skateboarding becomes a source of frustration and anxiety, you will not only annoy others but also eventually lose interest. People tend to do things they think are fun. If skateboarding becomes frustrating for you, makes you angry, and gives you temper tantrums, you should probably just quit doing it. Nobody wants to see you act like a baby. If you can keep skateboarding fun for yourself and those around you, there's a good chance it will become a rewarding part of your life for many years to come.

As you become more confident on a skateboard, you will develop some positive physical characteristics. Not only will your leg strength and stamina increase, but your balance will too. Balance is an often overlooked aspect of physical health that influences your core body strength and posture. The largest health benefit of skating is the cardiovascular workout it provides. Most skaters don't care about the details of their health. They just know that the more they skate, the better they feel, and that is enough. Skateboarding is fun, and the physical benefits are merely an irrelevant by-product. Few people skate to get in shape, but it's unusual to find skaters of any age who are unhealthy.

As with any physical activity, there is a certain degree of risk. Many skateboarding tricks require a high degree of precision. Small changes in how a trick is done—whether it's the skater's stance or some external factor—can be the difference between success and failure. Every skateboarder falls; it's part of skateboarding. Learning how to fall and being aware of when a fall is likely to occur *before* it occurs comes with experience. This is why most skateboarding-related injuries happen to people within their first few tries at skating: They haven't learned yet to recognize the signs of a fall or figured out what to do to get off the skateboard without injury. We provide some tips on how to fall in chapter 3, but for the most part these skills come with practice.

As your skating skill increases, you may find that you gain confidence in other parts of your life. You can take pride in knowing you can do difficult things on a skateboard. You have found a way of challenging yourself physically and mentally that is fun and rewarding. You are lucky to be a skater. If you dedicate yourself to skating, as so many have, it will be a source of confidence and inner strength that will last a lifetime.

Despite the benefits that skaters experience, it's not uncommon to encounter people who believe skateboarding is unhealthy. Criticism of skateboarding usually falls into two categories: social deviance and physical risk.

As we discussed previously, concern about the skateboarding culture is based on generalizations and fictional stereotypes. It takes only a few minutes with real skateboarders to realize they are as individually unique as nonskaters. Sure, there are some unsavory characters in skating, but you'll find some of those in every other subgroup of society. You skate for your own reasons, and you will find that other people skate for reasons you don't share. That's okay. There's room enough for everyone.

Skateboarding can be physically risky, particularly during the first few weeks or when done in places that present external hazards such as traffic. But every sport or physical activity presents certain risks; with skating, as with football or gymnastics, for example, it's possible to be smart and manage the risks rather than avoid the activity altogether.

PADS AND PROTECTION

What you wear while you skate can have a huge impact on your performance and your acceptance into the local skateboarding community. It's generally not considered fashionable to wear pads or a helmet while you skate unless you're really into vert. Showing up at the skatepark decked out in wrist guards, knee and elbow pads, and a helmet is a great way of getting everyone's attention. People will either expect some huge tricks that warrant all the pads or they'll assume you have overprotective parents. It's easy to say it doesn't matter what you look like, but we know that for most people it actually does. Nobody wants to be thought of as the dork with overprotective parents.

Shoes

Your shoes are the piece of clothing that will most influence your skating. In general, all skate shoes are excellent. They provide superb support, have padding in all the right places, and are built up where they will be getting the most wear and tear. Skate shoes have become so comfortable over the years that many people who stand all day as part of their jobs prefer them over ordinary tennis shoes.

Skateboarding tends to destroy shoes, and the more you skate, the faster you will be going through them. Buying skate shoes is a balance between support, comfort, style, and budget. Skate shoes generally start at $40.

Different shoes have varying amounts of grip. More grip isn't necessarily better. Some people like to move their feet around a lot on the board, so a less-grippy shoe may be better. Other people like lots of grip for better board control, so they would want a grippier shoe. Some companies are beginning to express their shoes' grippiness using what's called the NBS rating. A high NBS rating means the shoe will be softer and have more traction but less durability since the softer sole will wear out more quickly. A shoe with a lower NBS rating will be more durable but provide less grip. Remember: The NBS rating has nothing to do with the shoe's quality. It's merely there to help skaters identify what kind of shoe they like to use.

Another factor to consider when shopping for skate shoes is the sole thickness. A thicker sole will provide more stability and support and last a little longer. A thinner sole will allow you to feel the edges of the board more precisely but will wear out more quickly. Neither is better than the other; it's a personal preference that you will develop as you try different styles. If you are just beginning, you should look for a thin, grippy sole so you can tell where your feet are on the deck without looking.

The final important decision when choosing a skate shoe is the height. Skate shoes range from little more than slippers (slip-ons) all the way up to ankle-high lace-ups (high-tops) and everything in between. You will want a shoe that provides maximum support without hindering your movement. Vert skaters typically don't require as much ankle flexibility as street skaters and gravitate toward high-tops. Street skaters requiring a lot of ankle flexibility for flip tricks often prefer lower cuts.

Pads

It is nice to have a set of pads, particularly when you are starting out. Some skateparks require them, and they can protect your body from devastating injuries. Beginning skaters tend to try to stop their falls with their hands. This impact puts the wrists at risk. The most common injury among beginning skaters is to the wrists of skaters who are skating without protection and haven't learned how to fall properly. Until the habit of using the hands when falling is broken, wrist guards can be a wise investment. All modern wrist guards help keep the wrist stiff on impact. Knee pads are useful at first for protecting the knees, but for vert skaters they are an important device for coming out of unsuccessful tricks. When you are ready to try vert, it's practical to invest in a good set of knee pads. Elbow pads are less commonly seen but are often used by beginners and skaters with preexisting elbow injuries. Gloves are a good idea for just cruising around but won't work with most wrist guards. Longboarders like gloves with special plastic pucks attached to the palms for providing an extra point on the ground for stability on fast, tight turns.

When you go to a skatepark, you probably won't see pads being worn unless they're required. The most common reason cited is that some skaters feel that pads restrict movement. It's actually a matter of conditioning, or habit. Skaters have been wearing pads and helmets for years and performing well. Advancements in pad and helmet technology provide modern skaters with lighter, less restrictive pads and helmets than ever before. Wearing a cast also restricts movement.

The truth of the matter is that wearing pads and helmets isn't perceived as cool. Nobody wants to be the only person at the skatepark who looks like the Michelin Man. The pages of skateboarding magazines are filled with pictures of people doing incredible tricks without a helmet or pads. However, at a large halfpipe where pads and helmets are a common sight and socially accepted, most skaters throw them on without a second thought.

Like most other sports, skateboarding is inherently risky. You cannot remove the risk of injury, but you can manage it. Many people have skated all their lives and never gotten seriously injured. This isn't simply because they were diligent about padding up but because they managed the risk for the kind of skating they were doing. If you are just beginning, pad up. If you are planning on going fast, wear a helmet. If you are going to skate vert, wear a helmet and knee pads (at least). If you are going to do kickflips in the garage, maybe you feel comfortable not wearing any pads or a helmet. The bottom line is that you are responsible: Nobody will tell you that you have to pad up, but when you hurt yourself, you have only yourself to blame. If you don't wear pads and you bust something up, don't expect a lot of sympathy.

Many people who have had serious falls on a skateboard claim they don't know how it happened. Obviously they weren't trying to fall; it was an accident, and if they could have prevented it, they certainly would have. As a skater you need to consider this carefully. You will never intend to fall. Every fall can result in serious injury (even the small ones). Skate smart.

A BIG WORD ABOUT SAFETY

Skating safely isn't just about putting on a helmet and a bunch of pads. There are several things you can do to reduce the risk of a bad injury.

- **Skate within your limits.** You will have lots of opportunities to learn new tricks and skills. Some will be fun and easy, while others may be terrifying and risky. If you are not comfortable trying something, don't do it. You will prove nothing by hurting yourself while trying a trick you're not ready for.

- **When in doubt, pad up.** It's always a good idea to wear a helmet, but the fact is few people do. If you are going to try something risky, throw on a helmet. If you make the trick and it felt good, then the helmet wasn't necessary. If you miss the trick and you smack your skull, the helmet will have been an *excellent* idea. Which outcome would you rather regret: Wearing a helmet and making the trick or not wearing a helmet and smacking your noggin?

- **Don't be a jerk.** Shooting your board, not paying attention, or horsing around while people around you are skating is a sure way to get hurt or to hurt someone else. You can take skating seriously and still have fun.

- **Ask how.** If you want to try a difficult trick but are not sure where to start or what the risks are, ask people who have that trick mastered. They should be able to tell you how the trick can fail and what can go wrong so you can be prepared for the worst.

Most skateboarding deaths involve a motor vehicle. Skaters are killed when they are hit by vehicles. Some are killed while being towed by a car and fall. Getting hit by a car isn't always the skater's fault, but it is always preventable. Real skaters throw on a helmet when they want to bomb a huge hill. Falling while being towed by a car is such an unnecessary way to die, it's hardly worth talking about. Only dumb kids who want to hurt themselves get towed behind cars.

Helmets

A helmet is the single most important protective article you can wear. Many skaters wear one every time they are on a board. Some wear them at concrete skateparks. Some put one on only when they're trying high-risk tricks. Don't believe what you see in the magazines; the pros wear helmets too. In many cases a pro team will show up at a skatepark and skate for an hour while wearing helmets to get used to the place. When the cameras are all set up the helmets come off. That's the picture you see in the advertisement or video. It used to be the same way with BMX and snowboarding, but now it's completely acceptable to be doing either with a helmet. Unfortunately, in skateboarding helmets still aren't seen as cool. This is dumb. Sitting in a hospital bed unable to make complete sentences or change the channel by yourself is a high price to pay for being cool. Wear a helmet.

The grip of the helmet should keep it from moving around on your head. The strap should be adjusted so that it's snug but not tight. Wearing a helmet without buckling the strap is as good as not wearing a helmet at all. The most dangerous falls are backward when your head whips back and smacks the ground. This is the type of fall that knocks people out. If you don't buckle your helmet, your head will snap back, and the helmet will fly off just before your head hits the ground. It has happened before to experienced skaters, some of whom are no longer with us or able to ride a skateboard as a result.

Skateboarding helmets are the multi-impact style, meaning they have a hard outer shell and high-density foam inside. Some will have the hard foam (Styrofoam), and others will have a softer, spongy foam. Most people find that the spongy type is more comfortable, but both work well. The helmet should fit snugly on the head but be loose enough that you can easily squeeze two fingers between the helmet and your scalp. All better helmets will come with additional pads that can be inserted to adjust the fit.

CHAPTER 2

BUILDING AND
MAINTAINING A BOARD

There are lots of ways to immerse yourself in skateboarding, but the only thing you really need is a skateboard and a place to ride it. Because skateboarding has so few required devices, it's important that they function well enough for you to skate the way you want to skate. For downhill racers who require a high degree of performance, anything on their skateboards that might make them faster is inspected, adjusted, and tested. These skaters have little interest in their boards being durable or having pop. Street skaters on the other hand tend to ride rough terrain and land heavily on their boards. Compared with downhill racers, street skaters need their skateboards to have pop and be durable, but speed is not generally a concern.

What kind of board you get, how you improve it by replacing parts, and what you do to keep it in working order largely depend on the kind of skateboarding you plan on doing. It's probably safe to assume that you, like most skateboarders, are interested in street skating. Also, speed skating (e.g., downhill longboarding, slalom, and racing) is so technical that the type of equipment you use and how you tune or maintain it are dependent on your body type, experience level, personal skating style, and performance desires. These elaborate topics are beyond the scope of this book and are best explored after spending some time experimenting with different setups.

The skateboard is a simple device, but when it's not working properly, it can make the skating experience frustrating and unrewarding. Beginning skaters should be comfortable tuning their boards in different ways to find out what works best with how they like to skate. To tune the skateboard, it's important to know what all the parts are and how they work.

SKATING STYLES

There are lots of different kinds of skateboarding. You may find that you prefer one style over another. The tricks covered in this book are mostly street tricks, with a little miniramp thrown in for good measure. There are categories of skateboarding that have special boards and disciplines within

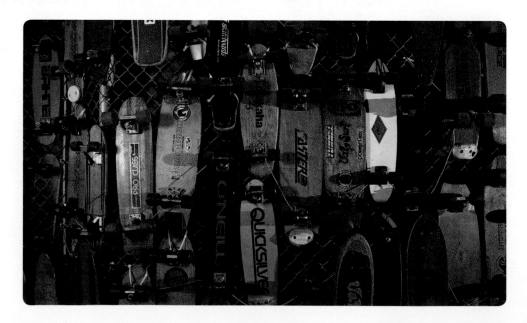

those categories. For example, if someone passed you on a sidewalk on a long skateboard with big, soft wheels, you could safely presume that he was longboarding. However, there are boards that serve this same purpose—just cruising around in style—that are shorter than an ordinary skateboard. This is where things get confusing. Is it the world's shortest longboard or something different? One of the greatest things about skateboarding is its tendency to avoid pigeonholes and definitions. The answer is that it's both a longboard and not a longboard. There's no wrong answer.

For the purposes of explaining how different board types are used, we must categorize the styles and boards. Remember, however, that skaters everywhere are working hard to blur the lines between street skating, longboarding, freestyle, and vert. By the time you read this, there may be a whole new popular type of skateboard.

Longboarding

Longboards are excellent for cruising around and are popular on college campuses and with people who aren't interested in trick skateboarding. Longboards are longer and usually wider than your typical street board. Their size provides more stability, and they are easier to ride. Skaters who use longboard techniques tend to turn on the front trucks so their weight is mostly near the nose of the board. This makes it similar to riding a snowboard.

Longboarding is easier so it may seem as if there is less risk. This is not true; a fall on a longboard is every bit as painful and dangerous as a fall on a street board. Beginners should always wear a helmet. Gloves are also a good idea.

There are many styles of longboards. Some are big, heavy planks while others are as short as an ordinary street board. Some drop down in the middle of the board to lower the skater's center of gravity, known as drop-through decks, and others, known as reverse camber boards, actually rise up in the middle and flatten out only when someone is standing on them. Longboards are often shaped into interesting and unusual shapes, and the more expensive ones may have inlays of exotic wood and other materials.

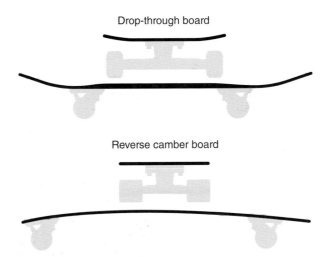

Drop-through board

Reverse camber board

Slalom and Downhill Racing

Slalom boards are usually the same size as a street board or a little smaller and are flat or slightly cambered (arced upward). The risers are wedge shaped so that the trucks are angled outward to sharpen the turning radius. Some racers put wedges under only the front trucks to prevent the tail from fishtailing and sliding out on tight corners. Most slalom and downhill racers geek out over the small improvements gained by a new product or small adjustment. If you want an earful about this type of skating, ask a racer. The slalom and downhill racing scenes are always friendly and open to newcomers.

Freestyle

Few people talk about freestyle today. This style was popular during the 1970s and early 1980s. The tricks are very technical and require incredible balance and strength. Over the years most freestyle tricks have been embraced by street skaters and adapted to new terrain. Tricks such as the ollie and kickflip were originally freestyle tricks.

Freestyle today is usually done on an ordinary street board, but freestylers used to have their own style of board. Freestyle boards were small and perfectly flat with squared corners. The smaller board required smaller trucks. What these boards lacked in size they made up for in weight and responsiveness.

WHO ARE OUR RACERS AND FREESTYLERS?

Everyone knows Tony Hawk, but who are the pros in freestyle and racing? Take this simple quiz by matching the pro with his style of skateboarding.

1. Danny Way	a. vert, street
2. Kevin Harris	b. vert, slalom
3. Steve Olson	c. freestyle, street
4. John Lucero	d. freestyle
5. Richy Carrasco	e. freestyle, slalom
6. Tony Alva	f. street, vert
7. Rodney Mullen	g. freestyle, vert

For answers, see page 27.

ANATOMY OF A BOARD

A skateboard is essentially composed of three parts: the deck, the trucks, and the wheels. Each of these parts has an impact on how the skateboard operates, and changes to any of these parts may end up requiring adjustments to the other components.

The deck is the wooden platform, usually maple, to which other parts are attached. The top is covered in grip tape so that the skater's feet don't slide around. Although the typical decks one finds in a skate shop look symmetrical, most have subtle differences that distinguish the front (the nose) from the rear (the tail).

Board or deck

Trucks

Wheel and bearings

Several aspects of the board will affect its performance. A wide board will provide stability but can be more difficult to maneuver. A narrow board will be more responsive and flip easily but will also be less stable. Most skaters who are interested in street skating, ollies, and kickflips get narrower boards, while those interested in going fast or who are physically larger tend to get wider boards. If you are buying your first board, a good rule of thumb is to choose a size that is slightly narrower than the length of your foot so that when your heel is even with one side, your toes stick off the other side by about an inch. By the time you've worn the board out, you should have a clear idea of what you're comfortable with.

A longer board will be stable but will not turn as sharply as a shorter board. The distance between the trucks, or the wheelbase, influences the radius of the board's turning arc. The wheelbase does not change how responsive a board will turn, only how sharply it turns when you lean on the side of it. (Adjusting the trucks is the main way to adjust how responsive the board is to your weight.)

The concave—the angle and depth of the parts of the board that bend upward—will allow your feet to feel the board and apply downward pressure more easily. Tiny nuances in concave will not have an impact on your skating, and for most skaters it is merely a matter of personal taste and comfort. Beginning skaters should be less concerned about the concave of the board than with the length and width.

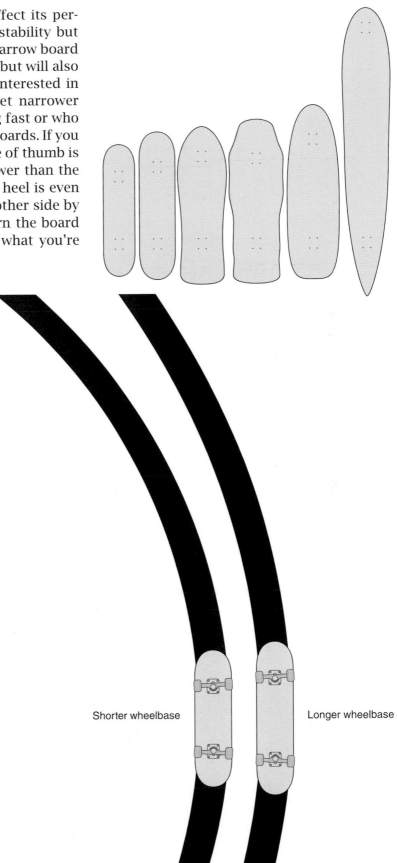

Shorter wheelbase

Longer wheelbase

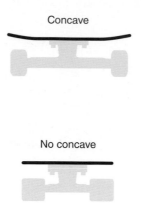

Concave

No concave

When choosing your first deck, place different decks on the ground in the skate shop and stand on them to test them with your feet. Find a board that is wide enough for your feet to fit comfortably. As you learn to skate, your preferences for board styles will emerge. These preferences come after hundreds of hours of skateboarding, so for most first-time buyers an inexpensive, basic street deck should be fine.

There are two sets of four holes drilled into the deck. Four bolts hold the trucks onto the board. The trucks are the most complex part of the skateboard. They are designed to rotate the axle as weight is applied to one side or the other. The portion of the trucks that mounts to the board is the baseplate. It has a large threaded pin sticking out of it called the kingpin and, near it, a small cup with a plastic bushing in it called the pivot cup. Around the kingpin are two rubber bushings. Sandwiched between the bushings is a portion of the hanger. The hanger also houses the axle that sticks out of either end. Holding the bushings and hanger assembly onto the kingpin is a bolt that can be tightened or loosened to adjust how easily the board turns.

Trucks, being metal, often outlive all the other components of a skateboard. When a deck breaks, the trucks are taken off and put on a new board. When the bushings wear out, the trucks are disassembled and new bushings are put in. Even when kingpins break they are usually removed and new ones are put in. The trucks themselves aren't replaced. Many skaters have gone through dozens of boards, wheels, and bearings with the same pair of trucks.

The width of the trucks is determined by the length of its axle and hanger. When the board is fully assembled, the outside of the wheels should be flush with or slightly inside the sides of the board. It is important that you know the size of the board before you pick out trucks. Your skate shop will

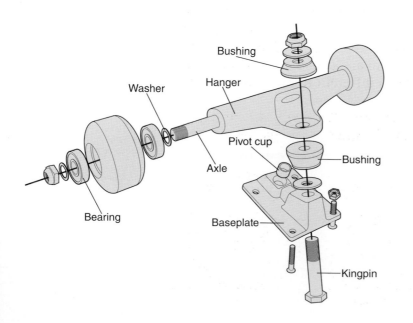

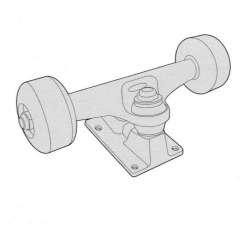

be able to help pair up the correct size of trucks to the board. Like decks, trucks come in all kinds of colors and styles, but they are all essentially the same until you get into special trucks for slalom and longboards. The size of the trucks (i.e., the length of the axle) is the main characteristic you should be concerned with. The baseplates are usually the same across a style of trucks regardless of their widths.

The two thick rubber pads between the kingpin and the hanger are called bushings. Any new pair of trucks will have bushings in them, but these may be replaced with bushings of different hardness. They may also need to be replaced when they become worn out and start to crack or chip. A softer bushing will provide less resistance and allow the board to turn easily, while a harder bushing will make the board stiffer to turn but very stable to stand on. Bushings take a few hours of riding to break in, so they can be difficult to assess before you buy them. Experimentation and experience are your best tools when shopping for new bushings.

The wheel assembly has several parts. There is the main polyurethane portion that touches the ground. This is the "wheel" part of the wheel assembly. Inside the wheel are two self-contained bearings that look like small steel collars. These fit snugly into either side of the wheel and allow the wheel to spin on the axle. A complete skateboard has eight bearings, two per wheel. Sometimes there will be an aluminum spacer inside the wheel between the bearings to help keep things aligned. Most skateboards assembled in a skate shop will also have small washers between the bolts on the axle and between the inner bearings and the hanger.

Choosing wheels can be complicated for first-timers. Two characteristics influence a wheel's performance: size and hardness. Most wheels have both the size and the hardness printed somewhere on the wheel graphic. The skate shop clerk will be happy to tell you about the different wheels.

A wheel's size is measured in millimeters. A typical range for wheels is between 50 and 60 millimeters. Smaller wheels will lower your center of gravity a little bit but won't be as fast or go over cracks and debris as easily as larger wheels. For your first wheels, 54 mm are a good place to start. As you learn new tricks and get comfortable on different terrains, your wheel preferences will emerge.

A wheel's hardness is measured in durometers. The hardness will sometimes have an *a* next to it. A 100 durometer rating is the hardest wheel.

> **I**f your board's nose and tail look similar you can use paint, a silver marker, or even colored grip tape to make a mark on a part of the board. That way you'll know which way it is facing. Some shops sell colored baseplate bolts for this very purpose.

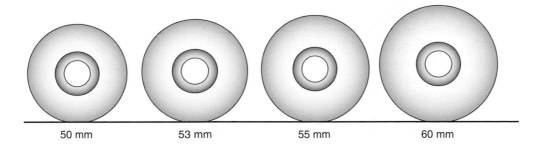

| 50 mm | 53 mm | 55 mm | 60 mm |

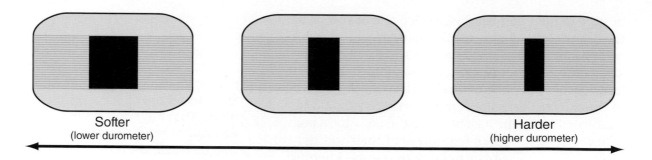

Softer
(lower durometer)

Harder
(higher durometer)

These will be very fast, but you will feel every bump and crack on rough terrain. A softer wheel such as a 92a or 94a will be smoother over rough terrain but won't be as fast. If you are unsure where to begin, 97a is a good place to start.

A softer wheel will provide more contact area with the ground and more grip. A hard wheel's footprint will be smaller and provide less traction. Hard wheels have less friction, which means less drag on smooth surfaces and, therefore, a faster ride.

To get the most out of your wheels, you need to know where you'll be using them and what you expect to do. If you do most of your skating at a concrete skatepark, a harder wheel will provide plenty of grip and speed. Soft wheels in a smooth concrete skatepark might feel a little mushy. If you are going to be skating on asphalt parking lots and sidewalks, a softer wheel will help absorb the roughness of the surface to produce a smoother ride and more grip. Hard wheels on a sidewalk will be loud and rough.

Not all wheel manufacturers follow these ratings. Instead, they've created "special formulas" for particular kinds of skateboarding styles and terrains.

THE SKATE TOOL

Any typical skateboard adjustment and assembly can be made with just one object: a good skate tool. The skate tool has different parts that fit with the various parts of your board. There will be a Phillips screwdriver for your baseplate bolts, two different sockets for your axle nuts and kingpin, and sometimes a few other features that make working on your skateboard easier. It's recommended that you pick up a good skate tool with your first board.

These are generally just marketing schemes, and you can ask your skate shop clerk to help compare the different wheels in easy-to-understand ways. For example, some companies have a "skatepark formula" wheel that is basically just a large, hard wheel.

Some companies saw a need for wheels that were even harder than 100a, so they created a *b* scale. The b-scale wheels are very hard. Where the a-scale stops, the b-scale starts.

The skateboard bearing is fully enclosed but has several different parts within it, including the actual ball bearings that allow the outer ring to turn in the opposite direction of the inner ring. Bearings are rated for the quality and smoothness of the bearing itself, but for most skateboarders the bearing is a disposable element.

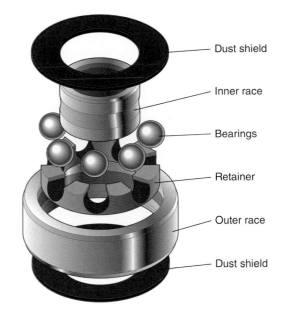

- Dust shield
- Inner race
- Bearings
- Retainer
- Outer race
- Dust shield

Bearings are rated by their ABEC (Annular Bearing Engineer's Committee) factor. A higher ABEC means a better quality (and usually more expensive) bearing. An ABEC 3 or 5 bearing should be fine until you are skating at a higher level.

Inserting and removing bearings from the wheel can be a knuckle-busting experience. There are several tricks for getting bearings into (or out of) wheels. A common technique is to push the bearing into the wheel with your thumb to get it started and then slide the wheel and bearing over the trucks' axle with the bearing closest to the hanger. If the bearing is seated evenly, you can press firmly down onto the wheel, and the bearing should slide the rest of the way into the wheel. When it's completely inserted, take the wheel off and do the other side. Some skate tools will have a small cylindrical protrusion for prying bearings out of wheels, but the end of the axle works too.

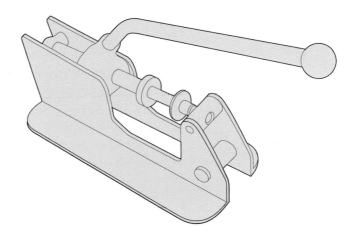

Better skate shops will have a bearing press for quickly putting pesky bearings into wheels. It is often worth it to have the clerk put new bearings into new wheels right in the shop. Your wheels will be ready to go, and you won't have to bust your knuckles monkeying with them.

A few skaters use a small plastic or rubbery pad between the baseplate and the deck. These are called risers. They help absorb shock and lengthen the life of the deck by protecting the wood from sharp impacts transferred through the wheels and trucks. Risers, as the name implies, also introduce more space between the wheels and the underside of the deck so that the trucks can be adjusted loosely without the wheels hitting the underside of the board (called wheelbite). The risers create a little more space between the wheel and the board to prevent this from happening. Risers also raise your center of gravity and can make flip tricks more difficult to land.

BUILDING A BOARD

We recommend that you get your first board from a reputable skate shop and have the staff assemble it for you. They have the tools and can quickly put it together without issue. But eventually you will need to replace something, and you will need to know how to do it.

The steps for building a board from the separate parts require a few simple tools. We will call out the tools needed within each step.

Grip-Tape the Board

To grip-tape your board, you will need

- grip tape;
- a board;
- a utility knife or single-edge razor blade or large, fine file; and
- an old pair of scissors (optional).

The tops of new decks are not covered in grip tape. (Complete decks are already gripped.) To grip your board, you will need a new board (or an older board with all the previous grip tape completely removed) and new grip tape. Grip tape is basically just a giant sandpaper sticker. It comes in big rectangular sheets and in rolls. When you buy your grip tape, it should be larger than the board you need to grip. Most precut grip tape sheets are large enough for a standard skateboard. If you are grip-taping a longboard, you may want to use a roll of grip tape so you can cover the board with one continuous piece. You don't need to use a single piece, though. Many people get very creative with their grip tape and cut different colors into patterns and pictures.

Gripping a board is complicated and time consuming if you don't have a lot of practice. This is why most people, when they buy a new board, have the skate shop staff grip the board right there. When it's done in a skate shop, it takes only a minute or two, while doing it at home can take quite a while and is easy to screw up.

With your board on a solid, stable surface, lay the grip tape sheet over the top to ensure it completely covers the board. The grip tape is a sticker, so you should be able to pull a bit of the backing sheet away to see the sticky underside of the tape. Gently pull away one end of the backing sheet until about 2 or 3 inches (5 to 7.5 cm) are revealed. Gently stick this part to the end of your board's top—nose or tail; it doesn't matter—so that the rest of the tape is aligned to the other end of the board. Reach under the sheet, and slowly pull on the backing sheet to reveal the sticky part of the tape with one hand while you tack the middle of the grip tape to the center of the board as you go.

Periodically smooth the tape out softly with the palm of your hand. You don't want to press too firmly in case you get a fold or a large bubble that needs to be pushed out. Eventually you will near the end of the tape. Smooth the entire gripped surface with your hand while doing your best to keep the tape flat and without folds or bubbles. It's likely that the first time you try this it will turn out poorly. That's okay. Practice makes perfect.

You should have a deck with a big square piece of grip tape covering the top. Using old scissors (do *not* use your good household scissors), roughly trim off the larger flaps of grip tape hanging off the ends and throw them away.

To make the ends of the grip tape flush with the sides of the board, use the file or razor to cut the tape. Using a file gives you a cleaner edge and is easier. Simply scrape the file along the edge of the board in a long, sweeping motion. Start with little pressure until you begin to see how much is enough to cut through the grip tape without filing into the edge of the board. As you make your way around the board you should be able to pull away the excess grip tape with your hand.

You can cut the grip tape with a razor by using the edge of the board as a guide. Be sure to cut against an appropriate surface. If you choose to hold the board while you do this, be sure to cut away from yourself. The razor will generally produce less attractive results than the file.

With the board fully gripped, stand all over it to press the tape firmly to the board and push out any bubbles that may have formed.

Using the tip of the razor, utility knife, or file, puncture the grip tape where the holes are to make inserting the trucks bolts easier. (It may help to gently push a sharp object up from the bottom of the board so you can easily tell where the bolt holes are.)

If the steps for gripping a board seem confusing, you can watch someone do it at a skate shop, and it will make sense.

Mount the Trucks

To mount the trucks you will need

- a skate tool,
- a Phillips screwdriver (or cordless drill with a Phillips bit),
- a set of trucks, and
- eight baseplate bolts and lock nuts.

Mounting the trucks onto the board is easy but time consuming. The job goes more quickly with a cordless drill.

Push a bolt through the hole in the board from the top of the deck down. It doesn't matter where you start. It may be difficult to get the bolt through the grip tape, but a light tap with the handle of the screwdriver is usually enough to get it started. Repeat for the other three bolts in the cluster. When you're done with this step, you should have four bolts sticking out through the bottom of the deck. It doesn't matter that the bolt heads are not flush with the grip tape. They will become flush later when you tighten them down.

It doesn't matter which of the two trucks you use, but it does matter what direction the trucks are facing. The kingpin and bushings should be facing the middle of the board, and the hanger should be facing out to the tail or nose. Slide the trucks onto the four bolts.

Thread the nuts onto the bolts with your fingers. Use the screwdriver and skate tool to tighten them the rest of the way. They should be tight enough that everything feels firm and doesn't wiggle but not so tight that the head of the bolt is below the surface of the grip tape.

Repeat for the other trucks, remembering to align it so that the kingpin and bushings are pointing into the center of the board. The trucks should be pointing in opposite directions, with the hangers closest to the tail and nose.

Insert the Bearings and Add the Wheels

To insert the bearings and put on the wheels, you will need

- eight bearings,
- four wheels, and
- eight spacer washers (optional).

Before you can put your wheels on the trucks, you will need to put the bearings into the wheels. It's usually difficult to put bearings into new wheels. The best way is to use a bearing press—a specialized tool specifically for inserting (and removing) bearings from wheels. Any good skate shop will have a bearing press and should be happy to help you out. There are some tricks for doing it yourself that will make it much easier.

Two bearings go in each wheel, one on either side. They will slide directly into the space made for them, but it will be a tight fit. You probably won't be able to push them into place with just your fingers.

Grab a wheel and one of the bearings, and try to push the bearing a little ways into the wheel. If the bearing has one metal side and one plastic side (a dust guard), you should have the plastic side facing outward and the metal side on the inside when you insert it. Some bearings have metal on both sides, so either way is fine. Keep the bearing even; you don't want it at an angle. Now slide the bearing and wheel over the axle of the trucks with the bearing closest to the hanger. By applying even pressure to the wheel, the hanger will push the bearing into its seat. You will know it when it's nested. You only need to get the bearing most of the way into the wheel. Now remove the wheel, and insert a bearing into the other side using the same process.

When you have both the bearings in the wheel, you can slide the whole ensemble onto the axle. On most wheels it doesn't matter which side faces out. If you like the printed graphics, you can have that side facing out. If you prefer a simpler look, you can have the graphic side of the wheel facing inward.

It's a good idea to put a washer as a spacer between the hanger and the inner bearing and another one between the outer bearing and the axle nut.

Screw the axle nut onto the axle as far as you can with your fingers, and then tighten it the rest of the way with the skate tool. If you were not able to get the bearings completely seated, you can screw the nut down tight and it should press the bearings fully into their place. Shops and performance-minded skaters don't recommend this method because it can be hard on the bearings, but many people do it without any noticeable issues.

When the nut is firmly tightened, back it off about half a rotation. The wheel should have just a little bit of jiggle along the axle . . . just enough that you easily feel and maybe even hear it. Naturally the wheel should spin freely.

Repeat this process for the remaining six bearings and three wheels.

You have just assembled your board!

TUNING YOUR BOARD

Whether your first board is new or used, you will eventually need to tune it. Skateboards are simple, and it's not difficult or time consuming to do a quick inspection to see if anything needs a quick adjustment.

Spin the wheels. They should spin easily, smoothly, and quietly. If a wheel stops spinning quickly, loosen the nut a little until you can move the wheel a tiny bit along the axle. If it still doesn't spin smoothly, the bearings may be dirty or old. Although you can soak the bearings in denatured alcohol and relube them, it's generally easier to buy new ones.

The board should turn when you lean on the sides. You can experiment with turning responsiveness by loosening or tightening the kingpin bolt on the trucks. You can even have your front looser than your back or vice versa.

On used trucks, you may find the kingpin so chewed up that adjusting the trucks is impossible. This is common on boards that have been ridden hard. There's not a lot to do about this except get a new kingpin or ride it the way it is. Bring your board into the skate shop, and if it's not busy, a clerk will often help you put the new pins in. (If you didn't buy your trucks or kingpin there, don't expect a whole lot of assistance.)

Kingpins break from time to time, so it's good to know how to replace them. Unfortunately it requires the trucks to be completely removed from the deck. On most types of trucks, the kingpin slides out from beneath the baseplate. The kingpin will usually be jammed and difficult to get out. A knock on the ground or tap with a hammer will sometimes pop the kingpin loose, but usually you will have to work at it for a while. Once it's out you can slide the new kingpin through. Make sure the kingpin's head is completely nested into the baseplate, and then reassemble the trucks. You may need a kingpin specific to your type of trucks since not all kingpins are universal. When the kingpin breaks flush with the baseplate, you can use an old screwdriver and hammer to pound it out. Watch your fingers and be smart.

Check the baseplate bolts and nuts to make sure the trucks don't wiggle. There should be four bolts on each trucks, although many people ride with three when one breaks and eventually replace the missing one when they can.

The deck itself should not have any visible cracks, and the nose and tail should not be ground down. When the tail is ground to a sharp edge, it's sometimes called "razor tail." Older decks can be ridden around the neighborhood, but you will find tricks very difficult to learn, and skateboarding probably won't be very rewarding. A fresh, new deck is much easier to ollie, turn, and stay on. When you're serious about learning skateboarding tricks, get yourself a board that is in good condition.

Set the board down and stand on it. Rock back and forth from your toes to your heels. The board should lean with your feet without the wheels lifting up until you really put a lot of weight on the side. New boards may creak when you do this. That's just the bushings rubbing against the trucks. Move your feet toward the middle of the board and bounce lightly. The board should feel stiff and strong.

STINK BAG

It is handy to have a gear bag to keep your pads, tools, and spare parts in. If something goes wrong with your board while you are out at a skatepark, you can make quick repairs and get back to skating within a few minutes. Even if your board works perfectly, there seems to always be someone asking if anyone has a skate tool. Here is a list of items you may find handy:

- Skate tool or socket set and Phillips screwdriver
- Spare trucks nuts and bolts (several lengths)
- Spare bearings
- Bearing lube and rag
- Extra kingpin and nut
- Pads
- Helmet
- Wax or spray lacquer
- Shoelaces
- Squeegee (for puddles)
- Small broom and dustpan (for glass and debris)
- First aid kit

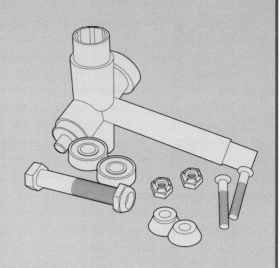

WHERE TO SHOP

There are three places to buy skateboards, but only one will deliver the best kind of experience and product for your needs. The best place to get a skateboard is at a dedicated skate shop.

When buying a new skateboard, you can either get a complete board that is ready to use right away (called a *complete*), or you can pick out the individual parts—deck, trucks, bearings, and wheels—and have the skate shop employee put it together for you (or assemble it yourself). The price will tend to be slightly higher when you choose the pieces yourself because shops tend to use inexpensive parts on the completes.

The big variety stores that sell clothes, bikes, soccer balls, and camping gear are not skate shops. You will see a few different kinds of skateboards (only completes) near the bikes and other sports gear. These might even be enclosed with some packaging and have an extra set of wheels or a set of pads. These are almost always terrible boards that use the poorest components. The boards are not designed for the kind of skateboarding you will read about in this book, and we do not recommend that anyone wanting to learn trick skating get one of these.

If you have never bought a new skateboard, it may be tempting to get the cheapest one you can find until you're sure you like it. (Well-meaning relatives are notorious for making this kind of purchase around Christmas.) It's fair to say that any new complete board for less than $50 is going to result in a lousy skateboarding experience. Rather than helping you learn to skate, these boards will impede your skills, and you will struggle while trying to learn rudimentary skills. These boards are mass produced, with little understanding of how they're used or what functions are most important to you, the skater. You can expect to pay between $60 and $100 for a serviceable beginner board. A high-quality complete will usually be about $130 or so. Unlike those cheaper boards, a decent beginner board is fully compatible with better components, so you can easily upgrade individual parts as they wear out or you decide you're ready to change things up.

The store in the mall that sells skate clothes and shoes and has a few decks in the back is *almost* a true skate shop. You should be able to find a serviceable board that meets your needs. These types of places probably won't have a workbench or the tools for tuning your board. Staff members there are often untrained on the differences in the stock and will either sell you what they like to ride or make an uninformed guess.

The best skate shops will have experienced skateboarders working in them. They should be happy to tell you about the different types of boards and help you pick out the one that will best suit your needs. At these shops you should find a wide selection of boards, trucks, wheels, and other accessories. The staff should also know where the good places to skate are and what might be going on around town for skate-related events. Some of these shops even have small indoor skateparks attached to them. It's worthwhile to seek out your area's better skate shops.

There are all kinds of boards to choose from. At the high end, there are performance components made of exotic materials. You can find boards made with high-strength polymers, carbon-fiber laminates, and other performance-enhancing materials. Decorative board materials, such as bamboo and mahogany, are often used in longboards since they don't get the same kind of abuse that a street board might. In some skate shops you can find collectible boards that aren't made of any special materials but have limited-edition graphics. Although these collectible boards can be used for skating, they tend to be slightly more expensive, and so most people buy them to hang on the wall.

Answers to the quiz on page 16: 1. f, 2. d, 3. b, 4. a, 5. e, 6. g, 7. c

CHAPTER 3

BALANCE
AND CONTROL

At the heart of skateboarding ability is balance. Missed tricks and falls are the result of losing your balance. Being born with good balance will help you progress as a skater. However, balance can be learned and improved with practice.

Balance is maintained by adjusting your center of gravity. Center of gravity is a term used to describe the place where the bulk of a person's or object's weight is concentrated.

When an object is at rest—be it a chair, alarm clock, or Labrador retriever—its center of gravity is spread across the width of its connection to the ground. This is why you have better balance when you stand with your feet apart than with your feet together. Think about a bowling ball: Its connection to the ground is a very small point, and so it's very easy to move the ball with a light touch even though it is heavy. It takes very little force to push the ball's center of gravity beyond its base. However, if you could find an object of identical mass and weight that was square, it wouldn't move with the same amount of pressure because its base is much wider—making it far more difficult to move its center of gravity beyond its base.

If you think about this principle in relation to skateboarding, it makes perfect sense. Any time the board contacts something that offers resistance or has changes in its pitch (such as a bank or a slope), your body needs to adjust. Hitting a rock, for example, can stop the board, but your body will continue moving forward. With a wide stance you have a better chance of adjusting in time and regaining your balance.

Center of gravity is also affected by its distance to the ground. When you're standing still, your center of gravity is right around your belly button. Bending your legs lowers your center of gravity and makes you more stable, whereas standing tall raises your center of gravity and makes you less stable.

When you are standing on a skateboard the same principles apply; standing tall with your feet together makes you unstable, while bending your knees with your feet apart improves your stability. When you are stable you can maintain control.

To see the benefits of a wide, low stance for yourself, stand with your feet touching each other and your knees locked, and swivel your hips as if you were using a Hula-Hoop. If you go crazy swiveling your hips, you may feel yourself losing your balance. Now try again with your feet about a foot apart and your knees bent. It is virtually impossible to throw yourself off balance with this stance. Keeping your center of gravity low and your stance wide is fundamental to good skateboarding.

You will find myriad balancing toys, mock skateboards, and devices that promise to improve your skating. The best way to improve your skateboarding balance is simply by riding a skateboard. This will prepare you for the small things that happen while skating and strengthen the muscle groups that skating requires.

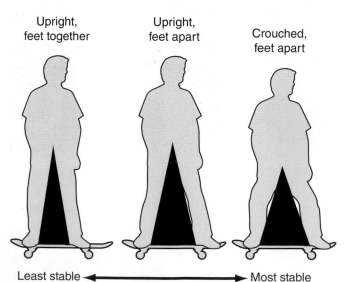

Upright, feet together

Upright, feet apart

Crouched, feet apart

Least stable ◀————————▶ Most stable

SKATEBOARDING TERMS

Loads of confusing terms are ingrained in today's skateboarding terminology. It's not important to know the lingo in order to skate, but it's helpful when you want to talk fluently about skating with other skaters. While talking about the tricks in this book, we've tried to use the same terms you would hear at a skatepark. We've also defined the terms and concepts that come up throughout the book here to make it easy to follow the trick instructions.

Nose and Tail

Nose will always refer to the front end of the board when it's rolling forward. When the board is rolling backward, the nose will be where the tail usually is, and the tail will be at the front of the board.

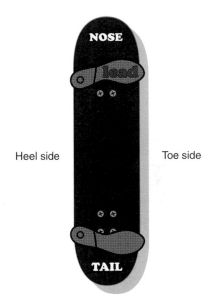

Heel side · Toe side

Toe Side and Heel Side

Toe side refers to the side of the board that your toes hang over. For regular-footers the toe side would be the right side of the board. Heel side would naturally be the side of the board closest to your heels. These terms aren't widely used in skateboarding, but they are helpful when describing how to do some tricks.

Regular and Goofy

Some people are right-handed, and other people are left-handed. In skateboarding, some people are right-footed (goofy), and others are left-footed (regular). Goofy-footers ride with the right foot forward, while regular-footers ride with the left foot forward.

In this book's instructions and diagrams, we use the regular stance since most skaters are regular, and including information and diagrams for both stances for every trick would be confusing and unnecessary. If you are goofy-footed (like one of this book's authors), you have our sympathy; you will need to flip the instructions and diagrams in your mind as you read. Like left-handers, goofy-footers are generally used to flipping things around!

Regular

Goofy

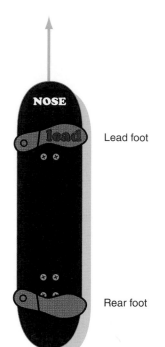

Lead foot

Rear foot

Lead Foot and Rear Foot

Your lead foot is the foot you normally have forward when you're just skating around. Many tricks will have you standing on your board backward, which will put your lead foot on the tail, or have your rear foot at the front of the board. When you see *lead* on the stance diagrams or in the text, think of it as your strong foot. When rolling forward normally, if you stand regularly, your lead foot is your left.

Backside and Back Side, Frontside and Front Side

Backside, one word, refers to a rotation of the board, skater, or both during a turn to the right (if leading with the left foot) or left (if leading with the right foot). Frontside refers to a rotation of the board in the opposite direction. For example, "Scoop the tail with your rear foot so the board spins laterally frontside" would mean you would scoop the tail away from you so the board rotates out in front of you.

Back side, two words, refers to a direction relative to the skater's current position. For example, "The board should be rotating so that the nose comes up under your foot from your back side." This would mean that the board is approaching your foot from *your* back . . . not that the board is necessarily rotating in a backside (one word) direction.

Backside is a direction your body or skateboard might go. *Back side* refers to your back. Make sense?

The same rule applies to the terms *frontside* and *front side*. Frontside describes the orientation of the skater in relation to the object being skated. Front side refers to the skater's front.

If you find this confusing right now, don't worry about it. As you read the trick descriptions later in this book and refer to the figures provided along the way, the distinction will become clear over time.

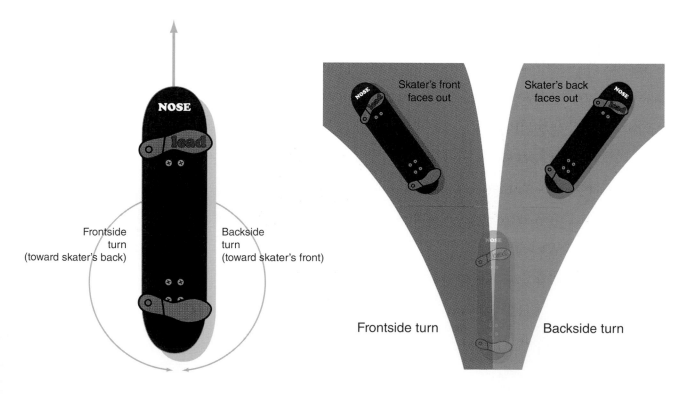

Frontside turn (toward skater's back)

Backside turn (toward skater's front)

Skater's front faces out

Skater's back faces out

Frontside turn

Backside turn

Scoop, Flick, and Sweep

In the ollie and shuvit tricks, you will be spinning the board using only your feet. There are lots of subtle motions involved, and so we've relied on a few terms to help describe these motions.

A **scoop** is when you use your foot to lift the board. This is done by scraping your shoe or the side of your shoe against the grip tape. When you scoop the board, you are trying to drag the board upward with your foot while exerting as little pressure against it as possible. A proper scoop is smooth and gentle and is part of doing an ollie.

A **flick** is a motion where you spin the board by flicking your foot in a certain way. Usually a flick is done with the outside of your foot or near your little toe, but some tricks require a flick from your heel. You will need to flick the board when doing a kickflip.

A **sweep** is a movement where you push the board to get it to rotate. Unlike in a scoop, you don't rely on the friction of the grip tape but actually push against the skateboard. A sweep is used in tricks such as the impossible.

Axis and Lateral Rotation

Throughout this book we refer to two types of board rotations. When the board rotates along its axis, it means the board spins along its longest dimension like a corkscrew. When a board is halfway through an axis rotation, the nose will be pointed forward but the board will be upside down. A lateral rotation is when the tail end of the board spins around toward the front—and the nose toward the back—like a Frisbee. During a lateral rotation the board is never upside down. Some complex tricks require the board to rotate both along its axis and laterally.

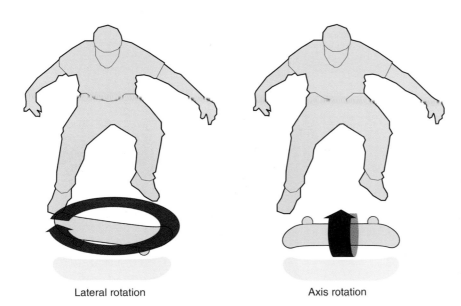

Lateral rotation   Axis rotation

Clockwise and Counterclockwise

When we use specific directional terms, we will remind you that the direction refers only to those who skate with the left foot forward (regular). Goofy-footers will need to reverse the direction. For example, when the instructions say, "The board should rotate laterally in a clockwise direction (regular)," if you are goofy, then you will need to replace *clockwise* with *counterclockwise*.

STANCE

A stance refers to the position of your feet on the deck. For basic pushing around on flat, there are two stances: pushing and standing. Most tricks, and particularly flip tricks, require very precise stances. The stance for each trick will be covered with that trick.

Before you explore different stances and how they affect board control, you will need to know which foot your body favors. Your favored foot will be positioned near the nose of the board and will be your lead foot. Your other foot will be on the tail and be your rear foot. If you already have some skateboarding experience, you probably know which of your feet feels right in front.

If your left foot feels more comfortable being the lead foot, you have a regular stance. If your right foot belongs in front, you skate goofy-footed. Neither stance is right or wrong, although regular stance is more common. Nobody will make fun of you for being "goofy."

Regular and goofy stance will change how different obstacles work for different skaters. A regular skater may have an easy time getting onto a particular ledge because she is facing it as she approaches. From the same starting point, a goofy-footed skater might struggle with it. At a different ledge it may be easier for the goofy-footed skater and difficult for the regular skater, so it all works out in the end.

When you are just starting out, pay attention to where your feet naturally like to be on the board. Many beginners stand on the skateboard with about one foot length between their feet and the lead foot pointed toward the nose of the board. This is an awful stance. Instead, put your rear foot squarely on the tail and your lead foot—whichever one is most comfortable being in front—over the front baseplate bolts. Now turn your lead foot so it's pointing almost completely sideways to the length of the board. This is a stable stance that you should be in whenever you aren't pushing or setting up for a trick.

Stance: poor form

Stance: good form

SWITCH

When you are skating backward, your lead foot is behind your rear foot. This is important to remember when tricks require you to start off backward. For old-school skaters, this is often known as fakie. For new-school skaters, it's called switch.

Some people argue that fakie is reserved for when the board and the rider are backward, while switch is when the rider is standing backward on a forward-traveling board. This presumes that the board's front and tail are critically different. On most boards this is not true, although usually a board will feel strange when it's going backward.

For the purposes of discussing tricks, you should just presume that switch is basically riding backward.

Normal   Switch

PUSHING

Pushing requires a major stance change that can be awkward for beginning skaters. The lead foot rotates on the board, while the rear foot comes off to push against the ground. This introduces a lot of changes to the skater's center of gravity. It's no longer over the board but rather split between the two legs.

The proper technique is to keep as much weight on the lead foot as possible. When the weight is split between the legs, pushing will look and feel uncoordinated. The body will "bounce" between the legs. Only as much weight as necessary to push the board forward should be put on the rear foot; the pushing foot shouldn't be holding up the skater at all. The proper appearance is a smooth, long push.

Push:
good form

Push:
poor form
(too wide)

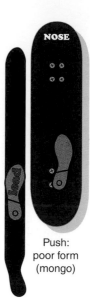

Push:
poor form
(mongo)

Good pushing technique basically balances the skater on the lead foot. This can be difficult and a bit frightening for beginners because it puts a skater's weight in a position that makes it difficult to steer the board or react to something going wrong. When you're pushing well, your rear foot should start ahead of you and the board, and the push should end with the rear leg fully extended out behind the board.

Some people push with the lead foot while keeping the rear foot on the board. This is commonly known as pushing mongo. There are a few famous skaters who push mongo, although most of them are skilled enough to push using either foot; they are just more comfortable with mongo. Because it takes more time to set your feet up for a trick after pushing mongo than pushing regular, it's best to learn to push regular if you can.

BRAKING AND SLOWING

Knowing how to get the skateboard moving forward is important, but knowing how to stop is critical. There are many ways to slow your skateboard. The best way depends largely on where you're skating, how fast you are going, and what your options are. The more ways you can skillfully slow or stop the board, the better equipped you will be in a variety of situations. It's good to practice all these methods.

Bail

The most common and easiest way to stop is to simply jump or step off the board. This is a reasonable option when you're going slowly, but whenever you're moving faster than you can run, bailing isn't going to be pretty. Braking at higher speeds will require some more advanced techniques.

Drag Foot

Most people brake by dragging the rear foot on the ground next to the board. This technique requires some strength and balance to perform, so practice is essential. You will basically be skating on one foot while you're braking with the other, so it may feel a bit awkward at first.

This technique could save your life, so it's worth learning.

While braking with the drag foot method, the sole of the foot is flat on the ground; you won't be dragging just your toe or heel. The foot should be placed as close to the side of the board as possible without getting in front of the rear wheel. To start, lightly scrape the sole of your shoe against the ground. The friction will tug at your foot. If it tugs too hard or kicks your foot out, you're putting too much weight on the foot too quickly. If your technique is correct, your foot should scrape the ground alongside the board. Gradually increase the weight on your rear foot until you can feel the friction transferring through your body. Remember, you're trying to stop your body mass, not the board.

Speed Check

One problem with dragging your foot to slow down is that it requires full commitment. It's the only thing your body can be doing, and it takes some drastic foot adjustments. When needing to lose only a little bit of speed, some people like to kick the tail out just a little. The friction can help lose that tiny bit of extra speed.

When you speed check your feet don't move from your ordinary riding position. You'll want to make sure your lead foot is at least over your front bolts or in the pocket of the nose. The rear foot should be on the low end of the tail. This technique is easier to learn if you are moving at a pretty good clip but not so fast that you feel uncomfortable or can't easily bail.

This isn't an easy technique. It will take practice, and you should be very comfortable bailing and braking by dragging your foot.

1. Look at the ground ahead and bend your knees slightly.
2. Ease onto your heels, with 70 percent of your weight on your lead foot. The board should start turning frontside.
3. As the board turns, extend your rear leg and kick the tail away from you. You are trying to slide the back wheels a few degrees.
4. Immediately after the wheels slide, let the wheels get traction and bring the board back under your center of gravity by steering the board backside so it is aligned with your body momentum. You might bring the front wheels off the ground a little to align the board more quickly.

Drifter

Sometimes called power slides, drifters are long four-wheel slides. They are great for losing a lot of speed. Similar to the speed check, you shouldn't need to adjust your feet from your ordinary riding stance. The drifter is executed by throwing your body mass to the side of the board as you turn it sideways with your feet, so you'll need considerable speed to pull this off correctly.

You should be going fast but not faster than you can easily bail out from. Drifters work better with hard wheels because they have less traction. The softer your wheels, the faster you'll need to go to pull off a good drifter.

Warning: This trick wears wheels out and can lead to flat spots. If you do a lot of drifters, you'll be gradually making your wheels smaller and smaller.

1. Look at the ground ahead and bend your knees.
2. Ease onto your heels with both feet so that you begin to turn frontside. You will want a little more weight on your lead foot.
3. As the board turns, push the board away from you hard enough so that you break the traction of the wheels. How hard to push depends on your speed, the wheels, and the surface of the ground.
4. Lean back and let the board slide sideways. The board may shoot out in front of you if you push away too hard. The board may not slide if you aren't able to break the wheel's grip, and you'll go over the board toe-side.
5. As the board slows, your body should start centering back over the board. When the board starts getting underneath you again, raise or slide the nose until the board is pointed in the direction of travel.

A B C D

180 drifter variation: Instead of bringing the nose back to the front, slide the tail around until you're going backward. Although this doesn't have a name, it's a stylish trick and a great way to control your speed on hills.

Backside drifter variation: When you're feeling bold, try a backside drifter by kicking your tail out behind you so that you slide backward. This is much more difficult because it's hard to moderate your slide by bending your legs.

WHEN YOU DO FALL

Everyone falls, and the more you push yourself to learn new tricks, the more often you will fall. Falling doesn't mean you don't skate well; it means you are challenging yourself to learn new things.

When you start falling, your natural instinct will be to throw your hands out to protect yourself. If you are moving slowly and aren't very high off the ground, this is probably fine. In most situations, though, you won't want to land on your hands. Catching your falls with your hands can easily lead to broken wrists.

Skateboarders fall a lot. If you watch experienced skaters, you will see that their falls look almost theatrical and dramatic. It's not that they're trying to make a big show of it; it's just that falling in such a way as to prevent serious injury often looks kind of elaborate.

It's a shame that you often can't see a fall coming until the split second before it happens. If you could, it would be easy to brace yourself. The reality is that you will usually fall when you're not paying attention . . . and this is when you are most likely to fall incorrectly. If you practice falling well even on small spills, you will develop good habits that will be even more useful when you need to rely on instinct.

The best way to fall is in a way that won't hurt, make you bleed, or break anything. This typically involves tumbling or rolling. Think about standing up right now, taking two swift steps, and launching yourself sideways into the air. How would you land? Maybe you would land on your hands and knees. This is what a hard fall on a skateboard might feel like.

Gymnasts are professional fallers. They can run across a mat, jump high into the air, and roll out of it. This is an intentional fall. Good news: You won't need a one-piece leotard to practice this kind of tumbling; you can do it while you skate. A great place to practice is anywhere concrete meets grass. Push once or twice toward the grass. When you hit it, the board will slow or stop. Let yourself fall forward and tuck your lead shoulder downward as if you were doing a somersault. This is a motion you will want to practice until it's instinctual. (You won't have time to remember how to do it when you're in a real fall.)

As you spend more time skating and falling, you will learn to cushion your forward falls with your forearm and shoulder. It's great to get in the habit of rolling through your falls early.

Falling backward is the riskiest type of fall because your head can snap back and hit the ground. This is how the most serious skateboarding injuries occur. Injuries caused by falling backward can kill you, leave you permanently brain damaged or paralyzed, or do any number of things that will seriously change your life. The best way to prevent riding in an ambulance is to wear a helmet. Most experienced skaters have personally witnessed situations where a helmet saved someone's life. Unfortunately there's little else you can do to prevent cracking your head on the ground when you fall backward. If you have any control in the matter, try to land on your rump.

PART II

Techniques and Tricks

Tricks are the very heart of skateboarding. The tricks you learn, and the style in which you do them, will define you as a skater. You might want to learn lots of tricks or specialize in a particular type of trick. Perhaps you want to be known for going big, or maybe highly technical tricks are more to your liking. Some skaters gravitate toward tricks that introduce some new innovation or creative element. No approach is better or worse than any other; it's all skateboarding! This section offers information and tips on all sorts of tricks. Work on the ones you find most interesting.

BASIC MANEUVERS

No journey, short or long, starts midway. It doesn't matter if you're taking a walk around the block, writing a term paper, or receiving a lifetime achievement award for piano mastery. In skateboarding, like most other things, there are no real shortcuts. But there are tips and tricks for learning a technique more quickly and for developing habits that will ultimately produce a cleaner, more flexible style, and we offer lots of them in this book.

If you're interested in skateboarding, and we know you are because you're already on chapter 4, then you probably have spent a little time on a board already. You began your skateboard odyssey the first time you saw someone skating and thought to yourself, *Hey, that looks fun!*

A lot of skaters want to skip all the boring basic stuff and jump right into kickflips. If that describes you, take a deep breath and think about where that skill comes from for a minute. Nobody is born a skateboarder. Every neighborhood ripper, every kid at school who seems to be better than everyone else, and every pro mastered the basics first. If standing on a skateboard and scooting up and down the block isn't fun for you, kickflips probably won't be fun either. (Sure, they may *look* fun, but it takes a lot of falls and painful landings to get them mastered.)

Building basic skills is just as much skateboarding as doing a backside heelflip over a seven stair. Any professional skateboarder will be much more stoked seeing you doing tic tacs with a smile on your face than watching you trying kickflips and getting angry. Do your best to enjoy building these basic skills because all of them can be turned into epic, mind-bending tricks later.

One hazard to keep in mind as you build a foundation of solid skills is becoming distracted by what people think of your skating. If skateboarding were a contest, the winner would be the person who enjoys it the most. If you are at the skatepark, and the kids who have a deeper bag of tricks than you are making fun of your tic tacs, remember that we think you're the coolest person there for not letting it get to you and just skating in whatever way brings you the most happiness. Those who get their kicks from belittling others won't stay skateboarders for very long, but the person who can find joy in just carving around the block will be a skateboarder for life.

Enough with the philosophy. Let's talk about tricks.

KICKTURN

NOSE

STANCE

Skateboards don't come with steering wheels. You steer by changing your weight on the board until the wheels are pointed in the same direction as your body's momentum. When the board is pointed in a direction other than the one your body is traveling in, you need to align the two or you will fall off.

The easiest way to turn is to lean on the toe side or heel side of the board. This method works when you're moving, but leaning the board is very difficult when the board isn't moving or is moving very slowly. This is when a kickturn comes in handy.

The kickturn is a short, controlled wheelie. If you ride a skateboard for more than a week, you will master the kickturn so that it becomes second nature. You won't even think about what you're doing after a while—you'll just do it.

The first and easiest kickturn is backside. You'll be turning to your right (if you stand with your left foot in front) or to the left (if you're goofy-footed, with your right foot in front). Stand on your board with your lead foot covering your front bolts or slightly in front of them. Your rear foot should be in the middle of the tail. Start learning this without moving at first—you can even practice on carpet.

1. Bend your knees slightly to lower your center of gravity. Check your stance to make sure your toes are pointed out to the side of the board and not forward and that your feet are far apart on the deck.

2. Lean forward slightly, and distribute more weight on the board's tail. The front wheels will become lighter until they come up off the ground. Try to keep the board's nose under you by rapidly putting it back on the ground so you feel balanced again. In other words, lift the front wheels and quickly bring the front of the board under your body weight.

You may have noticed that you rolled forward. When you lead with your body mass, you create momentum. When the board is pointed in the same direction as your momentum, you roll. Because of this, the kickturn is a great way to pick up a little bit of speed when you don't have the space or time to push. If you watch skate videos, you will see people do this all the time. They're not just trying to squeeze kickturns in between all their big tricks; they're picking up speed and directing the board where they want it to go.

Practice a few going frontside (turning toward your back). If you want to learn more complicated tricks, being able to kickturn comfortably is absolutely essential.

Take your kickturns up a notch by going for larger turns. At first your kickturns will probably be about 30 degrees or so. Try to take them up to 45 degrees (a quarter of a full circle) or even a full 180.

TIC TAC

If your kickturns are comfortable, you can chain them together to pick up lots of speed. These are tic tacs. There is nothing complicated about it; just do a small backside kickturn while you're moving, quickly followed by a small frontside kickturn, and so on.

Tic tacs are a great way to pick up speed. You can find fun challenges around your neighborhood. For example, try to tic tac around the block without putting your foot down. Try to tic tac up a small hill.

The secret of tic tacs and kickturns is not where you would expect to discover it. The secret is in the shoulders. You'll want to push your body momentum in the direction you want the board to go by leading with your shoulders. This is very important to remember, especially when you are struggling to figure out a new trick. The first question to ask yourself is, *What are my shoulders doing?*

STANCE

UP THE CURB

This isn't really a trick, but it can help you get around the neighborhood until you have your ollies on lock. It will also help develop good nose control for nose manuals and nollies later. This is a good, fast way to get up a curb without taking your feet off the board.

1. Position your lead foot up on the nose of the board. As you approach the curb, lift up the front wheels so they go over the curb.

2. While still moving forward (try not to lock your back trucks against the curb), quickly transfer your weight onto your lead foot to raise the tail of the board up so the rear wheels clear the curb.

3. Roll away.

With practice, you should eventually be able to use this technique consistently and without concentration. It's not very stylish, but it will help you with general board control and will be useful later when you start doing more difficult tricks.

FAKIE AND SWITCH

Fakie is backward. Some people call this switch, but as we mentioned in chapter 3, there's a small distinction. Switch is when your body is backward. Fakie is when your body *and* your board are backward. Most boards are pretty much the same forward or backward, so it's not really an important distinction. Plus, who really cares if you did a trick with the board backward or forward?

For some people, the true distinction between fakie and switch is in the stance of the skater. Fakie is rolling backward with your feet positioned as if you were traveling in the opposite direction. In other words, your lead foot is on the nose, and your rear foot is over the rear trucks bolts. Switch is standing in a forward-moving stance, with your lead foot over the lead trucks bolts and your rear foot on the tail, except that your body is backward. A better way to describe it is that switch is when regular riders skate goofy and vice versa (the feet are switched).

Riding switch is hard. Even experienced skaters can look like total noobs when they try to push around a skatepark switch. All the skills your body has will abandon you when you try to do them with the opposite leg.

Switch is a handy skill to have, particularly if you want to learn advanced tricks. One great thing about being comfortable in switch stance is that you can essentially double all your tricks. You will have the regular version of the trick and the switch version too!

The first (and maybe most difficult) switch skill is the simple push. If you are regular-footed (left foot leading), you'll start off with your right foot on the front bolts. You'll push with your left foot a few times and then bring the foot up onto the tail. This is guaranteed to feel weird, but it will build your skateboarding skills quickly. It's powerful medicine.

After a few minutes of kicking around switch, try some switch tic tacs or switch manuals.

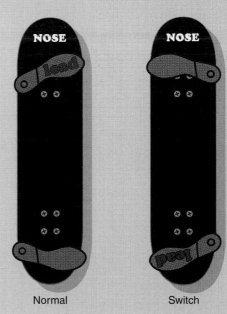

Normal   Switch

MANUAL

Manuals are easy to do and difficult to master. Solid manuals are a reflection of your balance and comfort on a skateboard.

There are lots of different types of manuals, but the place to start is with a classic wheelie. It will help to learn this trick on smooth ground without cracks such as a tennis court or a garage. It is easier to do these with a little speed, so kick once or twice to get going.

1. Stand normally on your board, with your lead foot angled slightly forward and just in front of the bolts. Raise your arms off your sides a little to help with balance.

2. Look at the ground ahead, and find a spot where you want to start your manual. When you get to that spot, press on the tail and shift your center of gravity toward your rear leg. It may help to bend your knees just a bit to lower your center of gravity.

3. Try to maintain the manual by adjusting the board forward and backward so that the rear wheels stay under your center of gravity. Keep looking at the ground just ahead of the board.

4. Your manual will be done as soon as your tail touches or the front wheels come down. Kick once and try it again.

STANCE

You can improve your manuals by using little landmarks to measure your progress. For some reason many people find it easier to manual longer distances if they are aiming for a target. When you can manual for 5 feet (1.5 m) or farther, try manuals along a broad arc instead of a straight line.

When you are ready to add style to your manuals, try moving your lead foot in so it's in the middle of the board.

Manual variations. There are lots of different manuals, and they are all cool. Manuals are the ultimate trick in terms of flexibility. They not only are excellent on their own, but they also add style to almost any other trick. When you are ready to take your manual to the next level, you can start with these fun variations:

Feet together
manual stance

Old-school
manual stance

One-footed
manual stance

SPACEWALK

The spacewalk combines a manual with a tic tac. Your manuals should consistently be 5 feet (1.5 m) or longer, or you may struggle with this trick.

There are two styles of spacewalk. One relies on rapid back-and-forth wiggles of the nose of the board while you are in a manual with the board traveling in a forward path. The other requires deep back-and-forth S-turns with the rear wheels while you are in a manual. The refined version of the spacewalk is the latter—deep and smooth. Don't forget to consider what your shoulders are doing if you are struggling. They should be pointing where you want to go, not where you are.

Spacewalk is a great skill-building trick that will help you control your manuals.

You should start learning the easier version of the spacewalk. Later you can improve your technique until it resembles the real version.

1. Push once so that you're moving slowly, and position your feet in your most comfortable manual position. Raise the front wheels off the ground slowly, with your knees slightly bent as if you were doing a standard manual.

2. Use your lead foot to point the nose of the board out to your frontside and then quickly back to center. Practice doing this until you can do it without losing the manual.

3. Immediately following the frontside manual, push the nose of the board to your backside and then back to center. This whole sequence is fast, and you should be able to do it within the space of 3 or 4 feet (about 1 m).

4. String the frontside and backside manuals together so that your board moves in a serpentine fashion, like a snake. Try as many back-and-forth motions as you can before you lose the manual.

If you do a hundred or so of these, they should start feeling pretty fun. Try slowing down the back-and-forth sweeps so that the board actually swerves through each turn. Eventually the turns should be slow and deep so that it feels as if you're going through a slalom course while doing a wheelie.

Spacewalks are super fun and worth practicing. A good spacewalk will usually be good for a laugh at the skatepark.

NOSE MANUAL

The nose manual is a staple trick for all experienced street skaters. In the nose manual, as you might expect, you do a wheelie on the front wheels instead of the back. It helps a lot to have your ordinary manuals down so that you understand the kind of body motion it takes to roll along on two wheels. The nose manual isn't much different once you get the hang of it.

The biggest challenge with nose manuals is that the weight of the board is behind your center of gravity. This makes it more difficult to use the board to "push" through little bumps and imperfections in your balance. As with ordinary manuals, the board sort of acts like a ballast or counterweight for your balance. When it's behind you, it becomes more difficult to make small, quick adjustments.

1. Start by rolling slowly on a smooth surface. Your lead foot should be squarely on the nose, and your rear foot should be near the tail or rear trucks bolts.

2. Keep your knees slightly bent, raise your elbows up and away from your sides, and press down on the nose so that the tail rises up. Try to bring the tail high enough so you feel your center of gravity over the front wheels. At first you will certainly go too far, and the board will dip all the way over. That's okay; it's how you learn where that perfect balance is.

3. When you feel as if you can bring the board up just to the tipping point, try to hold that position for longer and longer distances. Use your arms and hips to maintain your balance and pull the nose manual out to greater distances.

STANCE

If you are getting frustrated by continuing to tip forward and fall off, try experimenting with frontside 180 kickturns off the nose. (Pivot off your nose while bringing the back end around in the direction your toes are pointing.) Try to do these slower and longer so that the 180 turns are more like long arcs. You'll find that you are doing a nose manual while you turn.

WHAT DO THE NUMBERS MEAN?

A 360 is a full rotation because there are 360 degrees in a full circle.

90: Quarter turn
180: Halfway
360: Full rotation
540: One-and-a-half rotations
720: Two full rotations
900: Two-and-a-half rotations
1080: Three full rotations

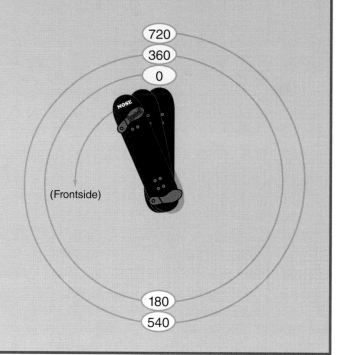

(Frontside)

180

The flat-ground 180 is a fundamental skill you'll want to be able to do comfortably. It's not really considered a trick, but it is very useful for getting around on your skateboard. Without being able to 180, every time you need to turn around you'll need to step off the board. The term *180* describes the number of degrees the board turns: half a rotation so that the board is pointed in the opposite direction. A 360 is a full rotation. A 720 is two complete rotations, and so on.

You can do your 180s moving slowly, but they're easier to learn standing still. You should start with a backside 180 (i.e., rotating in the same direction your chest is facing), as it allows you to better see where you are trying to go.

1. Position your lead foot on or just in front of the bolts. Your back foot should be squarely on the tail.
2. Before you begin, look over your rear shoulder (regular stance: right shoulder; goofy stance: left shoulder) so you can see where you want your front to end up. Bend your knees just a little bit and twist at your waist so you will be able to swing your arms into the spin.
3. Begin to unleash your spin with your body. When your body is untwisted, you should have some good momentum. Lift up the front wheels a bit. Your momentum should bring them around with your body.
4. As your body and board spin around, you may feel your balance begin to go. Set the nose down to regain your stability. If your spin was good, you should have made it a full half circle. It's likely that you weren't able to make it a full 180 degrees on your first try. Just keep practicing.

After you're comfortable with your backside 180, try it frontside. You'll turn the other way and load up your stance with a spin in the opposite direction. The hard part is that it will be harder to see where you want to go. Remember to look and point your lead shoulder where you want to go.

360

The flat-ground 360 is an actual trick. Most modern skaters are focused on ollie-based tricks, and it's uncommon to find someone who can bust out a bunch of 360s. In the 1970s it was a staple of the freestyle scene, with people routinely being able to easily do a dozen consecutive 360s.

Although the 360 may look like two 180s back to back, the body motion for the 360 is very different from the 180.

Your 360s are different because you have to balance on your rear wheels for a lot longer than in a 180. You can learn 360s easily by trying to pull your 180 out farther and farther. You may notice that you end up leaning more on your tail and that the spin is slower. Stay relaxed. You can experiment with holding your arms out wide while you do your spins, or pull them in close. When you pull your arms in it should speed up the spin, which can help get you around a few more degrees.

1. Position your lead foot on or just in front of the bolts. Your back foot should be squarely on the tail.
2. Before you begin, twist your waist and torso in the opposite direction that you want to spin, and bend your knees just a little. Don't rotate your head; keep it pointed in the same direction as it was before you started twisting. You are "loading up" the action that will cause you to spin in a circle.
3. Begin to unleash your spin with your body. When your body is untwisted, you should have some good momentum. Precisely at the moment when your body is open and in its normal riding state, lift up the front wheels a bit. Your momentum should bring them around with your body.
4. As your body and board spin around, concentrate on where your balance is over the rear wheels. If your spin was good, you should have made it all the way around.

It's likely that you weren't able to make it a full 360 degrees on your first try. That's okay—just keep practicing. This is one of the skills you should see fast improvement on. Practice a few 360s, and you'll get it.

NO COMPLY

The no comply is a contemporary and popular trick, but it's also practical for getting around the neighborhood. The no comply is a simple-looking trick, but you will probably bang up your shins as you learn it. It's easier to learn these on a curb or parking block at first. Once you can pop over a curb with a no comply, try some of the variations.

1. Position your feet in a normal stance, with your lead foot hanging a bit off the heel side of the board. Your knees should be bent, and your arms should be down.

2. Roll toward the curb slowly at a slight backside angle. You should approach the curb with it behind you a little bit.

3. When the curb is close, quickly slide your lead foot off the board and onto the curb. At first you may need to hop off the board, but sliding the foot is better technique.

4. Without your lead foot on the board, the nose should kick up. Keep your rear foot on the tail and scoop the board toward the curb while the nose is still in the air.

5. At first the rear wheels will probably hit the curb, and everything will stop. Keep trying, and try to lift the board up over the curb by speeding things up, getting your lead foot off the board smoothly, and scooping the board from the tail with your rear foot. Eventually the rear wheels should start clearing the curb.

6. When the board's tail has slapped the curb, ease off with the rear foot and hop from your planted lead foot back onto the board as the nose comes down. Then roll away. Good job.

Doing the no comply on flat is a little more difficult because the board doesn't have anything to bounce off of. Your rear-foot scoop needs to be smooth and precise.

STANCE

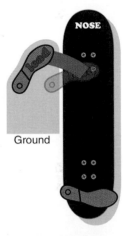

Ground

MOVEMENT

NO COMPLY 180

After you have your no comply over curbs on lock and the flat version is coming along, put a 180-degree rotation into the mix. This sounds complicated, but it's still considered a basic trick by most street skaters.

1. On flat and moving slowly, crouch into the ordinary no comply position.

2. Slide your lead foot off the board toward the heel side and let the rear foot scoop the tail.

3. Instead of pushing the board into a curb, push the tail slightly away from you. This will bring the front end toward you. Keep your eyes on this rotation and try to keep your lead leg out of the way. (The board may be on a collision course with your shin.)

4. Try to keep your rear foot near the tail of the board as it rotates around. All your weight should be on the planted lead foot.

5. Spring off the ground with your lead foot. You will need to time this so that your lead foot can trap the board as it comes around. This is more about timing than balance. Your body weight should be coming down just as your feet get over the board. Roll away in a switch stance.

TAKING THE BASICS FURTHER

The tricks in this chapter are the basic building blocks of good skateboarding. Without kickturns, tic tacs, and 180s, you will find the rest of the tricks in this book beyond your abilities. These are skills you will use constantly, whether you are going to the store or riding in the skatepark. Eventually you will stop thinking about these as tricks, and they will become "just skating." When you are comfortable with 180s and can experiment trying your basic skills in switch stance, you are ready to start learning some more difficult tricks.

CHAPTER 5

OLLIES AND SHUVITS

The ollie is the most significant trick to ever emerge in skateboarding. In an ollie, the board jumps into the air without the skater having to touch the ground with their feet or the board with their hands. Before the ollie, skaters rolled or kickturned into every obstacle. The ollie allows skaters to get onto things that previously had required a no comply, boneless, or some other grab. It didn't take long for skaters in the '80s to see the ollie's potential and make it the cornerstone of their whole bag of tricks.

A good ollie will allow you to get around the neighborhood in record time. You can ollie up curbs and over cracks. More important, a solid ollie will open up a whole category of advanced tricks. The nice thing about a lot of these tricks is that the ollie is the hardest part! The tricks are easy except for the ollie portion.

The ollie is also a benchmark for beginner skaters. It's the trick that everyone new to skateboarding wants to learn right away. For some people it's as if you're not a "real" skateboarder until you can ollie. That's absolutely not true, but an ollie will open up a world of skateboarding tricks that you might feel right at home in.

We have some good news and some bad news about learning ollies.

The good news is that once you learn what a successful ollie feels like, you'll know it. It's like riding a bike; you know when you're doing it right because you're doing it. The bad news is that explaining how to ollie is difficult. There are swift, subtle body motions going on in an ollie that take precise timing and the right amount of force, which is hard to explain in words. We're going to do the best we can, but what you'll need to do is practice, don't give up, and have fun every step of the way.

A shuvit is the ollie's cousin. Shuvits used to be an ollie with no pop; the deck's tail or nose never made contact with the ground. It was like an ollie, but you "shoved" the board where you wanted it. To confuse matters, people started doing "pop" shuvits to indicate that they were doing a shuvit but included a pop. This would then make it an ollie. Perhaps pop shuvit just sounded cooler than ollie. Whatever the reason, today we have ollies and pop shuvits, and they're virtually indistinguishable.

Having a second term has some value. The different terms can express different variations of a similar-looking trick. For example, a 360 ollie and a 360 shuvit are two different tricks, although the difference has nothing to do with shoving or the ollie. In a 360 ollie, the board and skater rotate 360 degrees together . . . usually off a drop. In a 360 shuvit, the skater kicks just the board into a 360-degree rotation and then lands on it when it's pointing forward again. (The skater doesn't rotate.)

QUICK WORD ABOUT LANDING

Whenever you are landing on your board, you put incredible strain on it. Although skateboards can take a lot of punishment, there are certain places on the board you can land that will dramatically increase the chances it will break or crack.

All your tricks should end in a clean, confident landing. That usually means having your feet right over your base-plate bolts. This is the strongest point on the board for landing since all your downward force is transferred through the board and into the trucks and wheels. The worst place to land is with one foot on either the nose or the tail and the other foot between the trucks. Land on the trucks bolts and save yourself a trip to the skate shop.

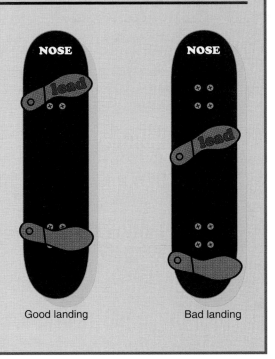

Good landing   Bad landing

OLLIE

The only things you need in order to learn great ollies are a skateboard, time, and a place to practice. It's hard to ollie on grass, carpet, or spongy ground. If you have a choice in the matter, avoid trying to learn ollies on old boards with the tail ground down. A new board is great because the deck is stiff and the tail is still whole. It's not worth running out to the skate shop for a new board, but if you have a choice of boards to practice on, grab the one that's in better shape.

A great way to learn ollies is with a friend. It helps to see your friend try and to think about what she is doing right (or wrong) and then have her do the same when you try. A friend who knows how to ollie can share tips and advice.

When you start learning ollies, don't roll forward. It may help if the concrete or asphalt is a little bit rough so the board doesn't roll around too much.

1. Ollies require a particular stance that may be a little uncomfortable at first. The rear foot is on the tail, but the heel is raised up. The front foot is flat in the middle of the deck or slightly in front of the middle, with the heel hanging just a little off the heel side.

2. Crouch low enough so that you can jump off the board straight up. Lower your arms to help with the jump. Try to keep your weight evenly balanced over both legs, but if you lean more heavily on one leg, try to make it the forward one. Keep your eyes focused on the nose of the board.

3. Jump straight up, but just as you jump and your weight is coming off the board, you need to kick the tail down hard with a snap. This is the ollie's central technique, and it requires a lot of coordination to time correctly. The confusing part for most beginners is that you are both jumping up and kicking down at almost the same time. Remember, you are jumping off the board and not off the tail when it's on the ground.

4. A split second later the board's nose will come flying up. Slide your lead foot, the one that is near the middle of the board, up the middle of the deck, scraping the side of your shoe against the grip tape. This scooping motion will help bring the board up. You can do an ollie without it and start with your front foot closer to the front bolts on the board, but your ollies will be smaller. As you finish the scoop, the board will come forward a little and level out. Your legs should be bent deeply, and your arms should be out.

5. As the board levels out under you, straighten your legs and let the whole thing land.

STANCE

MOVEMENT

Your first ollie attempts may feel as if you're just not getting it. This is very common because the body motion for good ollies is really strange. A lot of things can go wrong with your ollie that makes it feel as if it's not coming together.

- If the board is not staying under you, you are probably twisting your body before your jump or not jumping straight up. It's an easy mistake to make since our bodies have a natural aversion to landing on a board with wheels under it. (Your mind may be trying to get your body not to land on the board.) Keep your eyes on your board and focus on a smooth motion rather than going big.

- Sometimes the board may land sideways or at an angle. This is common and isn't a problem until you start doing ollies while you are rolling. You'll want to practice your ollies so the board lands in the same direction that you started. After your ollies consistently come off the ground, experiment with bending your body at the waist a little, and see what happens with the board.

- When the board just stays there and it seems as if you have just jumped off of it, try doing an ollie as slowly as you can while still catching a little air. Don't try to go big; just try to focus on loading up your legs for the jump, jumping smoothly, and then kicking the tail. You may be kicking the tail *with* the jump, which will result in the board just bouncing around a little but not actually getting off the ground.

When you can land an ollie every third attempt, do 500 more and then try a kickflip.

FRONTSIDE 180 OLLIE

Some people find that frontside ollies are actually easier than straight ones. This is probably because these people tend to twist their bodies while they jump. On the one hand this is good because the trick will come naturally. On the other hand it can make straight and backside ollies difficult if your body becomes too accustomed to one way of doing it.

The frontside 180 ollie—sometimes called a frontside ollie or a frontside 180—is an ollie where the board and the body rotate laterally halfway around to land backward. Your tail end (and rear foot) will swing around to your front side. It may feel as if your board's nose rotates around to the back, but most of the motion is from the tail end.

1. This trick is nearly impossible to do standing still. Roll forward and get into your ollie stance—rear foot on the tail with the heel up, front foot flat near the middle with the heel hanging off a bit. Drop your arms as you would normally do, but drop your lead shoulder toward your toes a bit so you are twisting at the waist. When you jump you'll be spinning your body, so this motion helps preload that spin.

2. Start to unwind your torso, and then pop your ollie—raising your body up as you kick the tail down. The timing is key here, and you'll need to experiment to get it right. Your ollie should occur in the split second that your untwisting body is in an ordinary straight ollie position. You should notice that your board follows your body naturally.

3. When you are at the apex of your ollie, you and your board should be sideways to your direction of travel, or squarely facing the same direction you are moving. In an ordinary ollie, you probably trap the board with your rear foot to land the trick. For the frontside 180 ollie, you'll want to trap the board with your front foot.

4. As you cross the apex of your ollie, bring your lead foot down and toward your back side to complete the 180. The tail should continue to come around so it is pointing forward.

5. Land and then roll away as if you've been doing this all your life.

If your ollies are good, the frontside 180 ollie shouldn't be too challenging. Landing them cleanly with all four wheels touching down at the same time and your feet over the bolts will take practice.

- If the board is moving away from you or you are falling off backward when you land, try putting more weight on your toes before you ollie.
- If the board isn't doing a full 180, your ollie may be too low, or you are not twisting enough during your crouch. If the board is making it almost all the way around, try landing on your front wheels a little before your tail comes down. That will give you a split second for the tail to make it around that last few degrees.

BACKSIDE 180 OLLIE

The backside 180 ollie is a bit more challenging than the frontside version for most people because the board has a greater tendency to move away from you. In the backside 180 ollie—or just backside ollie—your board will rotate 180 degrees in the air clockwise (regular) or counterclockwise (goofy).

1. Roll forward and get into your ollie stance with your rear foot on the tail and your lead foot somewhere near the middle of the board. Point your chest a bit toward the nose so you are twisting a bit at your waist. You are loading your body with twist.

2. Begin to untwist your body. Pop your ollie just as your left arm swings past your lead foot (regular stance). The rotation of your shoulders will bring your feet around in the same clockwise rotation.

3. Scoop the board with your lead foot. Although your lead foot will start rotating with your body just as you pop, try to guide the board with your lead foot so that it follows you around. As the board's nose comes up, continue your shoulder rotation. Bring your rear foot under you as you rotate. Keep your eyes on the ground where you want your front wheels to land.

4. When the ollie is at its apex, you should be halfway through your 180. You should be traveling backward.

5. As the board starts coming down, keep your lead foot in contact with the deck by pressing down. Your front wheels may touch the ground a split second before your rear wheels.

6. Roll away switch.

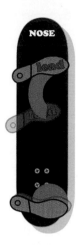

MOVEMENT

There's no doubt about it: Backside 180 ollies are hard. It is typical to struggle with this trick for a while before it starts coming together, so if you don't land it on your first try, don't get frustrated. Think about what you want the board to do and how your body should be helping it.

- If the board is shooting away from you, start your body rotation a little bit later so it coincides with your ollie instead of coming before it.
- If you are landing in a nose manual or on the nose, or if the board lands ahead of you instead of under you, lower your ollie a bit and watch the ground near your rear foot. It's likely that you're putting too much power into your ollie and losing control of the board. Don't worry about a full 180. Focus on your technique. Landing only slightly backside is better than not landing a full 180.

SWITCH OLLIE

If you can ollie, then you can do a switch ollie. Unfortunately your body may not want to cooperate. If you have nice ollies on lock, you may notice that you don't need to think about what your body is doing. This is muscle memory. When you try your switch ollie, your brain will be telling your body to ollie in a switch stance, but your body will try to do a normal ollie.

Switch ollies are an ordinary ollie while you are moving backward, and your pop comes from your nose. Another way of looking at it is that you are doing an ordinary straight ollie but in a goofy stance if you are ordinarily regular or regular if you are ordinarily goofy.

The secret (if you want to call it that) is to rely on everything you know about doing a normal ollie but with the opposite legs.

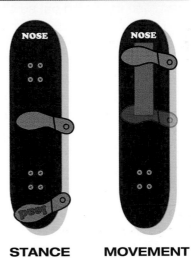

STANCE **MOVEMENT**

SHIFTY

The shifty is an ollie tweak where the tail end of the board drifts out a little while the board is in the air. The deeper the shifty, the farther out the tail end of the board is angled. A frontside shifty will swing the tail end of the board out to the side you're facing, while a backside shifty will swing the tail end out behind you.

To learn the shifty, your ollie needs to be on lock, smooth, and high enough that you have a moment in the air to make adjustments. If your ollie is low and quick, you will struggle to find time to make the midair adjustments that a good shifty requires. You must also be comfortable doing an ollie while you're moving.

While the board is rising, your feet will move the board laterally using only the friction of the grip tape and the contact provided by the rising board against the soles of your shoes.

A smooth shifty can be broken down into two main parts. The ascent is the part of the ollie where your lead foot is bringing the board up. The apex of your ollie is where you'll straighten the board out so it lands pointed in the direction of your momentum.

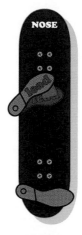

1. Build up a little speed and get into your ollie position with your rear foot on the tail and your lead foot near the middle of the board.

2. Pop your ollie. As your lead foot slides up the middle of the deck, direct the board to your left (regular stance, frontside shifty). The board should rotate as if you were doing a frontside ollie. Don't twist your torso; keep your shoulders and head pointed as if you were doing a straight ollie.

3. As the board levels out, move it forward slightly with your lead foot. This will bring the tail end back in line with the direction of travel. In other words, your lead foot is going to make a small S shape as you ollie.

4. Stomp your landing and roll away.

MOVEMENT

Shifties aren't easy, and it's important to not get hung up on your progress. Relax, have fun with it, and come back to it later if you start feeling frustrated.

○ If the board is landing sideways or at a steep angle, you may be twisting your body as if you were going to do a 90-degree ollie. Remember, the shifty is more about a small leg movement than a whole-body motion.

○ If it feels as if you have the motion down, and the ollie is solid but the board isn't shifting, it could be that you're doing them perfectly but you just can't see it. Ask a friend to watch and see if the board is moving laterally while you are in the air. You might already be doing them!

After you feel your shifty coming together, work on the other side. For a big shifty, try them off a bank hip or kicker.

OLLIE NORTH

If you can ollie, you may have already done an ollie north accidentally. They are easy to spot when they're done well. Even when done poorly, it will just look like a sloppy ollie. The trick isn't exactly a showstopper, but it is a way to add style to your ollies and an easy way to build on what you already know.

The ollie north is a straight, forward-moving ollie where the lead foot kicks out past the nose of the board when it's airborne. When they're done with a lot of energy, the front foot almost looks as if it is in position for some kind of one-foot ollie.

You don't need to be moving to learn the ollie north, but it may help you get a higher ollie. You'll need a little extra airtime for this trick, so having a high ollie will definitely help.

1. Crouch into your ordinary ollie stance but with your rear foot on the tail and your lead foot slightly forward of the usual spot. This may result in a lower ollie, and that's okay.

2. Pop your ollie and scoop your lead foot straight up the middle of the deck and right over the nose.

3. Stabilize the deck with your rear foot. (The board may be trying to rotate as for a heelflip or kickflip or even drop down into an endo.) Quickly bring your lead foot back over your board.

4. Your lead foot should be over the board just as you land.

STANCE   **MOVEMENT**

Most of the problems that occur during an ollie north have to do with the lead foot sliding off the board, so that's where you'll want to be looking if you think your ollie north isn't coming together.

Remember: Not landing the trick is part of skateboarding, and every pro has gone through exactly what you're going through now. Keep it fun for yourself and don't worry about what other people are thinking.

○ If the board is rotating on its axis (as for a heelflip or a kickflip), your lead foot may be flicking the nose of the board as it comes off. Experiment by lifting your lead foot up off the board rather than pushing it forward. When you can raise your lead foot off easily, start moving it out over the nose little by little.

○ If the board keeps landing on its tail and getting ahead of you, load more weight on your lead foot and check that your rear foot isn't "tippy toe" on your tail. You may be kicking the board forward with your rear foot and accelerating that motion with the scoop off the nose.

NOLLIE

When an ollie just won't do, the nollie comes in nicely. It's a great way to make any ordinary ollie trick extra special.

The nollie is an ollie done off the nose rather than the tail. If you've been working on your switch ollies, your nollie should be pretty close. The nollie is a lot like doing a switch ollie while rolling backward. The challenging part of learning to nollie is getting your legs to cooperate with your mind. You may understand what needs to happen when you nollie, but your body will struggle to overcome your ollie habits.

1. Since you'll be popping off the front of the board rather than the tail, position your lead foot far up on the nose and on the toes and ball of your foot so that your heel is hanging off the nose. Your rear foot should be between the middle and the back trucks bolts.

2. Crouch into an ollie position, with more of your weight over your rear leg. Drop your arms and look at the ground in front of the board.

3. Spring up off your rear leg and bring your arms up. As you come off the board, pop the nose into the ground with a quick snap. (Remember, you're not jumping off the ground but off the middle of the board.) The pop should be in a slight forward direction and not straight down as you might do in an ordinary ollie.

4. As the tail end of the board comes up, roll your rear foot inward so the outer part of your shoe slides over the bolts. In an ordinary ollie, you use your lead foot to scoop the board upward. In a nollie, you are doing the same thing but on a much smaller scale. The nollie scoop is little more than moving your rear foot back over the bolts.

5. When your rear foot gets over the bolts, the board should flatten out. Trap the nose end with your lead foot and get ready to come back to earth.

6. Land, smile, and roll away.

STANCE

MOVEMENT

Almost anything you can do with an ollie can be done with a nollie. Although many people think nollies make a trick look sick because it's harder, there's a practical reason they are gnarlier than an ollie. When you ollie an obstacle or stair set, the board can be coming up off the ground after the nose is already past the edge of the obstacle. With a nollie, the board has to come off the ground before you get to the obstacle. The result is that nollies must be done while traveling faster than ollies to clear the same obstacle.

If the board is shooting out behind you, there is too much force pushing the board backward. Try leaning onto your back leg more and focus on popping the nose down and forward. Don't worry about the rear-foot scoop until the pop feels solid.

ONE TIME AT SKATE CAMP . . .

A local ripper was approached by a beginning skater at a skatepark who wanted some advice on how to learn kickflips. The ripper asked the kid to ollie. The kid's ollie was pretty weak. It took him a few tries to land one, and even then it was just an inch or two (5 cm) off the ground. The ripper said to the kid, "Here's how to kickflip. Go over to that corner of the skatepark and do 500 ollies. I'll tell you the secret of kickflips when you're done."

The kid went to the side of the skatepark and started his ollies. After about an hour the kid came back. When the ripper asked to see his ollie again, it was a solid 6 inches (15 cm) off the ground, and the kid nailed it on the first try.

Then the ripper showed the kid how to kickflip.

Without a solid ollie, a lot of cool tricks will be unattainable. Practice those ollies!

KICKFLIP

This is a flashy trick that everyone wants to learn right away. Being able to ollie is usually enough proof to anyone that you are a skater, but being able to kickflip will remove any doubt.

The kickflip is an ollie where the board does a full rotation along its axis. The board rotation is caused by the lead foot sliding up the deck of the board at an angle. This motion is a quick, smooth flick of the foot.

You should have a solid and consistent ollie before you start working on your kickflip. The board takes time to rotate in the air, so it is best if you can comfortably ollie 12 inches (30 cm) or higher.

1. Roll forward and get into your ollie stance. You may need to position your lead foot a little more off the heel side of the board than for your regular ollie. Some people find kickflips easier with the lead foot pointed more toward the nose than usual.

2. Pop your ollie. As the board rises, pull it up with your lead foot. As your lead foot crosses the trucks bolts, flick your foot toward the heel side of the nose.

3. Keep your feet and legs clear of the board as it rotates.

4. As the top of the deck comes around, bring your rear foot down to stop the rotation, with your lead foot touching the deck a split second later.

5. Land the board, roll away, and pat yourself on the back.

STANCE   **MOVEMENT**

Like so many skateboard tricks, there are lots of things that can go wrong with a kickflip. Nobody gets it on the first try, and most people will still struggle with it after 100 tries. To master the kickflip, you will need to do hundreds of them, so it's in your best interest to keep it fun and low stress. Relax and think about what's going on with your body when you kickflip.

- The board may be shooting out in front of you. Try setting up your ollie with more weight on your lead foot. You also may be kicking the board away from you rather than flicking your foot to the side. It's a common problem. If the board keeps flying away from you, try a normal high ollie between each kickflip attempt.

- The board might rotate laterally while in the air so that it lands sideways. This is caused by the same reasons that your ollie may not be straight—you are twisting your torso before you pop the ollie. Relax, align your shoulders with your board, and visualize where you want the board to land.

- The board may not be spinning all the way around. When it lands on its side (primo) or upside down, the problem is either that your flick isn't smooth and quick—the board is rotating too slowly—or that your ollie isn't high enough and the board is running out of time. You may find that trying to flick the board more quickly introduces new problems, so focus on smooth and efficient body motions.

- If the board *still* isn't spinning all the way around, you might be separating the ollie from the flick by doing the ollie and *then* trying to spin the board with your foot. The good news is that this is called a late flip and is its own style of kickflip. The bad news is that it's harder, and you will probably still want to learn the standard kickflip. If your kickflip is turning into a late flip, try thinking of the pop of the ollie, the scoop of the lead foot, and the flick of the toe as one smooth action.

FRONTSIDE FLIP

The frontside flip combines your frontside 180 ollie with a kickflip. If you have both of those tricks dialed, you shouldn't have much trouble with this one. It's a great trick to have on lock for two reasons: It can be taken over gaps or off drops, and it opens up other more complicated tricks. If your frontside 180 ollies and kickflips aren't on lock, you should at least have a solid understanding of the correct principles behind them before attempting a frontside flip.

In the frontside flip, both your body and the board do a frontside 180 ollie but with a kickflip thrown in. You will land switch.

1. Get into your frontside ollie stance and crouch. Your lead foot should be just behind the front bolts. As you crouch, twist your body and prepare to rotate your body frontside (to your left if you are regular) as you jump.

2. Pop your tail and sweep it out in front of you. Scoop the board slightly with your lead foot. Your body momentum should bring the board around with you as you do the shuvit.

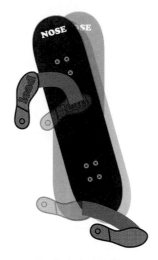

STANCE   **MOVEMENT**

3. Your lead foot will roll onto its side and flick the heel side of the board with the side of the toes. Bring your rear foot up over the board and aim to trap the board on those trucks bolts.

4. Your landing should be untwisted, with your shoulder aligned with the tail (which is now in front).

You may struggle with this trick if your 180 ollies aren't clean or if your kickflips are inconsistent.

If the board is rotating only about 90 degrees (so that you are landing sideways on the board), focus on sweeping the tail outward off the pop. This will help the board rotate. Your lead foot doesn't do any of the rotation since it's busy handling the kickflip.

HEELFLIP

If you can land a kickflip every now and then, heelflips should make a lot of sense. You won't have a hard time understanding the trick. It will just be a matter of practice and training your body to do the motions without your mind interfering.

The heelflip is identical to a kickflip except the board will rotate along its axis in the opposite direction. A kickflip spins the board toward your heel side (counterclockwise for regular, clockwise for goofy), while a heelflip spins the board toward your toe side.

The action is easy to understand. Instead of flicking the board with your toe to do a kickflip, you'll bring your lead foot off the toe side of the board so that your heel creates the flick. The hardest part about this action is that your legs don't like to move quickly in that direction, so it takes lots of practice before the action is smooth and the board starts responding in a desired way.

1. Push and get into your ollie stance. Position your lead foot slightly to the toe side of the board so that the front of your foot hangs off. It may help to point your lead foot toward the nose slightly.

2. Pop your ollie. As the board's nose rises, flick your front foot out to your front side. Try not to kick out with the heel of your lead foot because it will just send your board flying away from you.

3. As the board rotates along its axis and nears right side up again, lower your rear foot with your lead foot quickly following.

STANCE   **MOVEMENT**

4. Try to have all four wheels landing at once, with your feet covering your bolts.

5. Roll away. Be stoked.

○ If the board is flying away from you, try to coordinate your flick with the scoop so that they are almost one smooth, continuous action.

○ If the board isn't leveling out or getting off the ground, you are probably neglecting the ollie portion of the trick and focusing too much on the flick. Throw some straight ollies into your mix to keep your body tuned to the ollie.

M-80 (OLD-SCHOOL KICKFLIP)

The M-80 is another basic freestyle trick that can serve as an inspiration for other flip and manual combinations for skaters who like tech skating on flat and manual pads. In the M-80, you flip the board as for a kickflip and revert immediately after the landing.

Old-school kickflips don't require an ollie. Instead, you place both of your feet in the middle of the board facing forward. Your rear foot hooks the underside of the board and flips it over while you jump so that it rotates as in a kickflip. You can practice just this portion of the M-80 alone if you want.

1. Flip the board around so you are riding switch, with your tail and rear foot in front.
2. Adjust your stance so your rear foot (which is now in front) is near the middle of the board and to the heel side. It will help if it's hanging off the side of the board slightly.
3. Bring your lead foot (which is behind your rear foot because you are in a switch stance) up near your other foot and pointing forward. Find your center of balance, and crouch slightly.
4. Hook the inside of your rear foot against the edge of the board next to where it was just standing and prepare to spring off your lead leg. This is a quick action; you shouldn't be rolling around with one foot hooked under your board or else the weight of your lead foot will start turning the board in a big circle.
5. Spring up and flick the underside of the board with your rear foot. This will send the board spinning along its axis to the side. Pay attention to how far it moves before the wheels are pointed down again. This is where your feet need to be.
6. Once you can match the distance and rotation of the board with your leap, try to trap the board. You'll notice that you need to rotate your hips so you can land in a wide stance with your feet over the bolts. You should be landing in a wide switch stance.

7. So far you've done a switch old-school kickflip. To make this a true M-80, you need to revert (quickly slide the front of the board into its forward-facing direction) or pivot off the tail as you land. This is a quick frontside 180 off the tail of the board. At first you will find that landing the old-school kickflip alone is hard enough. To include the revert you will need to land more heavily on your rear foot so that the board is trapped and lands in a fakie manual. As the wheels touch the ground, immediately twist at your torso so the board spins around and points forward, with your lead foot on the nose.

You will land twisted up. In fact, the M-80 requires a lot of quick leg movement. From the waist up you won't be doing much.

- With the M-80, timing is everything. Most of the problems you'll encounter at first are in timing the different parts of the trick so they sync up correctly.

- The old-school kickflip is not a difficult or high-risk trick, but you may find it difficult to get the board to rotate fully. If the board underrotates, or lands primo, check to see how your rear foot is against the underside of the deck. You should be hooking the deck with the corner of the sole of your shoe right by the arch of your foot. The top of your shoe shouldn't be touching the board at all.

- The quick revert is much easier if you can consistently land in the fakie manual. Focus on your landing stance so your weight is over the rear trucks. (Remember, because the board is rolling backward, the tail is in front.) If you are struggling with this portion of the trick, you can practice it by itself by trying frontside 180 ollies while trying to land in a fakie manual and then quickly reverting back to normal.

PRESSURE FLIP

The pressure flip is a sweet trick that looks cool and isn't too difficult to learn. For many people the pressure flip is the trick they learn right after their ollie. Low pressure flips are cool. Later they can get big and gnarly, so build good habits as you learn them the first time.

In a pressure flip, the rear foot scoops the tail toward your back side so that the board does a 180 and half a heelflip. All this motion comes from the scooping motion of the rear foot. (Also, your heel will have nothing to do with it.)

1. Push and crouch into a pre-ollie stance. Point your lead foot at less of an angle than normal so it is pointing more toward the nose of the board. Your rear foot placement is important. Your rear-foot toes should be halfway off the board at the base of the tail just behind the rear wheels, and your foot should be pointed slightly forward.

2. Spring out of your crouch. Pop the tail as you would for an ollie. Because of your foot placement, the tail of the board should bounce out toward your back side. Furthermore, because you popped on the side of your tail, the board should begin to spin along its axis.

STANCE   **MOVEMENT**

3. At your body's apex, the board will be upside down and sideways to your direction. There's nothing to do but keep your legs up high and out of the way.

4. When the board starts to finish its rotation, you should see the tail coming up under your lead foot and the nose coming around under your rear foot. Trap the board with your rear foot first while you aim to position your lead foot over the bolts. Return your seatback to its upright position and prepare for landing.

5. Land.

If the board is just spinning away from you, concentrate on trying not to scoop the board with your rear foot. If you've been working on impossibles, your foot may be reverting to that action. Keep your pop clean and hard off the base of the tail.

FRONTSIDE POP SHUVIT

The frontside pop shuvit is an intermediate trick that will open up a whole family of other tricks. It's a staple trick for most street skaters. Many people can do it without much concentration.

Consider the frontside pop shuvit as a frontside 180 ollie but without rotating your body. Only the board does the 180 and lands rolling backward. You will land with your lead foot forward, and it will be on the tail of the board.

1. Get into your ollie stance and crouch. The ball of your rear foot should be on the tail, with your heel hanging off a bit.

2. Pop with a forward motion. Unlike an ollie where you would pop straight down with a lot of force, here you want to pop in a diagonal direction toward the toe side of the tail. The lead foot doesn't need to scoop as much for this trick as for a straight ollie. Some people like to help the lateral rotation by scooping the lead foot slightly toward the heel so that the lead foot scoops to the back side while the rear foot sweeps to the front.

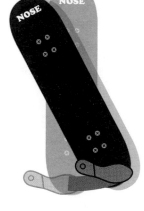

STANCE   **MOVEMENT**

3. The board should be rotating in a counterclockwise direction (regular), with the tail coming around your front side. Some people use the lead foot to keep the board flat while it's in the air. The cleaner technique is to keep your lead foot clear of the board. Keep your eye on the tail of the board.

4. When the tail gets close enough, trap the board with your lead foot and land with your feet over the bolts.

5. Roll away.

6. If you're feeling really slick, do another one to return the board to its normal nose-first orientation.

You can warm up to this trick and get a good idea of what the board is supposed to do by popping the board with your rear foot while standing behind it. Pop the board at a downward diagonal angle and watch it do its 180. That should help you figure out how much pop and angle you will need.

If the board lands primo or upside down, move your lead foot more toward your toe side. It may be accidentally scooping and flicking the board off the heel side. Your rear foot may be popping the tail off the side, causing the board to begin to rotate on its axis.

BACKSIDE POP SHUVIT

The backside pop shuvit is a standard trick that can become the foundation for other more complicated tricks. It's a great trick to have on lock.

The backside pop shuvit is almost identical to the frontside pop shuvit except the board will rotate laterally to your back side. The nose will come around in front of you before you trap it with your rear foot. Like the frontside pop shuvit, you will land with your lead foot forward and the board backward (or tail first).

1. Get into your ollie stance and crouch. Your lead foot won't be doing much, so it should be near the middle of the board and not hanging off either side too much. Your rear foot should be ready to pop directly in the middle of the tail.

2. Pop with your rear foot at a slight heel-side angle. This will start the board spinning laterally in a clockwise direction (regular). Your lead foot doesn't scoop the board as it might in an ordinary ollie.

3. Watch your nose as the board rotates in a clockwise (regular) direction under you. When the board has almost completed its airborne 180, trap it with your lead foot.

4. Bring your feet down, and land on your bolts.

STANCE   **MOVEMENT**

Some people claim the frontside and backside 180 shuvits are easier than the normal ollie. You be the judge.

⊙ If your board is rotating along its axis and landing primo or upside down, your rear foot is popping the board unevenly. Make sure you are popping in the middle of the tail. If the board is consistently rotating in the same direction, try experimenting by moving your rear foot a few degrees off-center to see if this corrects it.

⊙ If the board is flying away from you and just going crazy, slow down. The backside pop shuvit is not fast and twitchy but more big, smooth, and almost slow.

BACKSIDE 360 SHUVIT

This is a stylish trick that separates the occasional skater from the hard-core one. If your frontside and backside 180 pop shuvits are starting to feel clean, you may be ready to start looking at this "bigger" version of those tricks.

The backside 360 shuvit looks like the backside pop shuvit except the board spins 360 degrees underneath you. Your body doesn't rotate at all. Unlike the backside pop shuvit, the 360 shuvit is popped off the front wheels instead of the rear. You'll want to be comfortable doing short nose manuals before trying this trick.

1. Place your feet into a nose manual stance, with your lead foot ahead of the front trucks bolts. Your rear foot can be anywhere from near your tail to the middle of the board, whatever feels most comfortable for you.

2. Lift the tail end of the skateboard up slightly so you are in a low nose manual. Hold it until you feel perfectly centered over your front wheels.

3. Crouch slightly to give yourself enough spring to flick the tail end of the board to your back. You'll be kicking the board out into a clockwise rotation if you're regular, counterclockwise if you're goofy. You will have to flick the board out the moment you feel the stability over your front wheels. You will need to jump high.

STANCE   **MOVEMENT**

4. Clear your feet so the board can spin freely. If you can't jump high enough, you can try to clear your feet up and to the sides, although this is more difficult than just raising your feet straight up.

5. Watch the board as it spins quickly below you and catch it as the nose comes around to where it started. This is more about timing and keeping the shuvit consistent than waiting for it to come around as if it were in a slow orbit. The trick is quick, and you won't be off the board for very long.

6. As you land, the board should be aligned underneath you.

You may find yourself trying to get the 360 shuvit consistent by landing the trick with one foot as a safety precaution. This technique, known as "chicken foot," is a way of testing a trick to see that the board does what you want it to do without committing to landing on it with both feet. When you're sure the board is rotating enough and at the proper speed, you can try stomping it with both feet or landing with one foot slightly before the other. The problem with trying new tricks using a chicken foot technique is that you may eventually train your body to try *not* to land it.

- The skateboard may land sideways by rotating not enough or too much. You can make adjustments to your shuvit on the fly, but try mixing in a few backside 180 shuvits too, just to regain your sense of consistency.

- When the board seems to rotate along its axis and land upside down or primo, pay attention to where your rear foot is starting. The rotation is probably caused by the position and flick of your rear foot. It should remain in the middle of the board and not out to the side.

- If the board has a tendency to fly out and away from you—usually slightly ahead of you to your back side—time your shuvit to coincide with a very slight frontside turn. This will help your body get back on your heels slightly and keep the shuvit from flying out.

360 KICKFLIP (TRE FLIP)

This hot trick is also called a tre flip and makes frequent appearances during games of SKATE. It is a fast trick, and it's hard to tell what is going on when it's done well, but when you break it down into its individual parts it all makes sense.

The 360 kickflip combines a 360 pop shuvit with a kickflip. You'll want to have both of these tricks down before you start getting serious about your tre flip. Your body doesn't rotate, but your board will spin around laterally *and* along its axis. You can do this trick stationary, but if you're moving you will have more control over your board.

1. Push and get into your ordinary ollie stance. Adjust your lead foot so it's pointed slightly more forward than usual and your rear foot so the ball of your foot is squarely on the tail and your toes hang off just a bit.

2. You will begin to pop your ollie, but instead of clearing your rear foot off the tail to allow it to come straight up, you'll kick the tail to your backside. Your lead foot will scoop as usual. Your lead foot will do all the work in this trick.

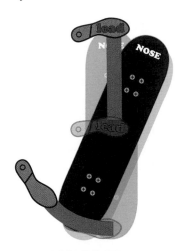

STANCE   **MOVEMENT**

3. As the board's nose comes up and the back end swings around behind you, flick the board with your lead foot. Because the board is rotating laterally, it should already be pointed a bit sideways by the time your lead foot is ready to flick it. So flick your lead foot forward rather than to the side as for a kickflip. Your foot should be leaving the board in the same place as if you were doing an ordinary kickflip.

4. Keep your feet clear and your eyes on the board. Unlike the kickflip, you will have to start to trap the board before you see much grip tape. The nose will be coming up behind your lead foot, so try to trap the board with your lead foot and your toes pointed down a little.

5. Land like a fighter pilot with your feet over the bolts.

This trick takes practice and patience. Your body is doing a lot of different things at once, and any adjustments to one part can change what may be required elsewhere. Concentrate on keeping those parts that are working and making small changes to those parts that aren't.

- If the board is flying forward, you may be flicking it too hard with your lead foot. Try to adjust your flick just a little to the heel side (like in an ordinary kickflip) until you are only spinning the board and not actually moving it.
- If the board isn't spinning around laterally all the way, try to land it just shy of the 360 and then drag the front around the rest of the way.

BIGSPIN

The bigspin is a cool trick that you see in a lot of contests and demos. It's a difficult trick that comes with some risk since you are moving backward while you are airborne, so if the board isn't cooperating and you have to bail, you will need to be quick on your feet or land on your rump to avoid a nasty fall.

The bigspin is easy to understand but hard to do. In a bigspin, your body is doing a backside 180 while the board does a backside 360 pop shuvit. Your body will land switch, and your board will land with its nose forward. Make sense?

1. Crouch in your backside shuvit stance but with your rear foot more toward the pocket of the tail. Your lead foot should be hanging off the heel side and up near the trucks bolts. Even though you will be doing a 180 with your body, most of the twist is at your waist, so you don't need to load up a bunch of body momentum.

STANCE   **MOVEMENT**

2. Pop the tail toward your heel side at an angle. This will send the board into a lateral spin. You will need to pop hard and jump high. Don't scoop your lead foot, but rather lift it straight up off the deck right after the pop. This will help keep the board spinning flat like a pizza and not rotating as in a kickflip or heelflip.

3. Move your legs out of the way, and let the board make its full 360 lateral rotation. Keep your eyes on the board.

4. As the tail comes around to its original position, trap it with your lead foot. Your rear foot will trap the nose of the board. You'll be twisting at your waist to get your rear foot into position.

5. Land with your feet somewhere near the bolts and roll away switch.

This trick is easier to learn if you're moving. You won't want to go too fast because it will probably take a lot of failed attempts before the board and your body start getting into position consistently. If you're going slowly, you can bail backward without a problem.

○ When the board doesn't rotate all the way around, you are not popping the shuvit hard enough or are trapping the board too early. Try a harder pop with more sweep on your rear foot and jump higher to give the board more time to rotate around.

○ If the board is flying out at some crazy angle, you should mix up your bigspin attempts with a few backside pop shuvits and 360 shuvits. This will help remind your body what it should be doing.

VARIAL KICKFLIP

The varial kickflip is like the inward heelflip's cousin. The two tricks are almost identical except the varial kickflip is flicked with the toe of your lead foot, hence the kickflip, whereas the inward heelflip is flicked with the heel. Reading the inward heelflip instructions will help you learn this trick. These are two good tricks to learn at the same time.

1. Get into a kickflip stance. The heel of your lead foot should be hanging off the board, and you may find it easier to angle your lead foot slightly toward the nose. Your rear-foot heel should be hanging off the tail as much as you can while still providing enough traction for you to sweep the tail toward your back side (behind you).

2. Crouch and then pop. As you are coming up off the board, sweep the tail behind you to get the shuvit started. Scoop the board with your lead foot at the same time so that the flick happens just a split second after the pop. In an ordinary kickflip you would flick off to the side, but because the board is rotating laterally from the shuvit, you'll be flicking your lead foot straight ahead. (The board will be at an angle so that your flick comes off the board just behind the nose over the front wheel.)

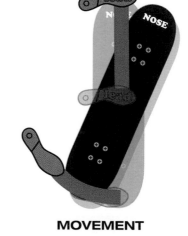

STANCE   **MOVEMENT**

3. While the inward heelflip looks like a scissor kick, the varial kickflip looks like a forward flying karate kick. Your lead foot is kicked out over the nose while your rear leg is behind you.

4. Keep your eyes on your board and your legs clear as it spins.

5. You should see the tail of the board coming around to the front from your backside as your feet start coming down.

6. Land with your feet on the bolts and your lead foot in front.

Like the inward heelflip, there's a lot that can go wrong, but most problems are easy to diagnose.

○ If the board is landing upside down or primo, try flicking a little harder with your lead foot. It could be that your timing between the flick and the shuvit is off, so consider also where the board is in its lateral rotation when you flick it.

○ When the board isn't doing a full 180 (or overrotating beyond 180), adjust your shuvit. It may help to do a few clean pop shuvits to remind your body what needs to happen there.

INWARD HEELFLIP

The inward heelflip is a combination of a pop shuvit and a heelflip. It looks similar to a pressure flip but garners more respect. (Pressure flips are not very popular anymore.) You should have landed a few heelflips and pop shuvits before working on this. The lead foot is used to flick the board into a heelflip while the rear foot pops the board into a backside 180 shuvit. Your body doesn't rotate with the board.

One nice thing about this trick is that you can learn it without the board doing a full 180. You can get away with a 90-degree shuvit and slide the front end around the rest of the way after you land. If you stick with this way of doing them, you will never be able to do them while going very fast, so try to develop your inward heelflip into a clean 180-degree shuvit as soon as you can.

1. Get into a heelflip stance. The heel of your lead foot should be near the middle of the board, and the toes should be hanging off. You want to angle your lead foot so it is pointing more toward the nose than usual. Your rear-foot heel should be hanging off the tail as much as you can while still providing enough traction for you to sweep the tail toward your back side (behind you).

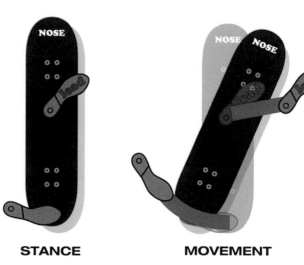

STANCE   **MOVEMENT**

2. Crouch and get ready to jump. This is a shuvit trick, so it's not quite an ollie and more like a sweep or scoop of the tail. You'll still need to jump high enough to do three separate things at nearly the same time.

3. Pop the tail like an ollie. As the board's nose comes up, you'll need to do two things together. Your lead foot will kick out toward your front side in order to flick the board with your heel. This will send the board spinning on its axis. Your rear foot will be sweeping the tail back behind you. This will send the board into a lateral spin (in other words, a backside 180).

4. You should have jumped high enough that it's easy to keep your legs clear of the spinning board.

5. Just after you've done the scissor-kick motion, bring your legs down as the board finishes its rotation. The tail should be coming around to the front from your back side as you start coming down.

6. The board should land backward with you landing on it forward.

The biggest challenge with the inward heelflip is getting the pop shuvit to come around 180 degrees consistently. As you're working on your inward heel, throw a few clean backside pop shuvits in there to keep your legs fresh with the memory of that technique.

- If the board doesn't come around all the way, try landing it short and then dragging the front end (the tail) the rest of the way around. It won't look as nice, but it will give you something to improve on.

- If the board lands upside down or primo, concentrate on the flick. It's going to be difficult to concentrate on the shuvit *and* the heelflip, so mix a few straight heelflips in there.

IMPOSSIBLE

The impossible is not only possible but also a trick you can learn to do consistently. It's a great trick to have in your bag for games of SKATE because it's common enough that a few people will know it but not so common that everyone does.

During the impossible, the board does a backflip motion while it is midair. It's like a forward flip but with the nose flipping over backward. Because the board is doing a flip along its longest dimension, impossibles take a lot of confidence. You can't do "half" an impossible and expect to land it. To help the board spin around, your rear foot provides the scoop to help it along.

1. Push and get into your ollie stance but with your rear foot squarely on the tail rather than just the balls of your feet.

2. Your rear foot is going to do something a little different than if this were an ordinary ollie. Start the pop as for an ordinary ollie, but instead of snapping the tail down, you will sweep the tail into and under the board. This is the secret—you don't wait until you're in the air to do this trick.

STANCE   **MOVEMENT**

3. As you are sweeping the tail under the board, clear your lead foot. The board should be turning over along its axis, and the nose should be rotating in front of you.

4. Midway through your apex, the board should be upside down with your rear foot under it. Bring your rear foot up so that both your knees are tucked into your chest. This motion should help finish the board's rotation.

5. As gravity pulls you back down to earth, the board should be coming around to a right-side-up orientation even though you shouldn't be able to see it. Land with your feet somewhere on the board, and roll away.

○ If the board just flies out in front of you, then try to prevent your lead foot from flicking the board while it's coming off near the nose.

○ If you are landing with your feet too close together, try pulling your rear foot up higher into your body.

HARDFLIP

Impossibles aren't impossible, but hardflips are actually hard. The hardflip combines a frontside 180 pop shuvit with a kickflip, so you should be comfortable doing both of those tricks before you get into this one. The biggest difference is the tail comes under the board so that it flips almost end over end rather than in a lateral rotation. Your body does not rotate; you will land with your lead foot forward.

Seeing pictures of a hardflip or even seeing one in person can be confusing. It's difficult to understand exactly what's happening with the board. If you are confused about what the board should be doing, it will help to move the board through the action with your hands so you can visualize the trick clearly before you try it with your feet.

1. Get into your frontside 180 pop shuvit stance so that your rear foot is right on the tip of the tail and your lead foot is in the middle of the board.

2. Pop at a diagonal angle toward your toe side with your rear foot. This will send the board into the frontside lateral 180.

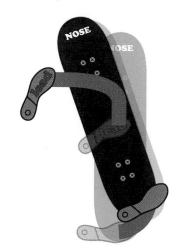

STANCE　　　**MOVEMENT**

3. As you pop and the nose rises up, scoop and flick the board with your lead foot. Because this is a kickflip, you will be flicking the heel side of the board with the side of your toes. However, the board will be rotating frontside laterally, so you may need to flick out to the side (behind you) more than at a forward and diagonal angle.

4. Raise your knees high to give the board lots of room to rotate. Keep your eyes on the rotation. Because the board's tail is almost coming up under the board rather than from the side, the kickflip flick doesn't need to be too aggressive.

5. As the board flattens out, trap it with either foot (although your lead foot may be easier).

6. Land and roll away.

You'll be landing with your lead foot forward, and that should make any adjustments to a sloppy landing easier to do.

○ If you are landing sideways or diagonally, try to slide the front around and ride away. This may not be the cleanest way to do hardflips, but it's enough to improve upon. If you demand that they be clean, pop the board harder to give it more lateral rotation. (Remember, the lead foot is controlling the axis rotation, and the rear foot is doing the lateral rotation.)

○ If the board is landing primo or doing an endo, flick your lead foot out behind you toward your back side instead of out at a forward diagonal angle. The board will be rotating, so your lead foot is probably coming off over the nose rather than off the side of the board near the wheels.

TAKING OLLIES AND SHUVITS FURTHER

There are lots of places to explore once you have your ollie and shuvit fundamentals down. All the tricks you've just read about can be finely tuned until you can land them cleanly most of the time. You can take them over gaps and off stairs or just push them farther on flat. Even the simple kickflip can be challenging when you try its own host of variations: double kickflip, late flip, nollie kickflip, switch kickflip, manual to kickflip (and kickflip to manual), and kickflip up curbs and ledges.

This book can't take you to all the places that experimentation and practice can. When you are struggling and frustrated, remember these fundamental skateboarding truths:

- Point your shoulders in the direction you want to go.
- Analyze what your body is doing. You can do *any* trick that has ever been done. . . . You just need to learn it.
- You are doing this to have fun, so don't let a hard trick and grumpiness ruin it for you.

CHAPTER 6

LIP TRICKS

All the tricks covered in this book so far can be done on flat ground. When you go to your local skatepark with its quarterpipes and halfpipes, you'll want a few tricks for these fun structures. Although you can have a rewarding time with skateboarding as strictly a tech skater, broadening your bag of tricks to include different kinds of terrains will help all of your skills. In other words, learning some lip tricks will help your flip tricks and vice versa. It can be disappointing to arrive at an awesome new skatepark only to find out that you don't know how to skate any of the types of structures there . . . and end up doing kickflips in the parking lot. Skaters who can ride anything are sometimes known as ATVs, or all-terrain vehicles, and they are ready for anything they encounter. When you can go anywhere and skate anything, you'll never be bored at any skatepark.

Lip tricks are skills and maneuvers you do at the top of a quarterpipe, miniramp, or halfpipe. The lip is the coping at the top of a ramp, so any trick where the board touches the coping could be considered a lip trick. You'll also find some basic skill-building exercises in this chapter that will help you learn how to skate on transition structures like a pro.

KNOW YOUR STRUCTURES

You don't need to know all the parts of a skatepark or ramp in order to rip it up, but it will help you when you want to talk with other skaters about a structure's characteristics. A few key terms and concepts follow.

Curved structures—ramps and bowls—all fall into the transition family. Transition typically includes quarterpipes, miniramps, halfpipes, bowls, volcanoes, tacos, cradles, and snake runs. This category of structures— sometimes called *tranny* for short—also describes the kind of skater who prefers this type of skating. If someone is known as a *tranny skater*, it means

STREET TERRAIN

TRANSITION TERRAIN

he excels at skating on curved walls, although it's not important to define yourself as a skater in this way. Some skaters refer to curving transitional walls, like you might find in the corner of a bowl, as *roundwall*.

Another term that some skaters use to describe tranny is *vert*. This is incorrect. Not every transitional element is vert. Only those structures that curve all the way to a vertical angle—that is, straight up and down—are vert (or vertical) structures. Miniramps and quarterpipes are not vert, and neither are most skatepark halfpipes. Their curved walls may arc up to 70 or even 80 degrees, *almost* vert. Professional-size halfpipes and most bowls more than 8 feet (2.4 m) deep have vert. Cradles, full pipes, and some pockets go "oververt," meaning they actually arc back inward. Imagine you are looking at a clock face where the 6 is the bottom of the halfpipe or bowl. Anything from the bottom up to 3 on one side and 9 on the other side is not vert. Anything precisely at 3 and 9 is vert, and anything beyond (above) 3 and 9 is oververt.

Oververt structures include cradles, clamshells, and full pipes because they all have overhangs that enable the skater to literally skate upside down by using centrifugal force. It is important to understand that all vert is tranny, but not all tranny is vert.

As you learn some lip tricks, there are some terms you'll want to be familiar with. On a typical miniramp you'll have the deck, coping (or lip),

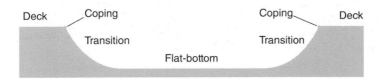

BACKSIDE AND FRONTSIDE ON THE RAMP

The terms *frontside* and *backside* are easier to keep straight on a miniramp than on flat. On flat, the terms are used relative to your lead foot. On the mini the terms are used relative to the ramp—and since the ramp doesn't move around, skate switch, or spin in circles, you will always have a reference point for the two terms.

One good way to keep backside and frontside straight is to think about how those terms were used in the early days of skateboarding, when contests often took place in bowls. The judges sat on the deck next to the bowl with the rest of the audience, just like today. When a skater did an air near the judges, if her back was to them it was a backside air. (Her front faced the bowl.) If she came out and the judges could see her front, it was a frontside air. Whichever side of your body is facing the deck (or audience) when you get to the coping determines whether the trick is frontside or backside.

The terms *frontside* and *backside* originated with surfing. When surfers move along the curl with their backs to the crest, it's called backside. If they are facing the wave, it's frontside.

---

transition, and flat-bottom. The deck is where people stand and wait their turn. The coping is the metal tube at the edge of the deck. The tranny is the section that curves from the coping to the bottom of the ramp. The flat-bottom is the span of ramp that connects the two opposing sides.

In this chapter we talk about these tricks as if they are being attempted on a miniramp or a small halfpipe. From flat to coping, miniramps can be between 3 and 6 feet (about 1 to 2 m) tall. Any taller and you're probably looking at a full-size halfpipe.

Every miniramp is different. Some are fast and challenging, while others are slow and easy. There are three qualities that can change how a miniramp feels to ride.

1. **Material.** Wood, steel, and concrete miniramps all ride a little differently. Wood is usually the slowest but most comfortable to fall on. When you ride a wood ramp, keep an eye out for screws and chips. Steel ramps are about as fast as concrete and are usually the smoothest. This makes reverts and slides easier but also provides less grip when you want it. When crafted by a professional, concrete is both smooth and fast but also hard as a rock, so don't forget your helmet. For most skaters concrete is the perfect balance of speed, smoothness, and grip.

2. **Size of tranny.** There are two sizes used to describe tranny. The first is the height of the ramp (i.e., the distance between the flat-bottom and the deck). The second is the radius of the curve. A smaller radius will feel more "whippy" than a larger radius. You'll hear this type most often described as "fast tranny" and larger-radius ramps as "slow" or "easy." Most experienced skaters have preferences regarding what kind

WOOD, STEEL, AND CONCRETE RAMPS

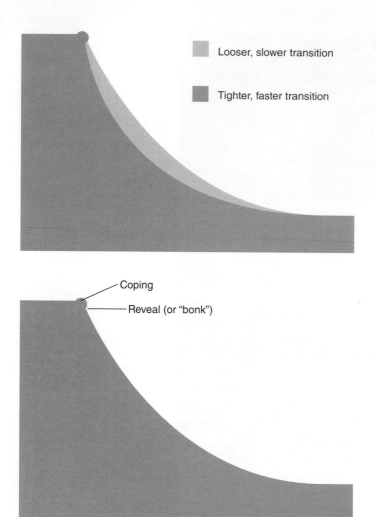

Looser, slower transition

Tighter, faster transition

Coping

Reveal (or "bonk")

of transition they like, although there are plenty of miniramp champs who are comfortable on anything. When the transition of a ramp feels uneven or has bumps in it, it's "kinked." This can make the ramp very difficult to ride.

3. **Amount of bonk.** The lip of the ramp has a role to play on the miniramp. Some ramps have no coping; the tranny just ends in a corner with the deck. When there is no coping, it's sometimes called *noping*, short for *no coping*. The coping should stick out from the tranny face of the ramp a little bit. The amount it sticks out is the amount of bonk it has. A lot of bonk would be big coping that sticks way out. You'll find this in pool replicas that feature concrete block coping (or pool coping). Smaller coping may offer only a little bonk. The amount of bonk is important because it helps your board interact with the lip of the ramp. The term *bonk* is not widely used, but it's an important consideration as you experiment with different types of coping.

FINDING THE RIGHT MINI

Not all miniramps are created equal. When you are ready to start learning lip tricks, you can make your life a lot easier by finding the right kind of transition. Tight transition is much more difficult to learn on but tends to be fast and gnarly. Slower transition (or longer tranny) is a lot easier to skate and much less intimidating, but it will be harder to keep your speed. Something in between is best.

If you haven't spent a lot of time on miniramps, you may not know what's tight and what's slow. Slowly move your board up and down the transition; if at any point the nose or the tail touches the surface, you should find a better miniramp or quarterpipe to learn these tricks on. At the other extreme, if you can roll the board from the deck and into the transition without the coping ever touching the underside of the board, the mini is probably too slow to really learn much on.

The best way to find a good mini is to look at what kinds of tricks the other skaters are doing on it. Most wooden-style ramps are designed to provide a balance between speed and ease. In concrete parks there tend to be more variations, so try out the different parks to see what is most comfortable for you.

MINIRAMP ETIQUETTE

The tech tricks we discuss in chapter 5 can be done on a sidewalk, a quiet street, or a parking lot. There's always plenty of space, and you don't usually need to wait your turn to do a kickflip. When you are dealing with a specific structure that skaters are sharing, you may wonder how a bunch of people who don't know each other are going to share a single small space without a lot of discussion and negotiation. This is where skatepark etiquette comes in.

There is an order to the activity at the skatepark and at the mini. Just like when you're skating with your buddy on the sidewalk comparing tricks, at the miniramp you typically take turns. On the mini your turn is sometimes called a run. If there are a lot of people waiting to take their turn, you should wait to go until the person you went after last time has taken his run. Your "number" has come up, and it's now your turn. This isn't a hard-and-fast rule, and getting seriously stressed out about whose turn it is would be worse than cutting ahead of someone.

When people don't understand the system or aren't paying attention to their place in line, it's called snaking. A snake will go whenever she wants or will barge in and go quickly before the person who deserves to go next has gotten into place. Occasionally you will come across a crowded ramp where there is no order. This is a "snake session" and usually indicates a high, energetic level of skating. Because snake sessions require a lot of confidence, there is usually little patience for people who are skating slowly and practicing basic skills. During snake sessions, an aggressive skating style is rewarded. If you aren't feeling confident with your miniramp skills, you may want to wait until the ramp session isn't quite as intense.

It's also polite to keep your run length appropriate to the number of people waiting to take their turn. If there are three or four people waiting for you to finish, going back and forth 10 times is about right. With fewer people you can probably skate a little longer during each run because each person is getting plenty of turns at the ramp. When there are more than five people waiting, your runs should be shorter to allow others to take their turns without having to wait too long. When there are lots of people and someone consistently takes long runs, those who are waiting may start getting irritated, particularly if the person skating isn't bringing fresh tricks to each run. Even when a lot of people are waiting their turn, though, you should never feel rushed. If your runs are reasonably short and someone is hollering at you to get out, it's possible that the person is just a jerk. Don't let anyone ruin skateboarding for you, but try to be sensitive to where you're going and who else is sharing that space with you.

If all the skaters at the session are friends, sometimes a person can take two runs back to back. This usually happens when the person drops in, goes up the opposite wall, and falls off while trying a trick. The run was so short he didn't really get his allotted time in the ramp, so it's polite to let this person go again if he wants to. Some people call this a "rebate." Aggressive skaters who fall may presume that because they screwed up so quickly they'll just take another turn and immediately set up to drop in again. This is the fine line between snaking and having a good time. It's all part of the natural rhythm of the miniramp session.

PUMP

Skating the miniramp is different from skating on flat in one significant way: You don't push with your feet. All of your speed is controlled by pumping and counterpumping. It's a lot like a swing; you can start with one good push and then use your body mass to get going higher and higher. The same is true in the miniramp. By compressing your legs and applying more weight to the board at critical moments, you can pump to get going faster and faster. You can also apply weight or lift up at certain times to suck up speed and slow down. This is known as counterpumping and is an essential skill to have before you can learn any of the more complicated tricks in this chapter. You will need to know how to manipulate your body mass and the board so that you are approaching the coping with the right amount of speed for each trick. On the flat you have the luxury of kicking one more time to speed up or dragging your foot a little to slow down; on the ramp you'll do all this through pumping and counterpumping.

You might understand how to pump, but you'll need to practice until you do it subconsciously. Eventually it will be second nature, and you won't even think about it. You'll just do it.

When you press down on your board, for a brief period you increase the force exerted on the board, and you pick up speed. Imagine that you are rolling toward a very large, smooth speed bump and you barely have enough speed to make it over. Just before you start going up, you lift your body and try to make it as light as you can, almost as if you're jumping up the slope. When you get to the top of the hill, your body is compressed, and you slowly roll over the top. As you start going downhill, you pick up speed and press down hard on your board as you straighten your body. You are probably going a lot faster than you were before you got to the hill. This is pumping.

Let's try it on a miniramp. You should be comfortable rolling backward (in switch stance) before trying this.

1. Start at one side of the miniramp flat-bottom. Push hard once with your lead foot, and quickly get on your board. Pay attention to your stance. Your feet should be at least over your bolts or even farther out toward the ends of your board.
2. Roll up the tranny a ways and come straight back down backward (fakie).
3. Roll up the opposite tranny a ways and come straight back down forward.
4. Keep going until you run out of speed. Throw in a quick push when you can.

After a while you may find yourself getting pretty high on the ramp. This is good. When you are comfortable going back and forth like this without feeling as if you're about to fall any second, start bending and flexing your legs at different places on the ramp. You should notice that when you pump on some places on the ramp you pick up speed, and at other places you slow down.

Keep practicing. Eventually you should be able to pump and maintain a consistent height without having to push with your foot.

- If you feel off-balance over the nose or tail every time you reach the apex of the tranny, it could be that your feet are too close together. Widen your stance by moving your feet farther out toward the nose and tail, and then bend your knees a bit so you are lower on your board. This should improve your stability.
- If you keep falling off the side or the board veers away from you, you are probably skating with tight trucks. It can be difficult to learn how to pump when you can't easily steer. Either loosen your trucks or practice skating switch on flat ground for a while until you're confident in steering while rolling backward.

Keep practicing pumping until you are able to build speed. After a while you should be able to get the wheels almost to the coping on both sides of the ramp—the front wheels when you are going forward and the back wheels when you are going backward. When you can do this, you are ready to drop in.

DROP IN

There aren't many tricks that require as much bravery and commitment as dropping in. Many people who feel a desire to learn it will stand on the edge of the ramp for minutes trying to get psyched up. There is no doubt about it: The first time is scary.

Are you ready? Probably. The technical requirements of successfully dropping in are tiny compared to the amount of bravery that is needed. Dropping in is a mind game. The good news is that everyone who skates transition knows exactly how this feels and has passed this challenge. There is only one way to do it, and that is to just do it. For almost every skater, dropping in is something of a rite of passage. When you can't do it, it hangs on you like a curse. After you can do it, you feel liberated and ready to explore miniramp tricks at whatever pace you like.

Several techniques will make your dropping in experience successful right away. Make sure you are comfortable pumping on the transition and that rolling down the ramp is something you aren't afraid of. Lots of people think they need to learn how to drop in before they know how to pump. This isn't true. You can learn all kinds of lip tricks on the mini by starting at the bottom of the ramp and pumping your way to the coping. Eventually you get to the point where you want to learn how to drop in and be done with it.

To get ready to drop in, start with your board hanging over the edge of the ramp, and then shift your body so you are standing fully balanced on the board at the top of the transition. When you drop in the board does very little, but your body weight does a lot.

1. Place the board's tail on the deck, with the rear wheels beyond the coping and the nose sticking out over the ramp. Keep the board in place with your rear foot on the tail and your lead foot on the deck.

2. Balance on your rear foot, and move your lead foot up just beyond the front bolts. You are ready to drop in. Do your best not to seize up mentally at this point. From the moment you put the board down, you should be focused on a smooth attempt without a lot of mental deliberation.

3. Without changing the position of the board, lean out over your lead foot. It's critical that you put nearly all your weight onto your lead foot. Don't push the board down with your lead foot, but lean your leg and hip into it. It may help to reach down and lightly hold the nose of the board with your forward hand to help bring your weight in.

4. As your weight is transferred to the nose of the board, stomp it hard onto the surface of the ramp. This is very important. The transfer of your weight to your front wheels must be committed and aggressive. You cannot "kind of" commit to stomping your front end.

5. The board should roll down the transition with you balanced on it. You did it! Pop out of the other side of the mini, grab your board, and set up to do it again.

The biggest challenge of dropping in is facing the fear of falling. Starting from your board sticking out into midair and ending by rolling down a curving decline is about as unnatural as skateboarding can get.

○ When you let your fear take control of your technique, you will have a tendency to lean backward as you drop in. This is a very common problem for people. When you lean back it may seem as if you're preventing yourself from slamming, but what you're actually doing is ensuring that you *will* fall. The board will roll down the transition in a wheelie, and you will fall backward, maybe even over the coping. The solution is to stomp hard on the front wheels immediately.

○ Sometimes—though rarely—a skater will drop in with her body weight slightly to the side of the board and fall off to the toe or heel side at the bottom of the slope. This may be a subconscious reaction to the fear of putting your body onto a rolling board pointed down a steep slope, or It could just be poor board control. Whatever the cause, you can fix this problem by focusing on a point on the opposite side of the mini that you want you and your board to reach. Keep your eyes focused on this point and don't let the board tell you where it wants to go; you tell the board to go to the point you've selected.

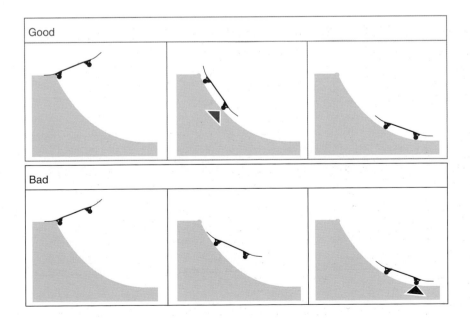

As you become more comfortable, you can experiment with cool ways to set up for dropping in. Some people like to ollie and land in a tail stall (your starting position for dropping in). Another good way is to roll along the deck up to the coping and then kick the board into the tail stall with a tiny manual. When you start enjoying blazing miniramp sessions, you will see all kinds of variations.

Eventually you will want to learn to drop in switch. This is like learning to drop in all over again because your mind will understand exactly what your body should do, but your body may not cooperate. When dropping in switch, you'll start with your nose on the deck and the tail hanging out into the ramp. Your lead foot will be firmly on the nose, holding the deck in place, while your rear foot will be lightly placed out near the tail of the board. When you're ready to drop in, lean into the ramp and stomp the tail down. (If you've already been doing fakie rocks as described on page 129, you might find it easier to be in a forward stance so that you come off the nose with your body pointed in the direction you are coming from.) Dropping in from your nose is essential for nose stalls and will improve your overall confidence and abilities on the mini.

READY TO DROP IN?

"It's easy! Grab your nose! Slam your front trucks down! Don't think about it! Hurry up! Don't lean back! Everyone falls the first time! *Do it!*"

Once a month or so at our local skatepark, a kid will show up who wants to learn how to drop in. While he stands with his board perched over the coping, a half dozen other skaters shout out advice. When the kid decided he wanted to learn to drop in, he wasn't thinking he'd have so many people paying attention and telling him what to do. This isn't intentional abuse; it's a rite of passage.

People who can drop in know something that other people don't. Dropping in is the easiest scary thing you can do in skateboarding. It's 90 percent jitters and 10 percent skill.

When a group of people stand around yelling advice to the kid perched on the edge of the mini, it doesn't help. Nobody likes to fall with a big audience while trying something that should be easy, but dropping in is a rite of passage, and maybe an audience wouldn't be so bad.

You get to drop in the first time only once, so make sure the time and place are right for you.

ROLL IN

Rolling in is a classy way of getting into the mini. Instead of perching on the coping in a tail stall, you push once or twice on the deck and roll right over the coping and land on the transition. This method will eventually allow you to roll anywhere around the skatepark without pushing. You can just roll in, out, and back into whatever bowls you like.

Similar to dropping in, rolling in takes confidence and commitment more than a particular skill. Learning to roll in requires a strong desire to succeed, the ability to comfortably pump on transition, and not much else.

Rolling in requires that you start a short distance from the ramp. A word of caution: Other people using the ramp may not be aware that you intend to roll in. Make sure people know where you're going so two of you don't drop in at the same time.

1. Start on the deck about 6 to 10 feet (2 to 3 m) away from the coping. You need enough room to get one good push and get your feet solidly on the board.

2. Push once and get on the board. Approach the coping head-on. Lots of people prefer to roll in with a bit of a frontside turn (with your back a little bit to the ramp).

3. When you get to the coping, lift your front wheels up just enough to clear it. Although this is a very short manual, you'll want to keep your weight evenly on your board or slightly forward as if you were dropping in from your tail.

4. At the moment your rear wheels hit the coping, push down with your lead foot to point the board in the same angle as the transition. Your board will bounce a little off the coping. This should feel a lot like bouncing over a crack in the sidewalk; lift your weight so the board bounces over the coping easily.

5. Straighten your legs to stomp the board firmly onto the transition and roll the rest of the way down.

Because rolling in requires commitment, it is scary the first few times. If you are struggling to find the bravery to try it, find a quarterpipe or miniramp with very small or even no coping. Without the coping, you will have one less thing to worry about. After you can roll in on quarters without coping, find one with coping to practice on.

o When the back wheels hang up on the coping, it's probably because your body weight isn't clearing the coping. You should try approaching the coping a little faster and concentrate on bonking over the coping with your rear wheels. A common problem is to go too slowly. Some beginners think that going slowly will make the trick easier to bail from, but all it does is ensure that they will have to bail. If you go too slowly, you won't be able to roll in.

o If you are still hanging up and you think you have plenty of speed, focus on bouncing your rear wheels on the coping. Lift your front wheels as you approach the coping to do a short manual. You can practice this on any area of flat ground where there's a small raised crack, like a sidewalk near a big tree. Roll at the crack with a little speed and try to bounce the board off the crack with the rear wheels as if you were doing an ollie without the pop of the tail. This is the same feeling you should be having when you roll in.

o If the board slips out sideways as you land on the transition, approach the coping at a straighter angle. You may be landing on the ramp at a diagonal angle. By going straight in, you simplify the landing angles.

OLLIE IN

The most dramatic way to start your run is to ollie in to the ramp. Like rolling in, you'll need some speed. Pay attention as you approach the ramp to see that someone else isn't setting up to drop in, or you could risk a collision. Ollieing in is challenging and scary, but it looks terrific.

There are lots of ways to get used to this trick. You should know how to ollie while keeping the board straight and pointed forward every time. If you're unsure whether you have the skills to ollie into the miniramp, try to ollie onto a flat-bank from the top or over the hip of a pyramid. If you can land with all four wheels on the bank at the same time, you should be able to ollie into the transition without difficulty.

1. Push once on the deck to approach the coping with it to your back side and with enough room to position your feet into a small ollie stance. Don't load up a monster ollie while you're just learning this trick.

2. Just before your front wheels bonk the coping, pop a small ollie. Prepare yourself for landing in the transition by loading your lead leg with more of your weight than usual. This will help you tilt forward in the air and land with all four wheels simultaneously on the downward slope of the transition.

3. As your rear wheels pass the coping, press your front wheels into the transition so that all four wheels land together.

Like dropping in, this trick is another one where the fear can outweigh the difficulty. Some people will be comfortable trying this trick without much deliberation, and others may grapple with their fears for weeks before their first attempt. There's no shame in taking your time. When the anxiety of learning a trick outweighs the fun of challenging yourself, it's time to put that trick aside and focus on the kind of skating that is fun for you.

- If your ollie lands sideways or at an angle on the transition, your ollie isn't straight and needs correcting. You can work on either straightening it on flat ground or adjusting your approach to the coping. For example, if you consistently land in the tranny with the board at the same angle, change your approach to balance this so that your board lands straight. A technique such as this will help people who have the common tendency to ollie slightly frontside.

- As you get comfortable ollieing in, you might try an ollie to tail on the coping. You may have seen people do this before. It's a small frontside ollie on the deck that you land on the coping in a tail stall as if you were dropping in normally.

BACKSIDE KICKTURN

Now that you can get into the miniramp and keep your speed, you will need to learn how to turn the board around. Going back and forth—forward and fakie—gets boring pretty quickly. The next technique you'll want to get comfortable with is the backside kickturn.

The key to the backside kickturn is to start small, well below the coping, and get accustomed to repositioning your front wheels in toward the direction you want to go. The backside kickturn on transition is a fundamental skill required for dozens of tricks, so you'll want to concentrate on developing good form. It shouldn't take long to be able to do backside kickturns with a relaxed posture and casual confidence.

In the backside kickturn, you will do a backside 180 so your back will be toward the deck. You will probably start learning your backside kickturns with a much smaller angle at first, rolling up the transition at an angle (with your back to the coping) and then doing a small kickturn and coming back down the transition at an angle. As you build confidence, you can start approaching the transition more directly and doing a bigger kickturn. Eventually you will be able to roll straight up the transition, do a perfect 180-degree kickturn, and roll straight back down the transition.

1. Start with a few pumps and fakies until you are midway up the transition. As you approach the transition and are ready to try a backside kickturn, steer the board a bit until it is rolling up the slope at a backside angle. You shouldn't be going straight up the tranny the first few times you do this trick. It may seem counterintuitive, but many people find that doing a kickturn midway up the transition is easier than doing one near the bottom because kickturns are easier when you have some speed and momentum to work with.

2. Before you reach the apex of your carve, turn your head and look directly in the direction you want to go. Lift the front wheels slightly (without looking at them) and reposition the board so it is pointed where you are looking. You can even slide the front wheels if that is more comfortable for you. Don't lift your front end so high that your tail touches the ground.

3. As you pick up speed and begin going back down the transition, correct the direction of the board until you're well balanced.

At first your backside kickturns may be about 45 degrees, but as you get better at them, you should try going straight up the transition and straight back down along the same path. You might even pick out a seam in the ramp or use a landmark on the ramp to measure your progress. If you want to take this further, you can try rolling up the transition in a frontside carve direction and doing a backside 270-degree kickturn. This is sometimes called an alley-oop.

Keep practicing backside kickturns until you can do them high enough on the transition that the front wheels go over the coping. This is the beginning technique for learning the backside 5-0 grind.

FRONTSIDE KICKTURN

In the frontside kickturn, you will roll up the transition and do a frontside 180 below the coping. You know it is frontside because your front side will be facing the deck and anyone who is standing on it as you reach the coping.

Use your shoulders to help steer your board. This is the single most important gesture to understand when learning smooth frontside kickturns. Using your shoulders doesn't mean keeping your body aligned to the board; it means really throwing your shoulders into the kickturn before your board does anything. Lead with your shoulders and point your chin where you want to go. It's easy to spot kickturn novices on minis and quarters as they grapple with underrotations caused by not leading with their shoulders. They look stiff and off-balance.

The frontside kickturn is more challenging than backside for most people because it's harder to see where you are going. It's also harder to bail because your heels are downhill. Like backside kickturns, it's typical to start learning them by approaching the transition at a frontside angle, then doing a small kickturn on the wall, and coming down at an angle. By practicing these arcing kickturns first, you will build an understanding of how to get your body and board through the turn without feeling off-balance. With practice your frontside kickturns will get narrower until you are going straight up the transition, doing a flawless frontside 180 kickturn, then rolling back down the transition in the same place you came up.

1. Start with a few pumps and fakies until you are midway up the transition. As you approach the transition and are ready to try a frontside kickturn, steer the board a bit until it is rolling up the slope at a frontside angle. You shouldn't be going straight up the tranny the first few times you do this trick.

2. Before you reach the apex of your carve, turn your head and look back over your lead shoulder to the direction you want the board to go. Lift the front wheels slightly (without looking at them) and reposition the board so it is pointed where you are looking. It may help to turn your body toward the coping a little bit before you lift the front wheels.

3. As you pick up speed and begin going back down the transition, correct the direction of the board until you're well balanced.

TAIL STALL

The tail stall is a fundamental skill that is important to learn. It will open up lots of other tricks and provide a great way of resetting your feet and clearing your head before your next trick. When you dedicate yourself to learning a smooth, comfortable tail stall, it will become the go-to trick for when you need to set up or "start over" midway through your run.

In a tail stall you approach the coping backward (fakie) and lift the board up on its rear wheels so the tail laps over the coping and onto the deck. Your body weight then rests on the tail as it's resting on the deck, as if you were prepared to drop in. This stall requires enough speed in the ramp to get you over the coping, so you must have strong pumping technique and feel comfortable going fast enough to reach the coping.

1. Fakie back and forth a few times in the mini and pump to maintain enough speed that your wheels almost touch the coping.

2. As you get to the apex of a forward pump and start coming down, pump hard enough that when you roll up the other side backward (fakie), your rear wheels will easily go over the coping. You don't actually lap your board over the coping, but you will need this speed to do the tail stall.

3. When you approach the coping fast in a fakie direction, lift the front wheels just as your tail crosses over the coping. You don't need to stall at first; just focus on tapping the tail against the coping. You'll develop the true stall later.

4. Set the front wheels down hard against the transition and roll back down the transition forward.

A proper tail stall puts all your weight onto the tail while it is flat against the deck, almost as if you were dropping in all over again. Instead of keeping your body low, you'll need to get your body mass up and above the coping. Practice the little nose lifts and tapping your tail against the coping until you can get the tail pressed against the deck—as just outlined—a few times, and then try the following steps to get into a proper tail stall:

1. As you approach the coping switch, transfer your weight onto your tail so that all of your weight is on your rear foot. The trick here is timing your transfer so that the tail dips down onto the deck just before the rear wheels hit the coping. It's all about the timing and properly judging exactly when the tail should be lowered so that it comes to rest on the deck before the wheels cross over the coping.

2. Come to rest with both your feet on the board and 90 percent of your weight on your tail.

The first dozen or so times you try this, it may be difficult to get your weight up and onto the deck. That's okay as long as you are coming back into the ramp on your board. Your stalls may be small at first, but you can build on them and increase their duration by practicing getting more of your weight to come to rest on your tail.

- If you can't seem to get your body weight up onto the deck, work on pumping really hard on your approach from the other side of the ramp and almost throwing yourself up onto the deck. Concentrate on where your hips and torso are during your attempts. You might try to intentionally throw yourself off-balance toward the deck so you have to take your front foot off to catch your balance. Now that you know what the two extremes feel like, dial it in until you can hold your tail stall for as long as you like without taking your feet off the board.

- When the rear wheels bounce over the coping, adjust your timing so that you are lifting up sooner. Face the coping as you approach it, and try to drop your tail down right on top of the coping. Look at the spot where you want to put your rear foot.

- If the end of the tail is hitting the face of the coping and stopping the board, you are obviously starting your tail stall too early. This usually happens when people are tired or not paying attention, but if it's happening to you all the time, return to the small tail taps on the coping to adjust your timing so you can consistently lower the tail over the coping and not under it.

NOSE STALL

Nose stalls are far more challenging than tail stalls. Don't attempt this advanced trick until you've gained a lot of experience on your board. Many people think that dropping in from the nose—which is basically what you are doing to get out of a nose stall—is like learning to drop in all over again. It's scary. The process for learning nose stalls is exactly the same as for the tail stall except that you approach the coping in a forward direction and roll away from the stall backwards. By the time you've done hundreds of tail stalls, you already "know" how to nose stall. You just need to train your body.

When you approach the coping fast in a forward direction, lift the rear wheels just as your nose crosses over the coping. Then set the rear wheels down hard against the transition and roll back down the transition backwards, or fakie. As with the tail stall focus on tapping the nose against the coping at first, then work up to a full stall over time.

Nose stalls feel so weird and scary for people trying them the first time. To warm up to the feeling and build confidence, you can try pumping a few times below coping then lifting the rear wheels off the ground at the apex of each forward pump.

REVERT

Reverts are a great way to turn your body and board around to either set up for your next trick or add some flair to the end of a trick. In a revert, you slide one end of the board 180 degrees. Reverts are identical to kickturns except you don't lift your wheels but slide them on the surface of the ramp instead. You can revert frontside or backside. Depending on how you are starting, you'll be going from switch to regular or vice versa.

Reverts are really easy to learn because you can do them on a smaller transition at first to get used to the feeling and then start taking them higher. You can also do them on small quarterpipes or even flat-banks until you're ready to take it up a notch. Let's start with some low ones. Like kickturns, reverts are all about your upper-body rotation. You won't be able to revert if you don't lead with your shoulders.

1. Pump a few times until you are midway up the transition. Keep your stance wide and stable. Approach the transition in a forward direction. (You can do fakie reverts later.)

2. As you reach the apex of your pump, rotate your head and shoulders in the direction you want to revert. Slide the front wheels around 180 degrees until they're pointed back down the transition and roll away.

Do this a few times and then try kicking the tail end of the board up the transition so that part of the slide is on your front wheels and the other part is on the back. This is like splitting the 180-degree turn between both ends of the board so that the nose end will do 90 degrees downhill while the tail end does the other 90 degrees uphill. You may need to lift your body weight up off the board slightly to allow the wheels to break their grip on the surface of the ramp.

After you know how much pressure it takes to slide the wheels on the surface, you should try a revert from a tail stall.

1. Get into an ordinary tail stall position and prepare to drop in.

2. As you drop in, rotate your shoulders to your front side. (Backside reverts are a little easier for most people than frontside.) As you transfer your weight to the nose of your board to drop in, your torso should be rotated so that your shoulders are aligned with the coping and your chest is facing the transition.

3. Just before the front wheels hit the ground, push the tail end of the board down and toward your front side. You need to slide the tail end all the way around, a full 180 degrees, so that you roll away backward.

Some people find that learning reverts from a stall is easier by starting from a nose stall. If you try it this way, you'll be sliding the nose around backside (to your right if you're regular) and rolling out of the revert with your lead foot in front. You might find this more comfortable.

○ When the board doesn't seem to want to slide, practice a few reverts without the stall so you can dial in how much pressure it will take to break the wheels' grip. You might have to work harder than usual at reverts if you are riding with soft wheels or if the surface of the transition isn't smooth.

○ If the board is overrotating and bucking you off, put less pressure on the slide. Underrotation is usually okay, especially with backside reverts, because you can just step off the board if it's not cooperating. If you are underrotated, try to ride it out and correct the board's direction on your way down the transition.

ROCK TO FAKIE

Even though it isn't very flashy, rock to fakie is a hard trick to learn. It is worth the effort because it allows you to set up for dozens of other tricks that require you to approach the coping rolling backward.

In a rock to fakie, you roll up to the coping high enough that the nose of the board laps over onto the deck. After a second you roll back into the transition backward. The fear of this trick is usually justified because it's easy to screw up and fall in a way that is difficult to jump away from. Getting into the rock to fakie is easy; getting out of it is hard at first.

Take a close look at the miniramp or quarter that you want to learn rock to fakie on. Lay the board across the coping and roll it up and down to see the wheels clear the coping. Some coping will have lots of bonk and will be less forgiving than smaller coping. The best ramps to learn the rock to fakie on don't have too much coping.

1. In your forward stance, roll toward the coping with enough speed to get your front wheels to lap over the coping and go onto the deck.

2. When you approach the coping, lift the front wheels so they clear the coping and come down onto the deck. You can also just roll your front wheels right over the coping, but it's better form to lift the wheels. This practice will develop good habits and help keep you from hanging up as you come back in backward.

3. As your front wheels go over the coping, your board should become high-centered and "rock" on the lip. If the board goes way up onto the deck with the back trucks slamming against the coping on the transition side, you may want to bail and try again with a little less speed. You can improve your rock to fakie by pushing the board into this fully committed position later.

4. Pause here briefly and let your weight begin to come back into the transition. As you feel your body starting to go back down the transition, lift the weight off the nose end of the board a bit so it clears or rolls over the coping as it comes back in. The entire operation should take only a split second.

If the board clips and hangs up when you are coming back in, widen your stance so your feet are firmly on the nose and tail. It will help to get in the habit of lifting your front wheels over the coping when you're going into the rock to fakie and lifting them a split

second later as you come back into the transition backward. You can practice this technique below the coping by lifting your nose high, balancing for a second, and then putting it back down against the surface of the transition. You can do the tail too on the opposite wall. This will help your body get used to that lifting motion.

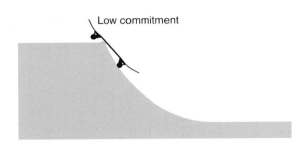
Low commitment

Your first successful rock to fakie attempts will probably have the board lapping up over the coping just a little bit. The front wheels might even be touching the top side of the coping. As you get more confident, the board will go up higher onto the deck. The most committed rock to fakie will slam the back trucks into the coping, with the nose of the board all the way up on the deck.

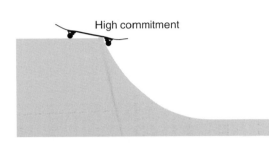
High commitment

FAKIE ROCK

The fakie rock is the exact opposite of the rock to fakie. You enter the fakie rock backward and exit the trick rolling forward down the transition. Most people find this trick a lot easier than the rock to fakie. The problem is that you basically need to know how to do a rock to fakie to get into a position to even try a fakie rock because it requires going into the trick backward. If your pumping technique is good, you can probably try fakie rocks by just getting into it from a good solid pump.

1. After coming out of your rock to fakie, pump hard to give yourself enough speed to roll halfway over the coping. (You should be moving backward.)
2. With your lead foot firmly on the nose, as you reach the coping lift the rear wheels up slightly so they go over onto the deck without touching it. Allow the tail of the board to come back down immediately on the other side so that the coping contacts the underside of the board.
3. Pause for a split second and allow your body to begin falling back into the transition. As you feel yourself coming back in and the board begins to move, lift the rear wheels again so they clear the coping. (This isn't a nose manual but rather just a quick lift.) Even raising the rear wheels a little will remove enough weight from them that if they accidentally bounce over the coping it shouldn't matter.
4. Roll down the transition forward and prepare for your next trick.

BACKSIDE ROCK AND ROLL

The backside rock and roll—sometimes called just backside rock—is a classic trick many skaters like to learn early on. On most miniramps it is easy to learn, and it doesn't take any complicated motions to pull off.

The backside rock is like the rock to fakie except you do a 180 kickturn from the rock position instead of rolling in backward. There are two secrets to backside rock and rolls. First, push the board into the rock ahead of your body weight so you are not completely up on the board when it's against the coping. The second secret is absolutely required to do this trick: Lead with your shoulders.

1. Approach the coping with the same amount of speed as you might for a rock to fakie. You'll need enough speed to get the board over the coping so that the front is on the deck and the back end is still in the transition.

2. Before you reach the coping, rotate your shoulders so your chest is pointed toward your tail. This is the single most important motion your body must do. You'll be turning backside, so rotate your torso in the direction your board will soon need to go.

3. Lift the nose slightly so it crosses the coping smoothly. Once the front wheels are past the coping, let the nose come down so that the front wheels rest on the deck. This is a very quick motion; you just want to quickly tap the front wheels to the deck. There is no stall to this trick, at least not at first.

4. Immediately lift the nose of the board up and bring it around in a backside 180. You may feel the rear wheels slide down the ramp as you bring the nose around. This is okay as long as you keep rotating.

5. As the front wheels come down, make your adjustments and roll away.

It may seem at first as if nothing can go right with your backside rocks. Most of the problems people have are easy to fix.

- If the front wheels clip the coping as you bring the 180 around, work on a few backside 180s below the coping and without the rock. Try to do your 180s so that you are traveling straight up the transition, doing a perfect 180, and then coming straight back down. Pay attention to what your shoulders are doing. Try to do the 180 as the board comes to a stop and not while it's still rolling up the transition.

- If the front wheels are still clipping the coping when you're bringing the front end around, you may be getting up too high onto the rock. If you find you can pause for a second while the board is lapped over the coping, you are probably too high. To fix this, try to push the board forward so the front wheels tap the deck quickly and then are immediately pulled into the 180 kickturn. The motion should be quick.

- If the board comes about only halfway around the 180 and stops sideways, you need to rotate your shoulders more. If you can slide the front wheels the rest of the way around, that's fine, but improve your upper-body technique as you practice. Under-rotating your body is the main reason most people struggle with their rock and rolls.

FRONTSIDE ROCK AND ROLL

The frontside rock and roll—or frontside rock—is the more respectable version of the two rock and rolls. (You seldom see backside rocks in magazines and videos, but front rocks are all over the place.) One of the many cool things about the frontside rock is that it's easy to learn but can be taken to gnarly terrain and styled in interesting ways. Frontside rocks never go out of fashion and will always be cool.

In the frontside rock, the board laps halfway over the coping and then is immediately brought back into the transition with a frontside 180. It's basically the backside rock's prettier sister.

1. Approach the coping with enough speed to get the front wheels easily up and over the coping. Try to get the board to lap up onto the coping a little bit. You may need a little more speed for the frontside rock than you would for a backside rock.

2. As you approach the coping, twist your shoulders deeply to your left (regular) or right (goofy) so that your back shoulder is almost over the nose. You need a lot of prerotation. More than any other trick, the twisting motion during the frontside rock is pretty extreme.

3. Lift the front wheels a bit so they easily clear the coping and quickly tap the wheels on the deck.

4. After tapping the deck, immediately lift the front wheels and bring them around in a frontside 180. This will feel as if the board is trying to catch up with your body. If your technique is reasonable, the board's front end should come down right below your body mass.

5. Make any adjustments as you roll down the transition.

It cannot be stressed enough that the secret of the frontside rock is in the prerotation of the shoulders. Lapping over the coping should be kept to a minimum at first; there's no stall on the coping. As you improve this trick, you can jam the board way up onto the deck and stall briefly before bringing it back in.

- If the board consistently slips out beneath you as you bring it back in, you are probably too high on the coping. Try to keep your body weight leaned out over the tail as the board laps over the coping.

- If the front wheels clip the coping when you do the frontside 180, practice doing some clean frontside 180s below the coping. Focus on going straight up, doing the 180, and coming straight back down. After this feels consistent, try to do them just after the apex so you are almost coming down backward before you start them. This may feel weird at first but should provide you with a good sense of what the frontside rock feels like when it's done properly.

OLLIE TO FAKIE

The ollie to fakie and its cousin, the fakie ollie, are both fundamental maneuvers that can become the basis for more complex tricks.

The ollie to fakie is simply an ollie on transition. You will roll straight up the tranny, ollie, and then land and roll back down backward. There is nothing complex about it. If your flat-ground ollies are good, you should be able to get some pretty high ollie to fakies in an afternoon of practice. The best technique for learning big ollies on transition is to start small and dial in your balance first and then progressively take them larger and higher.

1. Roll up the transition at a moderate speed but well below the coping. Position your feet in a wider than ordinary ollie stance so your lead foot is closer to the nose than if you were doing an ollie on flat.

2. Pop your ollie as usual. Use your lead foot to level the board out; don't worry about trying to scoop the board.

3. Push the board hard into the transition so that all four wheels hit at the same time.

You can warm up to bigger versions of this trick by honing your technique on the lower part of the transition. Gradually bring it higher up the wall and focus on a clean ollie that lands straight more than trying to get a lot of air. If your rock to fakies are comfortable and the ollie to fakie is coming along, you can combine them in a way that should be apparent.

If the board lands too far forward and you fall off the tail end, pop your ollie later so it happens almost when you are at a stop. Try to keep your weight higher than the board so it comes down below you rather than into the side of the transition.

FAKIE OLLIE

Most skaters believe the fakie ollie on transition is more difficult than the ollie to fakie. You might find otherwise. It's virtually the same trick except you are rolling up the transition backward and then rolling out of your ollie forward. One nice thing about the fakie ollie is that you can practice it by rolling up the transition until you come to a complete stop, and it will feel like a plain old "standing still" ollie on flat ground. If you pop your ollie in that split second just before you stop moving, it should feel comfortable and not particularly scary.

1. Pump up to a comfortable height on the transition and get your feet into a good ollie stance. Unlike the ollie to fakie, you can probably put your lead foot nearer the middle of the board as if you were doing the ollie on flat ground.

2. Make sure you are well below the coping. As you near the apex of your pump, pop the tail down as for an ordinary ollie. The transition should rise up to meet your tail, so you should feel the pop earlier than you would on flat ground.

3. Scoop the board with your lead foot as much as you are comfortable. You will be landing on a downhill slope, so you will need to bring the nose of the board down farther than usual.

4. Land, roll away, reposition your feet, and prepare to do it again.

There are two ways of training your body to land your fakie ollies clean. One method is to concentrate on pushing the board back into the transition behind you so your ollie is slightly uphill. The other way is to ollie and scoop the board out in front of you so you land downhill from where you started. The method that works best will be determined largely by the timing of your ollie. If you ollie as the board is moving up the transition, you will find that pushing the board down behind you will work best. If you wait until the board is almost completely stopped, the board will naturally land lower on the transition. Either method is fine; try both approaches to see what works best for you.

If the board doesn't seem to pop or get airborne, don't sweat it. Keep working on the timing and landing. Eventually the height will be there. It's much better to have a clean technique that produces smoother, smaller ollies consistently than to have a lot of height with low success.

FRONTSIDE OLLIE

The frontside ollie on transition is a versatile trick that every miniramp skater should be able to do. When the frontside ollie is done skillfully, it's an impressive trick on its own. The frontside ollie also leads to other cool tricks such as the disaster, lipslides, and even some cool tricks imported from the flat such as bigspins and tre flips on transition. You can't do any of these on the miniramp or bowl without a decent frontside ollie.

As they say about chess, the frontside ollie is easy to learn and difficult to master. In the beginning these will feel uncoordinated, but eventually they will start to smooth out. One important thing to understand while you visualize doing this trick is that you are not doing a frontside 180 ollie. Instead, you will be rolling up the transition at a frontside angle, popping your ollie with only a little frontside rotation, and then landing on the transition at a downward diagonal. After your landing, you can steer the board through the rest of the descent and prepare for the next wall.

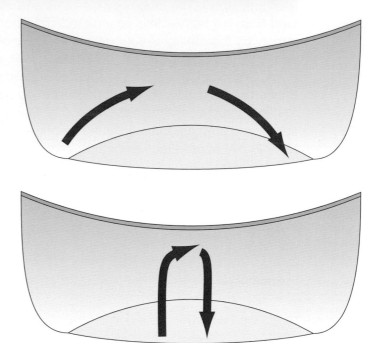

Adjust the arc of your line across the transition to make your ollie easier or more difficult.

1. Pump up some speed by doing a series of frontside kickturns. Keep the board comfortably below the coping for now. Keep your line in a large looping pattern rather than going straight up and straight back down. The larger your turns across the transition the better.

2. When you are ready, move your lead foot over or slightly behind the front bolts. You want to be in a wide ollie stance. Since most of the ollie height will come from the curving transition, a large lead-foot scoop across your board won't be necessary. The curvature of the ramp will be doing a lot of the work for you.

3. Roll up the transition at about a 45-degree angle, with your toes pointed toward the coping. Keep your weight lower on the transition so the board is riding a little higher than you.

4. While you are still moving forward at a reasonable speed, pop your ollie with a very small frontside rotation. You may not need any conscious effort to bring the board around frontside; you may do it naturally.

5. Land diagonally on the transition or as much pointing straight down the transition as you can.

When you are starting to learn frontside ollies on transition, don't worry about getting big air. Focus on popping your tail with a lot of snap and bringing the board around so it lands squarely under you. (Remember, on transition having the board "under" you doesn't necessarily mean the board is "below" you.)

○ If the board's nose doesn't rotate in a frontside direction, use your shoulders a bit more to lead it around. Start with a bit of a pretwisted posture as you begin going up the transition and rotate your lead shoulder to your left (regular) or right (goofy) as you ollie.

○ If the board just doesn't seem to want to get off the ground even though you are doing everything correctly, find a flat-bank and try a frontside ollie there. If you can ollie on a bank, there should be little challenge doing it on a small transition.

BACKSIDE 50-50 STALL

This stall is one of the first lip tricks many people learn. With a little practice, your 50-50 stall will become one of those tricks you don't think about; you just do it when you need to turn around. The 50-50 stall is required if you want to learn long, stand-up 50-50 grinds.

It looks simple, but there are some complicated body weight transfers that can be difficult at first. There are two types of 50-50 stalls: frontside and backside. The backside 50-50 stall is easier to get into, and for most people the frontside 50-50 stall is easier to get out of. You can experiment with both and see what feels right for learning first. Then challenge yourself with the other one afterward. We'll explain the backside 50-50 stall first.

1. Roll straight up the transition or at a slight backside angle, with enough speed to get your body weight fully onto the coping. Imagine you are going to roll on your board right up and stand on the coping perfectly.

2. As you near the coping, rotate your shoulders a bit so your chest is facing the coping. This is a tiny bit of prerotation to help get your body started into the backside turn.

3. As the front wheels pass the coping, do a 90-degree backside kickturn and drop the front trucks heavily onto the coping in one smooth motion. The back trucks should be resting, or locked, on the coping. You should now be standing on your board with the frontside wheels (or toe side) hanging over the coping in the ramp and the backside wheels (or heel side) on the deck.

4. Pause for as long as you need to until you start to feel your body fall back into the transition. If your body weight was not firmly planted on top of the coping, this may be right away. Conversely, if you had too much speed, you may need to take a foot off and plant it on the deck to regain your balance over the board.

5. Lift your front trucks off the coping and bring the wheels out over the transition. Your weight should bring the board out so it dips down in the ramp. Quickly plant the front wheels onto the transition under your body weight. The rear wheels should fall off the coping easily.

6. Roll away.

The problems people have with 50-50 stalls are usually rooted in how their body weight is distributed while they do the trick. Many people struggle to get their body weight all the way up onto the board, which results in a 50-50 stall that doesn't look as much like a stall as like a quick front-trucks kiss on the coping.

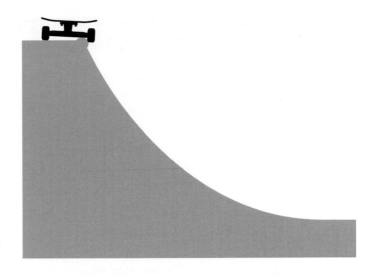

- If your 50-50 stall is too quick and doesn't stall, try to get your butt all the way up onto the coping over the board. This will help put your body up into the stall position. If you can throw your butt weight onto the board, the rest of your body should follow. Experiment with trying to get your body weight all the way past your board as it lands in the 50-50 position so that you need to take a foot off and put it on the deck behind you. This should give you a sense of the motion you will need to get your body fully onto the board.

- If the board hangs up when you bring it back in, slide the rear trucks into the ramp just before you drop back in. If you watch people do 50-50 stalls and 50-50 grinds, you'll often see them slide the tail of the board into the ramp a bit just before they reenter the transition. This helps the rear wheels roll over the coping easily instead of hanging up and rolling back onto the deck of the ramp.

- The front wheels may land on the deck rather than the trucks landing on the coping. You will know if you used your shoulders correctly if you land the board on the coping without feeling twisted. If you put your front trucks down and your arms are out over the deck and you feel as if your shoulders aren't facing the same direction as your board, you will need to lead with your shoulders better. Start your kickturn with more prerotation of your shoulders.

- If the front trucks are landing on the deck instead of on the coping and your torso doesn't feel twisted at all when you land, you can adjust the board with your feet by lifting or sliding it onto the coping. If the front trucks land on the deck, you can also just drop in from that position by bringing the front end back into the transition.

FRONTSIDE 50-50 STALL

For frontside 50-50 stalls, you reverse the kickturn when you reach the coping. Instead of approaching the coping and then turning backside—with your back to the deck—you will turn frontside so you're facing the deck and your back is to the transition.

Bringing the board back into the transition from a frontside 50-50 stall is easier for some people because the board tends to align under the body weight with less effort. Many people reenter the transition from a frontside 50-50 stall with a slight hop of the body to help the wheels come off the coping without getting hung up.

1. Roll straight up the transition or at a slight frontside angle, with enough speed to get your body weight fully onto the coping. Imagine you are going to roll on your board right up and stand on the coping perfectly.

2. As the front wheels pass the coping, do a 90-degree frontside kickturn and drop the front trucks heavily down onto the coping in one smooth motion. This should be a 90-degree kickturn, with the back trucks resting, or locked, on the coping. You should now be standing on your board with the backside wheels (or heel side) hanging over the coping toward the transition and the frontside wheels (or toe side) on the deck.

3. Pause for as long as you need until you start to feel your body fall back into the transition. If your body weight was not firmly planted on top of the coping, this may be right away. Conversely, if you had too much speed, you may end up stepping onto the deck. If this happens (and it will lots of times), the trick is over. It's better to approach the FS 50-50 in one smooth motion than to pick up where you stepped off.

4. Lift your front trucks off the coping and bring the wheels out over the transition. Your weight should bring the board out so it dips down into the transition. Quickly plant the front wheels onto the transition under your body weight. The rear wheels should fall off the coping easily.

5. Roll away.

If the board feels as if it's hanging up when you bring it back in, bring the board back into the transition with a bit of a hop. With backside 50-50s, you can rotate the board and it should come right back in. With frontside 50-50s, on the other hand, many people think it feels better with a slight hop.

5-0 STALL

In this fundamental trick, you roll straight up to the coping in a regular stance and do a 180 with your rear trucks on the coping. It is essentially a 50-50 stall in which the front trucks hover over the coping while the board rotates on the rear trucks. The 5-0 stall is fundamental for learning 5-0 grinds and pivots.

You'll need enough speed to comfortably roll up onto the coping. You should start with the backside 5-0 stall rather than the frontside.

1. Roll straight up the transition with enough speed to get your body all the way up onto the deck. As you near the lip, prerotate your body backside to help give it that extra spinning motion when you are on the coping.

2. As the front wheels cross the coping, do a 90-degree backside kickturn so you are facing the ramp. The nose of the board should rotate around with your body. Keep your balance over the rear trucks as if you were doing a slow 180 on flat ground. If you feel as if you are losing your balance, you can quickly set the front wheels down until you regain your stability.

3. As the nose crosses the coping and you are ready to drop back in, let your body weight begin to move back into the transition. Lead with your body and push the front wheels quickly into the transition. It may help to spring off your board just a little bit to get some weight off the rear wheels.

4. Roll down the transition and set up for your next trick.

The 5-0 stall can be difficult for people who have grown accustomed to keeping their body weight below the coping. A clean 5-0 stall requires you to transfer your body weight from the board while it's on the transition (using centrifugal force to stand "on" the board), all the way up onto the board when it's on the deck (using gravity to stand on the board), and then back again to the board on the transition. All this weight transfer can be difficult to get used to.

○ If you can't seem to get your body up onto the board, work on your 50-50 stalls to get used to the weight transfer. Try some 50-50 stalls while leaning back a little and lifting the front trucks.

○ When the rear wheels land all the way on top of the deck, they will tend to roll back as you bring the front end around. The board will fall into a rock or disaster position so that both rear wheels are up on the deck and the board is bottomed out on the coping. To help fix this, concentrate on letting your body weight fall back into the transition before your board instead of leading with the board. You should also fix your eyes on the exact spot on the coping where you want the rear trucks to land. This should help you time the kickturn so it's on the coping rather than after it.

PIVOT

A pivot is a simple but stylish trick that adds a lot of flavor to any miniramp run. It's a fundamental maneuver that has many variations and can easily lead to some killer grinds and rocks.

In a pivot, the board does a quick 5-0 stall and then reverses the motion to go back into the ramp. The pivot is identical to a 5-0 stall except there is no 180 rotation on the coping. Instead the board begins the rotation—anywhere from a few degrees to more than 90—and then reverses and reenters the ramp in the opposite direction.

1. Roll up the transition in a forward direction with a wide stance and enough speed to get the rear trucks onto the coping. You won't want to get your full body weight onto the deck, as you might if you were trying a 5-0 stall, so try to keep your body weight within the ramp.

2. Lift your front wheels over the coping and let the board continue to roll up. Just as your rear trucks get to the coping, rotate the nose of the board out to the side so the rear trucks lock onto the coping just as it would in a 5-0 stall.

3. As soon as you feel the trucks on the coping in a stall, wait for your body weight to begin falling back into the transition. This should take just a split second. When you feel your body is moving back into the ramp, straighten the board slightly so the trucks pop off the coping. You should be moving backward into the ramp.

4. Ride the rear wheels into the ramp until the front wheels have cleared the coping. This takes some practice and timing and is truly the scariest part of this trick. The front wheels and trucks never touch the coping, deck, or any other part of the ramp.

5. When the front wheels are clear of the coping, set them down and roll away backward.

Pivots are scary because you must commit your body weight before you are sure the board is going to be cooperative. You can warm up to them by rolling straight up the transition, letting your front wheels ride straight up in the air, and then rolling straight back down. This looks like a rock to fakie without the rock.

- If the front wheels clip the coping when you are coming back in, try moving the board off the stall sooner. But don't wait until your body weight is too far into the ramp or else the board must rush to catch up with you. (If the wheels clip the coping before the board is under you, your mass can't help the board bounce off the coping, and the board is more likely to hang up in a bad way.) Try to keep your body weight mostly centered over the board throughout the whole pivot.

- When the board seems to lock onto the coping and doesn't come back into the ramp with your body, concentrate on riding the rear wheels into the ramp as for a small manual. This will help keep your body weight over the important part of the board. You should not have any weight on the nose portion of the board when you are coming back into the ramp from your pivot.

After you have done a few successful pivots, try kicking the nose of the board out to the opposite side for the other pivot. For example, if you were most comfortable twisting the nose into a frontside pivot, try pushing the nose the other way for a backside pivot.

After you are confident with these pivots, you should try rolling up into the pivot in a backward direction and reentering the ramp forward. These will be your switch pivots, and these too can be done backside and frontside. There are basically four different types of pivots you can learn.

If the pivot seems too much for you, you can try rolling into a backside 5-0 stall and then coming back in forward. This variation will have you rolling up backward toward the coping and then lifting the nose of the board up and to the side just as the tail trucks get onto the coping. This takes a lot less commitment and is much easier to roll out of than the full-size pivots. It's not technically a pivot, but it relies on many of the same kinds of body motions.

DISASTER

This scary-sounding trick is easy to pick up right after the frontside or backside ollie. It is easy to imagine how the disaster was named—if you found yourself with the board in that position while on vert, it would truly be a disaster. To the untrained eye a disaster looks like the worst rear-trucks hang-up happening right in front of you. On miniramps, disasters aren't nearly as risky because locking up is less likely. Today, disasters are common tricks you'll see at your local skatepark and in pro contests.

In the disaster, you ride the transition and pop a 180 ollie just below the coping. After rotating in the air, you land with the board across the coping, with the tail end up on the deck and the nose end out over the transition. With a quick lift of the tail, you clear the coping and roll down the transition forward.

You can do frontside or backside disasters, but the frontside is easier for most people because frontside ollies are easier. There are lots of disaster variants waiting for you after you have normal disasters on lock. For example, you can do disaster rocks, shuvit disasters, kickflip disasters, and more. You may notice while learning disasters that they are similar to rocks, whether it's a rock and roll, fakie rock, or rock to fakie. The only difference is the ollie before the rock. Because of these similarities, some of these tricks may be called rock and roll variants in your area.

1. Start by rolling up the transition with enough speed to hit the coping. Position your feet in a wide ollie stance.
2. Prepare to spin by loading up your shoulders and bringing your lead shoulder (left if you're regular, right if you're goofy) toward your chest.
3. As you begin to pop your ollie, unload your shoulders to start your rotation. You will need to ollie *up* the transition slightly, so don't wait until you are barely moving before you ollie. The ollie will need to be high enough for the rear wheels to clear the coping and land up on the deck.
4. Once the board is rotated and the tail end is across the coping, stomp the board and trap it against the coping. It shouldn't matter if the board is at a bit of an angle

or whether the tail wheels are way up on the deck or barely over the coping. You can make this trick look clean and smooth later. For now just concentrate on keeping the board under your center of gravity.

5. Once you have the board trapped in a rock position on the coping, you should have a second to make sure your footing is good and your balance is over your board. If it all feels good and your lead foot is more forward than your front trucks bolts, lean into the transition to start the board on its path back into the ramp. Coming back in from the disaster is exactly like coming in from a fakie rock.

6. As the rear wheels near the coping, lift the tail end of the board by pressing your nose slightly. It's best if you can completely clear the rear wheels so they don't touch the coping at all, but most people usually bonk over the coping on their way back in. It's not as clean but works for lots of skaters.

7. Roll away with a smile.

Although disasters aren't generally considered a high-risk trick, a few things can go wrong. You will usually know what you need to work on since the disaster is actually a sequence of three individual steps: 180 ollie up the tranny, land in the rock, clear the coping to roll back in. Each step is distinct, and you can revisit any of these parts independently if you need to.

○ If the board lands with one or both of its trucks on the coping in a grind or stall, you'll need more rotation in your ollie. You might try a few 180s below the coping, making an effort to get as much straight up, straight down rotation as you can. Once you see that your rotation is dialed, try it with some speed to get it above the coping.

○ If the board hits the coping and slides away on the coping faster than a racehorse, you are landing too far back on your heels. This is caused by pushing the board up onto the coping instead of keeping it under you. To fix this, as you approach the coping, find a point on the coping where you will aim to put your feet *and* your board. Don't chase the board with your feet by trying to land it wherever it happens to come down. Keep the board under you.

BLUNT (TO FAKIE)

The blunt is a miniramp staple. It's a great trick and will demonstrate your mastery over the ramp. The blunt unlocks a handful of variations that are all cool in their own way but it's a difficult trick to learn.

In a blunt you roll up forward onto the coping until your rear trucks have lapped over the coping while keeping the tail flat against the transition just under the coping. A quick pop off the tail brings the rear wheels back over the coping and onto the transition. You bring the board down the coping on the rear wheels for a short distance before setting your front wheels onto the ramp. You can imagine the risk involved as you bring the board back into the ramp. Your body is fully committed to riding the board back down the transition, but if the front wheels clip the coping, the board will stop and you'll splat. There's no way to hedge your bets with this trick; you simply have to develop a solid technique and learn what works.

1. Roll straight up the transition with enough speed to get your rear wheels over the coping. Your stance should be wide and stable.

2. Lift the nose and push the rear wheels over the coping until they lock onto the deck side. The tail should slap against the coping on the transition side, with the board sticking up in the air. Keep your body weight off the top of the board so the board doesn't roll up onto the deck; keep your tail against the transition below the coping. This is the big secret behind the blunt: Don't put your body weight up on the coping.

3. Immediately after you feel the tail slap against the transition below the coping, pop the end of the tail against the transition. This will pop the nose of the board out toward you. The rear wheels should clear the coping. This is not an aggressive pop (like an ollie) but smaller. You want enough pop that the board rises up and away from the lip but not so much that it's hard to control.

4. When the lower (rear) wheels are past the coping, press them into the transition. This will help you guide the rest of the board down the slope. Keep your weight favored on the lower end of the board so the higher wheels can clear the coping without touching it.

5. A second later when the nose wheels pass the coping set them down and roll away.

There's a shortcut to learning blunts more easily. Instead of coming out of the blunt with a pop back into the transition, many people pop off the blunt into a rock position, with the board lapped halfway over the coping onto the deck. This is a much more stable position to reenter the ramp from and can take some of the risk out of the trick. Try this method at first, and then when you're ready you can go straight into the transition and skip the rock.

1. Instead of popping the tail against the transition and bringing the board downward, immediately push the nose of the board down onto the deck so the board falls into a rock. You will need to adjust your body weight a bit for this to work; instead of keeping your weight below the board and out over the transition, get your weight a little bit higher on the coping. The nose may dip down so that more of your board is on the rear wheels and the deck.

2. Pop the tail and try to bring the board down into a rock so the board is halfway on the deck and the tail end is out beyond the coping.

3. Roll your body weight back onto your tail end so the rear wheels contact the side of the transition and the board begins to slide back into the transition. The weight transfer during this motion is challenging, but if you have been working on rock to fakies with the rear trucks locked against the coping, then you should have this maneuver down easily.

4. As the front trucks near the coping, lift the wheels up and over so they don't clip and stop the board. Put the front wheels back down as soon as they're past the coping and over the transition. Roll away backward. You've just done a blunt to rock.

After you have blunts down, try getting into nose blunts by rolling up switch and locking onto the nose of your board. You'll pop off the nose, do a slight nose manual, and roll down forward.

There are many other variations to experiment with. One popular version is the blunt to backside 5-0. To do this, pop off the blunt with your weight high on the board and bring the board 90 degrees backside so you land in a perfect 5-0 stall facing the transition. If you're feeling technical, consider a blunt to rock and roll so you come out of your rock with a rear wheel 180 or even a backside 180 right off the tail of your blunt. Later you can experiment with kickflips into the blunt, kickflips out of the blunt, and the counterparts off the nose blunt.

FOOTPLANTS

Footplants can be done on flat-banks, on miniramps, or on vert. They're versatile and fun to do. There are three related tricks that all involve taking a foot off your board and then jumping back onto it as you drop in. The sweeper, boneless, and fastplant all require essentially the same type of skills. These three tricks can all be considered footplants because you will plant your foot on the deck of the ramp.

There are all kinds of footplant variations. The three most popular are often confused with each other because they look similar. The two differences between the different types of footplants are the hand you grab the board with (lead or rear) and the foot you plant on the ground (lead or rear).

The challenging part of the footplant family on the ramp is dropping back in. There is no graceful way to set the board up into a tail stall and drop in normally. The footplants all take you higher than the coping and require you to jump or drop back into the ramp or onto the bank from a standing position.

There are many ways to become comfortable with dropping in like this. One of the simplest ways is to find a flat-bank and jump from the top onto the side of the bank while holding your board under you. (You'll let go of the board at the last second.)

In the footplants, you will plant your lead foot on the ground either in front of you (to the toe side of the board) or behind you (to the heel side of the board). Being able to jump back onto your board from either of these positions is useful.

Footplants can also have you grabbing the board at different places and with either hand. Where you grab, which hand you grab with, and which foot comes off the board are the variations you should experiment with.

Boneless

The boneless is a great flat-land trick and can be practiced in your driveway, on a flat-bank, or even on the mini. Learn the boneless technique on a flat patch of ground first and then take the trick to flat-banks. Before long you'll be ready to take it to the vert ramp or deep bowl.

The key to doing a boneless is to grab the board with your rear hand before you take your front foot off. You'll put just enough weight on your hand to keep the board on the ground as you slide your lead foot off to the heel side. Without your leg's weight on the board, its front end should rise up. While the board's nose is popping up, plant your lead foot on the ground. Lift the board off the ground with your hand while keeping your rear foot on the tail, and spring off your planted foot. The higher you jump off your lead leg, the more time you'll have to get that foot back up onto your board before it lands on the ground.

To do a boneless on the ramp, reach for your board just as you get to the coping. You probably won't need to actually grab it before the board comes out of the ramp. Depending on the angle of the ramp at the coping, the board should shoot straight up. You can lead the board out of the ramp with your rear foot while stepping off with your lead one.

You will find yourself standing one-footed on the deck near the coping while holding the board against your rear foot. You can slow down at this part of the trick if you want.

To drop in from a boneless, you don't have to do much more than just lean into the transition and hop slightly off your planted foot. With your rear hand still holding the board, pull the board under you as you "fall" back into the transition. When you can see that the board is going to touch down underneath you, let go and get your lead foot over the deck.

FRONTSIDE BONELESS

BACKSIDE BONELESS

Fastplant

In a fastplant you grab with your lead hand and boost into the air with your rear foot. Grab onto the frontside (or toe side) of the board; step off the tail of the board with your rear foot; and plant your foot on the coping, bank, or ledge.

Beanplant

In a beanplant you grab the nose of the board (or the side of the nose) with your lead hand while stepping off with your lead foot toward the toe side of the board. Beanplants are easier for many people than the boneless because you're using your lead hand.

Sweeper

Sweepers are a footplant variation that "sweeps" the tail of the board across the deck until it comes back to the coping. They are a bit different to do on a bank than on a miniramp or halfpipe, but you can learn them on either. The angle of the ramp can shoot the board into your hand. On a bank you must pop the board up from the tail and then grab the board while it's in the air.

To do a sweeper on transition, roll up to the coping with enough speed to shoot the board upward. Approach the coping at a very narrow frontside angle (almost straight up the ramp but angled a little so you are facing the coping).

As the board's rear wheels cross the coping, step off with your rear foot and let the board come upward into the air. As the board flies up, grab the nose with your lead hand. Try to grab the board with your whole hand; don't just grab the nose with your fingertips. You need a good grip on the board.

Keep your lead foot against the board and your rear foot on the deck or coping. Your back should be to the ramp. You'll have to bend your lead leg deeply to grab the nose of the board and keep your foot against it. It will feel awkward the first few times you try it.

Your frontside momentum should rotate your body around and toward the transition. This is where the sweep comes from. Bring the board's tail back toward the ramp and rest it on the coping as for a tail stall. Hop off your rear foot and onto the tail at the same time as you throw your weight over your board. Don't forget to let go of the nose. You should land firmly on the board just as the front wheels touch on the surface of the ramp. Focus on technique, and the smoothness will follow.

If you are feeling stiff and nothing is coming together with your sweeper, focus on perfecting each stage of the trick independently. Popping the board up and into your hand while you keep your lead foot on it is the first stage. Bringing the board around to rest its tail on the coping is the second. Then jumping onto the board as it falls back into the ramp is the final stage. Each one is important and can be practiced on its own.

Russian Boneless

The Russian boneless is an odd but stylish trick that can be used on mini-ramps, in halfpipes, on flat, or to get up onto ledges. It's an early-grab boneless, so you will start by grabbing the board with your lead hand just behind your lead foot's toes. Lean onto your lead hand slightly to take some of the weight off your lead foot. This will allow you to slide your lead foot off the board and onto the ground on the heel side.

With your lead foot planted and a firm grip on the board with your lead hand, sweep the tail forward and lift the board up with your hand. It may be difficult at first, but try to keep your rear foot against the tail the whole time. The board should be in front of you.

After the board is off the ground, spring off your planted lead foot and jump, one-footed, over the tail of the board and your rear foot; land on the other side of the board. Now the board should be behind you.

Jump again while you let go with your lead hand and land with your lead foot on the front trucks bolts. You've just done a Russian boneless.

When your leg gets stronger and the Russian boneless action becomes more automatic, you can do it up onto ledges or on the deck of a ramp.

TAKING LIP TRICKS FURTHER

Many skaters out there devote a significant portion of their skateboarding time to the miniramp. They are fun, versatile, and reasonably low risk. A few simple tricks on a mini can keep a person entertained for hours and even for years. There's little reason to pass on lip tricks and the miniramp when there's so much potential enjoyment at stake.

All the tricks in this chapter can be expanded, tweaked, and combined with other miniramp or street tricks to produce limitless possibilities. For example, you might kickflip into a rock, manual across the transition from one coping to the other, pop out to manual across the deck and then roll back in, or mash a tail stall with a shuvit and then revert back in. The miniramp is a laboratory for your skateboarding imagination.

CHAPTER 7

GRINDS AND SLIDES

Grinds and slides are types of skateboarding tricks that stand apart from all other tricks. The board is moving against its own "grain" and interacting with the structure, using parts that weren't originally designed for that kind of contact. Unlike most of the ollie-based tricks, grinds and slides all require speed. You cannot practice these tricks standing still. They all require bravery and commitment to attempt, but by starting with some good habits and a solid understanding of what your body is supposed to be doing, your success rate should be rewarding.

There are three types of structures you can practice your grinds and slides on. Each type has its advantages and disadvantages for each trick, and the quality and size of the structures will have a huge impact on how difficult that trick is to do.

If you can ollie well but are just learning grinds and slides, you should seek out a ledge or rail that is between 8 and 14 inches (20 to 36 cm) high. The leading edge—that is, the corner or corners your board will be scraping (whether it's the trucks or the bottom of the deck)—should be smooth enough so the board doesn't hang up on any cracks or notches. Concrete edges are particularly prone to getting worn down so you can see the large pebbles in the cement mix. These are usually not good to learn grinds on because they're too rough.

You might find a ledge that is granite or marble. These are excellent materials for grinding. Marble is expensive, so be sure that the place is sanctioned for skateboarding. Granite is often found in newer skateparks, and it's becoming less necessary to trespass on private property in order to skate a good ledge. However, most great spots for grinds that you can find downtown are private property, and by skating there you might be risking a fine or having your board confiscated. Search for "skateboarder busted" on YouTube if you want a taste of what can happen when you skate in places where it's not appropriate.

Ledges may be fun, but use common sense when searching out a good place to skate. No ledge is worth a run-in with the law. The best place to find a great ledge specifically designed for skateboarding is in a skatepark.

LEDGE

A quick note about safety: Grinds and slides are the source of many skateboarding injuries. Serious injuries can happen doing this group of tricks, and lots of smaller injuries can happen through routine attempts on structures you are familiar with. It's possible to lose the board; slip out backward; and smack the back of your head on the ground, on the corner of the ledge, or against the railing. Any of these quick accidents can bring your skateboarding hobby to an abrupt end forever.

Wear a helmet and skate within your limits. There are a host of injuries you can't prevent. The longer you do these tricks, the more likely you are to eventually get caught by an accident. Some skaters call this "paying your tax," meaning you can avoid it for a while, but eventually you will fall, and it's going to hurt. When you ask a limping skater how she injured herself, she'll often start her story with "I was doing a trick I've done a million times. . . ." Be smart.

Ledges

They are all over town. Sometimes they are worn down and black with wax, other times they are untouched and look brand new. If you've been skating for a while, you are probably seeing curbs and ledges that have been waxed by skaters around your neighborhood. The best ledges for learning grinds and slides will be flat and between 10 and 14 inches (25 to 36 cm) tall. The edge should be smooth and free of chips and pock holes.

Rails

Like ledges, railings are all over town, but few will be appropriate places to skate. Most railings you'll find "in the wild" will be handrails next to stairs or slopes. If you are just learning grinds and slides, you'll want to search out a flat-rail—a low rail that is not at an angle. Good flat-rails of a suitable size for learning grinds are uncommon outside of skateparks. They are not difficult to make if you know someone who can weld, and several companies sell adjustable rails that can easily be set up in a driveway or on a sidewalk.

Ramps (Transition)

Most slides and grinds that you might do on a rail may also be done on the lip of a miniramp, quarterpipe, or halfpipe. The action is different though; on a rail you ollie into the grind or slide, while on transition you roll into the trick. It's very rare to find a good transition to learn grinds and slides on outside of a skatepark.

The instructions in this chapter focus on grinds and slides on ledges and rails, but most of the tricks can also be done on transition. The icons shown below appear next to the trick titles that follow to show where each trick is typically done. Even though the trick may be called the same thing whether it's done on a ramp, rail, or ledge, the trick technique is a bit different to learn. You'll find tips for doing the tricks on various structures included with the instructions.

RAIL

RAMP

KEY TO ICONS

Ramps   Ledges   Rails

BACKSIDE 5-0 GRIND

The backside 5-0 is a trick that can be done on a ledge, rail, or coping. However, the most popular place to do this trick is on a small ledge. In this section you will learn how to do a backside 5-0 grind on a ledge.

You will need to be able to easily ollie higher than the ledge you want to do your backside 5-0 grind on. You will find this trick very difficult to learn on a ledge that wasn't designed for skateboarding or hasn't been prepared with wax. You should also be comfortable with manuals. If you find yourself struggling with the backside 5-0 grind, you might try learning frontside 5-0s or 50-50 grinds first.

1. Approach with the ledge to your back side and set your feet for an ollie. If your approach is too straight-on, you will not grind along the length of the ledge. If your approach is too parallel, you might find it difficult to get the board to land perfectly on the edge of the ledge. The approach angle is important.

2. As you near the ledge, ollie slightly higher than the ledge.

3. Instead of landing flat like you might on flat ground, land with your back trucks straddling the leading edge of the ledge. Your trucks should slide along the edge.

4. Your momentum should carry the board along the ledge in a grind. The slower you are going, the shorter your grind will be. Try to keep the front trucks off the ledge and keep your balance as if you are in a manual.

5. Your body should be leaning slightly away from the ledge unless you have enough speed and balance to make it to the end of the ledge. When you feel that you've held the grind as long as you can, swing the front end of the board away from the ledge. The board should roll off the ledge easily.

6. Plop yourself on the ground and prepare for your next trick.

The 5-0 grind is a cool trick because it scales up nicely. At first they look like a 5-0 stall that slides just a little. The more comfortable you are doing them, the longer they get. Masters of the 5-0 grind can turn them into all kinds of gnarly variations. Any of these tricks are within your ability to learn.

The biggest challenge most people have with backside 5-0s is keeping the board in a manual. Some of this will have to do with the nature of the structure. Rough or sticky surfaces will provide more resistance, so you'll need to go faster or lean back more. Smooth steel will offer very little resistance and may even be faster than your wheels, so you'll need to keep the board under you as much as possible and prepare for it to pick up speed.

FRONTSIDE 5-0 GRIND

Some experienced skaters claim that "backside doesn't count." They mean the frontside version of any trick is the legitimate one, and the backside is its easier, less credible cousin. This isn't true; any trick on a skateboard is cool as long as the skater is having fun. There is no "better" trick.

In the frontside version, you will approach the ledge and turn to your left (regular; right if you're goofy) so you are facing the ledge. The grind feels the same as the backside version but aiming the ollie so that the back trucks land perfectly on the edge of the ledge is easier for most skaters.

1. Approach the ledge with enough speed to carry you off the end of the ledge (but not so fast that your ollie is shaky).

2. Approach the ledge at a slight frontside angle. Look at the spot on the ledge where you want to start your grind.

3. Ollie just high enough to get your rear trucks onto the ledge. Keep the nose high as if you were landing in a manual.

4. As the rear trucks straddle the edge of the ledge in the grind, your speed will carry you along. Hold your balance as if you were in a manual.

5. As you near the end of the ledge, simply push the nose down to flatten the board and fall off.

6. Adjust your feet and roll away.

The frontside 5-0 grind looks cool and is super stylish. When you have done a few and they feel good, you can take them to larger ledges and rails. For a real challenge, try them on pool coping.

- If the board slips away from you, try keeping the grind short so that you're popping onto the ledge and then quickly off again.
- If the 5-0 grind is difficult to hold, try faster 50-50 grinds on the same ledge and practice lifting the nose up during the 50-50.
- If the ledge does not have an end to pop off of, you will need to rotate your board off the ledge. This will require you to "fall" off the ledge to your back side and swing the nose of the board with you. The rear trucks should come off the ledge easily.

Imagine two skaters: The first is trying to learn frontside 5-0 grinds and keeps falling. Every time he falls, he slams his board on the ground and curses loudly and stomps around. The other skater is doing tic tacs around the edge of the park and smiling. He's having a great time and is stoked to be getting better. Who would you rather be? Who would you rather skate with?

BACKSIDE 50-50 GRIND

When people refer to backside or frontside grinds or even just grinds, they typically mean the classic 50-50. The 50-50 is the most fundamental grind you can do.

In a 50-50 grind, both trucks slide, or grind, along the coping, rail, or ledge. The technique for achieving long, solid grinds in a miniramp is having the trucks properly aligned on the coping and getting your body weight balanced up on the board.

1. Roll up the transition with enough speed to get your body weight out of the ramp. It may help to visualize the amount of momentum you'll need by imagining yourself flying right out of the ramp and onto the deck.

2. Approach the coping at a slight backside angle.

3. Lift the front wheels as they pass the coping and do a small kickturn so the front trucks land on the coping. At the same time, throw your body weight up onto the coping as well, so you are balanced on top of the board. This is the most challenging part of this trick.

4. Whether it's short or long, ride the grind with both trucks sliding along the coping for as long as you can. When you start slowing down (or even after you come to a stop), begin leaning back into the ramp.

5. When your weight is in the ramp, lift the front trucks off the coping and bring the wheels down hard onto the surface of the ramp.

6. Roll the rest of the way down the ramp and reset your feet if necessary.

○ If you can't seem to get your body weight up onto the board when it gets to the coping, try pushing your body up onto the board so much that you have to step off onto the deck. In other words, intentionally lose your balance just like when you learned 50-50 stalls. This should help you get a sense of how much momentum you'll need to get your body up onto your board.

○ If the front wheels land on the deck instead of the trucks hitting the coping, try approaching the coping at more of an angle so you are almost rolling right up onto the coping. This will reduce the amount of kickturn you need. This is a common situation, and you may find with practice that if your front trucks miss the coping and your wheels land on the deck, you can still try to bring the front end of the board back into the ramp and roll out of it.

If you have been practicing your frontside 50-50 stalls on the miniramp, the frontside 50-50 grind should not be very difficult for you. The frontside 50-50 is basically an extension of the stall.

Just like the backside 50-50 grind, both trucks slide along the coping, rail, or ledge. The technique for achieving long, solid grinds in a miniramp is having the trucks properly aligned on the coping and getting your body weight balanced up on the board.

FRONTSIDE 50-50

Frontside 50-50s on rails and ledges are very easy if you are comfortable doing ollies. You will need to be able to ollie higher than the obstacle you want to 50-50 grind on, so you should try your grinds on lower rails and ledges to get the grinding technique down. Once you understand what it takes to do the 50-50 grind, you can try it on larger obstacles.

50-50s are less scary on ledges than on rails for two reasons. First, ledges are usually concrete or stone. These materials are a bit rougher than steel, so the grinds tend to be slower. The slower the grind, the more time you will have to make tiny adjustments to the board and your balance. Rails, particularly round ones, are almost always smooth steel, and the grinds tend to be very fast, which gives you very little time for any adjustments. Second, and probably more significant, ledges have a flat top whereas rails just have air. If you don't land your front trucks directly on the lip of a ledge, you can either adjust your board or try to pop the whole thing off and roll away. If you don't ollie perfectly onto a rail, it will usually mean you have to bail out.

1. Approach the ledge at about a 45-degree angle and fast enough that you will be able to grind a short distance on the lip but not so fast that it will disrupt your ollie.

2. Crouch into your ollie stance and prerotate your waist so you'll get a little bit of a frontside rotation.

3. Pop your ollie as you lead with your shoulders. Concentrate on putting your rear trucks on the lip of the ledge.

4. At the moment your rear trucks land on the ledge, or a split second after, drop your front trucks onto the lip of the ledge.

5. Ride the grind for as long as you can. When you're ready to get off, pop off the ledge with a slight ollie. You won't need to actually pop your tail on the ledge. Getting off a ledge or rail from a 50-50 grind is a lot like a shuvit without any rotation.

6. Land with your feet over the bolts and roll away.

If you start learning 50-50s on curbs and low ledges first, you'll develop confidence and build good habits you can then take to higher, longer ledges and rails later.

To do your frontside 50-50s on a rail, follow the same directions but reduce the angle of approach so you're more parallel to the rail. You won't have any friction between the wheels and the top of the ledge, so your ollie must be precise.

- If your front trucks won't consistently fall directly onto the lip of the ledge, lean back slightly and try to concentrate on just dropping your back trucks on the lip as for a 5-0 stall. In other words, don't worry about the front trucks as much as perfecting your ollie so the back trucks land perfectly. When you use the "right" ollie, the 50-50 should come together nicely.

- If the board flips downward—and maybe even into your shins—off the ledge, it may be because you are not rotating the board enough during the ollie. To fix this, try approaching the ledge more straight-on, with more rotation in your ollie. This will help bring the back trucks solidly onto the coping by forcing the frontside rotation.

- If the board bounces off the lip of the ledge or doesn't grind because it's rough, find a smoother ledge or simply go faster and keep the grind short.

BACKSIDE 50-50

Backside 50-50s are a little different from their frontside versions in that you have to ollie with a backside rotation. It can be difficult to get a nice high ollie and backside rotation at the same time. As with the frontside 50-50, you should learn the backside 50-50 technique on a low ledge to begin with until you fully understand what your body needs to do before taking it to higher ledges and rails.

You should be comfortable with backside ollies before trying backside 50-50s.

1. Approach the ledge at a narrow angle so you are almost parallel to the direction of the lip.

2. Set your feet in an ollie position and prerotate your shoulders to prepare for a slight backside rotation.

3. As you near the ledge, ollie and unleash your rotation so the back trucks move away from you in the direction of your heels.

4. Drop the tail end down when the rear trucks are over the lip of the ledge. Because this is backside, you won't be able to easily see when this is. You will have to rely on timing and practice until you know how much ollie and backside rotation are required for that particular ledge.

5. The moment your rear trucks make contact with the ledge, drop the front trucks down on the lip and ride through the grind as long as you can.

6. As you slow down, pop your board off the ledge with a little hop and bring the board out and away from the lip.

7. Land with your feet on the bolts and roll away.

The backside 50-50 is difficult but can lead to some really cool variations. If you are comfortable with backside ollies, then you should definitely give this trick some practice.

FEEBLE GRIND

The feeble is the grind that most people learn by accident while trying backside 50-50s. In a feeble, the back trucks grind on the ledge or rail as usual, but the front trucks hang down near the rail on the opposite side that the skater approached from. For example, when you try a 50-50 grind on a ramp and the front trucks land on the deck instead of on the coping, that's a feeble.

Feebles are most popular on rails. That's where they look the best and—not surprisingly—are the most difficult. We'll start with the frontside feeble.

1. Approach the rail at a narrow frontside angle, with enough speed to carry you off the end of the rail but not so much that your ollie will be difficult to control. You won't need very much rotation, so drop into an ordinary ollie stance without a lot of twist.

2. Pop your ollie as you get to the rail while concentrating on putting your back trucks directly into a grinding position.

3. When you ollie without the rotation, the front of the board should go past the rail. Use the back trucks to redirect your momentum from the diagonal path that you approached the rail into a path to the end of the rail. You will need to keep your weight centered over your rear trucks. The front trucks should dip down on the far side of the rail.

4. Ride through the grind until you near the end of the rail.

5. When you get to the end, lift the nose up and toward you. As your rear trucks come off the end of the rail, the board should be pointed slightly upward.

6. Land and roll away.

The backside feeble is almost identical except you approach the rail at a narrow backside angle. Ollie "through" the rail, lock the back trucks against it, and let the nose of the board hang out away from you. As you near the end of the rail, bring the nose up and toward you so that when you drop off you land cleanly.

The challenges with feebles are mostly in the ollie. You need to have precise ollie control so that your ollie is neither too high nor not high enough, too far or not far enough. Your trucks are not very big, and you'll be using them to catch yourself and the board against the corner of the rail.

- If the board keeps landing in a lipslide position (with the bottom of the board resting on the rail), the ollie isn't quite high enough. Try the rail with a little bit of frontside rotation and some 50-50 grinds while landing your rear trucks first. After you have a few of those down clean, take out the rotation so the nose crosses the rail.

- If the board flies clear across the rail or the back wheels clip, you are probably putting too much ollie into it. Again, warm up with a few 50-50 grinds first while paying attention to your rear trucks.

SMITH GRIND

The Smith grind is sometimes confused with the feeble because it looks similar. In a Smith grind, the front of the board dips down next to the rail on the skater's side. (The feeble points the nose away from the skater.)

The technique for Smith grinds requires more body rotation than for a feeble. Frontside Smiths are easier to get into because you can see the rail clearly, so learn those first.

1. Approach the rail from a frontside direction. Get into an ollie stance with a prerotation for a frontside ollie.

2. Ollie high enough to get the rear trucks onto the rail. As you ollie, push the tail end out and onto the rail. Keep the nose in toward you as if the tail end is rotating around it (like a frontside 180 ollie).

3. Stick the rear trucks onto the rail. You can help stabilize the board a little by jamming the toe side of the board into the side of the rail.

4. Let your forward movement push you through the grind.

5. As you near the end of the rail or are ready to get off the rail, raise the nose of the board and push the board off the rail so it will land under your weight.

6. Land on your bolts and roll away.

Smith grinds feel a lot like 50-50 grinds except your body weight should be almost entirely on your rear trucks.

If you are struggling to drop your rear trucks right on the railing, you can practice the motion on a ledge. Approach the ledge slowly so you won't move on the ledge after you land on it. Try to just ollie onto the ledge with your rear trucks and then off again without the grind. After you have a feeling for rotating the board and aiming your rear trucks, return to the rail to try some Smith grinds.

CROOKED GRIND

The crooked grind—sometimes called just crooks—is a 5-0 grind on the front trucks, with the board's tail end hanging out away from the ledge or rail and under the skater. (When the back end is away from the skater and over the top of the ledge or rail, it is an overcrook.) Crooked grinds are mostly done on ledges because the underside of the board's nose slides while the front trucks are grinding.

The technique for getting into crooked grinds is a basic ollie into the rail, but instead of landing on your trucks, or just your back trucks, you'll land only on your front trucks. To get accustomed to the motion required to do this, you might practice with some flat-land ollies and try to land in a nose manual.

1. Approach the rail at a narrow backside angle (so you are facing away from the ledge) with enough speed that you can grind all the way off the end and drop into an ollie stance. Your ollie will have only a small frontside rotation, so you won't need to twist up too much.

2. As you near the rail, pop an ollie with just enough frontside rotation to bring the board onto the rail at about a 45-degree angle.

3. Jam the front trucks into the corner while slapping the underside of the deck's nose onto the top. Most of your weight will be on your lead foot. Your rear foot should only be stabilizing the board and keeping the tail out at an angle.

4. Slide through the grind. It should feel as if you are sliding more on your nose than on the trucks. (You shouldn't be trying to manual on the front trucks.)

5. When you get to the end of the ledge, pop your weight off the front end and lean back slightly to flatten the board. Land on all four wheels and roll away.

Sliding the board on both the trucks and the nose is not easy. You'll need to find the right combination of speed, pressure on the nose, and balance over the front trucks before your crooked grinds start looking smooth.

- If the board doesn't slide, it probably has more to do with a lack of speed than your balance. You can try speeding up or starting the grind later along the rail so it's shorter.
- Occasionally the board may slip and fall into a nose slide. Although you may be able to ride it out, you'll want to refine your technique so your ollie puts the board clear up onto the rail. Try to adjust the angle of the board so it is more parallel to the direction of the rail and not sticking out to the side too far.

You can take your new crooked grind into lots of variations. The overcrook grind, for example, has the tail of the board out over the top of the rail. You can mess around with variations such as this after you have your basic crooked grind on lock.

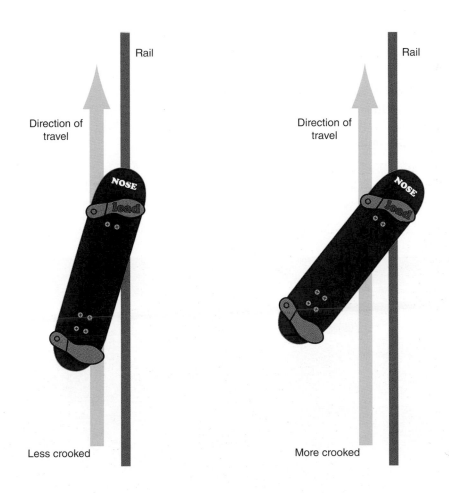

BLUNTSLIDE

The bluntslide has become a very fashionable trick lately. You see them frequently in magazines and in videos. They look like lipslides (or boardslides) except the board is sliding on its wheels, with the tail locked against the corner of the ledge.

Bluntslides are easy to learn on some structures and difficult on others, so choosing where to learn them is a big step in helping your first attempts yield positive results. Look for a ledge that is low enough for you to easily ollie over and that is slick enough to slide on. A short ledge that has a steel edge and is waxed up is perfect.

We'll start with a backside bluntslide so you can see where you are going.

1. Approach with the ledge to your back side and load up for a frontside ollie high enough to get your back trucks on top of the ledge. When you are just learning this trick, aim for the end of the ledge so the bluntslide will be short and you'll quickly come off the end. You can work on pulling them out longer as you learn what works and what doesn't.

2. When the timing is right, pop your ollie with a frontside rotation. Stick the ollie onto the ledge, with the tail firmly on the corner of the ledge and the nose sticking up high.

3. Your forward momentum should move the board forward as the wheels and tail slide along the ledge. Keep your weight on your rear foot so that most of the pressure on the board is on the tail portion that is against the ledge. The less weight you put on your wheels, the smoother the slide is likely to be.

4. As you reach the end of the ledge, pop the board off the ledge with a quick snap on the tail and bring the nose around with your lead foot.

5. Try to land all four wheels simultaneously, with your feet over the bolts, and roll away.

Frontside bluntslides require a lot more twisting in your torso. You'll be coming at the ledge with it in front of you, so you'll need a backside ollie to get the board into position. Sticking the ollie onto the ledge is almost entirely legwork; your chest doesn't turn with the board as it might if you were doing a flat-ground backside 180 ollie. When you're on the ledge in the bluntslide position, your lead foot is crossed in front of you and your shoulders are aligned with the direction of the ledge. In other words, if you are regular-footed you will be looking toward your left shoulder as you slide backward. When you get to the end of the ledge, bring the nose of the board around so it's pointing forward as it comes off the ledge.

- If the board hits the ledge and slips out away from you, focus on slapping the tail hard just below the corner of the ledge. You may not need quite as much ollie as you're giving it. (You can even practice ollies straight into the blunt position on the ledge to dial in how much ollie will be required before trying to slide it out.)
- When your rear foot slides off the tail, try to ollie higher onto the ledge so you are coming down onto the corner from an upward diagonal direction and not straight into it from the side. This will help you establish your balance on your rear foot over the corner of the ledge where it should be.

BOARDSLIDES AND LIPSLIDES

There is a lot of confusion between boardslides and lipslides. To many people, they look like identical tricks. In both tricks the skater approaches the rail, ollies, lands with the board sideways against the rail, and then slides along it until the end. This is where most of the lateral scrapes come from on the bottom of skaters' boards.

There are only two ways that skaters can slide along a rail or coping with the board sideways. They can either be sliding forward so they are looking where they are sliding, or they can be sliding backward and looking over the shoulder to see where they are going.

The difference between a boardslide and a lipslide is not quite as simple. In both tricks the skater ollies onto the rail, lands with the board straddling it, and then slides until the end. In a boardslide, the skater ollies straight up onto the rail so the front wheels go across the rail. In a lipslide, it's the back wheels that cross the rail. In other words, a lipslide is the simpler, easier version because it requires less rotation in the ollie. Remember, boardslide means the front trucks cross. Lipslide means the back trucks cross.

In a backside boardslide, you are sliding forward. In a backside lipslide, you will be rotating the board in a backside direction, and so you will be sliding backward. Yes, it's confusing.

Backside boardslide: Approach with the rail to your back side, ollie straight onto the rail, slide forward. People generally just call this a boardslide.

Frontside boardslide: Approach with the rail to your front side, ollie straight onto it, slide backward.

Backside lipslide: Approach with the rail to your back side, ollie high with a backside rotation so the tail end swings out over the rail, slide backward.

Frontside lipslide: Approach with the rail to your front side, ollie high with a frontside rotation so the tail swings out over the rail, slide forward.

The boardslide is fundamentally a rail trick. For skaters wanting to have a few railing tricks, the boardslide is where they usually begin. If you are sliding forward on the rail, it's a backside boardslide. If you are sliding backward, it's frontside. Remember, the way to identify the difference is in whether you approached the rail with it to your front (frontside) or back (backside).

You should learn this trick on a flat rail (one that is not sloped or curved). It should be short enough for you to ollie onto but tall enough that both of your wheels are easily off the ground. A rail about a foot (30 cm) off the ground is usually just right. If you have a choice, a square railing is better for learning boardslides than a round one because you have more surface to balance the board on. (Round rails are faster and make the sliding action easier than square rails.)

The backside boardslide is much easier than its frontside version, so learn that first. When you are comfortable with boardslides—particularly the frontside version—you can try the bigger versions where the back end of the board crosses over the rail before you slide.

BACKSIDE BOARDSLIDE

1. With moderate speed, drop into your ollie stance with the rail on your back side. The angle should be very narrow so that you are nearly parallel to the direction of the rail. Prerotate your shoulders for a frontside ollie.

2. Pop an ollie that is high enough for your front wheels to easily clear the bar. The ollie should have enough frontside rotation in it that the board lands across the rail at about a 90-degree angle.

3. Slide the board along the rail as far as you can. Getting out of a boardslide in the middle of a rail is very difficult, so try to get your slide far enough to pop off the end.

4. Just as the board reaches the end of the rail, rotate the board in whichever direction is most practical for you so that it lands in either a forward or switch direction. The closer you can get to a full 90-degree rotation at the end of the rail the better.

5. Land and roll away.

Most of the boardslide is done during the ollie. Once you're on the rail, there is not a lot you can do to adjust the board. When you're sliding, you are just along for the ride, making small adjustments to keep the board centered on the rail and your weight over the board.

○ If the board doesn't seem to get completely up onto the rail, you are not popping your ollie high enough. Your ollie needs to be clean, be high, and have almost a 90-degree frontside rotation. If you don't have these skills, you can practice on the flat until you're comfortable with them.

○ When you get on the rail but slide right off the other side, tighten the angle of your approach so you are almost parallel to the rail. Your body momentum is carrying you straight over the rail to the other side. It's possible to check your momentum against the rail as you land on it, but this will require you to stick the board against the front corner of the rail and then let the board and your weight roll up onto it as you slide forward. This is a great skill that will require lots of practice. The cleaner technique is to land on top of the rail in one motion without rolling the board up into the boardslide position.

○ Try to be prepared for the speed of the slide once you are on the rail. On round rails in particular there is very little surface area to provide friction and slow you down, so the board may have a tendency to shoot away from you. Just take it easy and anticipate it. With practice, you will become accustomed to the difference in speed.

○ It's fine to land sideways when you come off the rail at first. The ollie going into the boardslide is the most crucial part of the trick. Once your boardslide is on lock, you can perfect the landing. As the end of the rail approaches, the rotation is almost a flick. Most skaters land boardslides in a twisted posture because of the quick spin required by the exit.

FRONTSIDE BOARDSLIDE

The frontside boardslide—the version where you are sliding backward—on a rail presents an additional challenge because you must be able to cleanly ollie higher than the rail.

Frontside boardslides are more difficult than the backside version because you are sliding backward. It is more difficult to control your speed while sliding backward on a rail because your knees don't bend in the right direction. When you are sliding forward, you can use your knees and waist to keep the board under you, but sliding backward is much more difficult.

The key to keeping the board under you during a frontside boardslide is rotating your shoulders and looking at the direction you are traveling. If you square up your shoulders so your whole body is sliding backward, you won't know if you're squarely on the rail, and you will basically be "skating blind." Twist at the waist and watch where you are going.

The cleanest technique for getting into the frontside boardslide requires that you approach with the rail toward your front side and do an ollie with a backside rotation. The ollie must not only be high enough to get squarely onto the rail but also needs to have the perfect amount of backside rotation. When the board makes contact with the rail, it should be about 90 degrees across it, with your feet set in a wide stance.

1. With moderate speed, drop into your ollie stance with the rail to your front side. Prerotate your shoulders for a backside ollie.

2. Pop an ollie that is high enough for your front wheels to easily clear the bar. The ollie should have enough backside rotation in it that the board lands across the rail at about a 90-degree angle.

3. Slide the board along the rail as far as you can. Getting out of a boardslide in the middle of a rail is very difficult, so try to get your slide far enough to pop off the end.

4. Just as the board reaches the end of the rail, rotate the board in whichever direction is most practical for you so it lands in either a forward or switch direction. The closer you can get to a full 90-degree rotation at the end of the rail the better.

TAKING GRINDS AND SLIDES FURTHER

With your new selection of slides and grinds to work on, you are ready for almost anything the skatepark has to offer. If you've been working through this book in order, you have tricks for flat ground, the miniramp, and rails or ledges. If you were to stop reading here, there are still lots of variations and places to take these tricks. You can try higher, longer ledges for your crooked grinds. You might want to try nosegrinds on sloping rails, 50-50s on hubba ledges, or even combining grinds in a single trick such as a nosegrind to tail slide. Let your imagination and bravery be your guide.

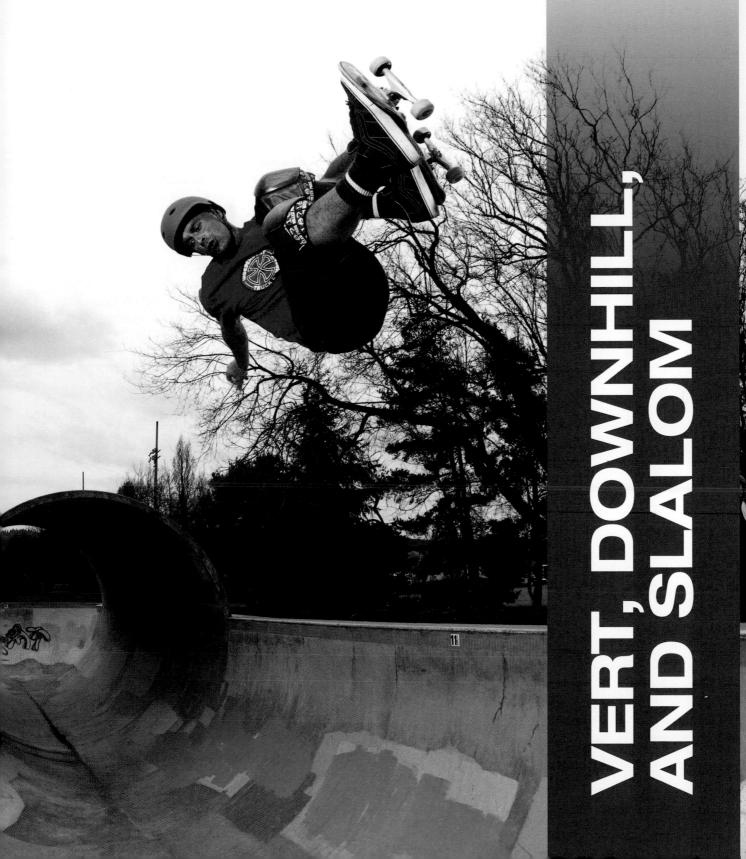

CHAPTER 8

VERT, DOWNHILL, AND SLALOM

Skateboarding is a broad definition for just about anything that involves standing on a board with wheels. There are skateboards for doing street tricks, skateboards for vert ramps, and skateboards for just cruising around the neighborhood. The challenges and possibilities are virtually unlimited. Consider some of the accomplishments of some of the big names in skateboarding.

For example, Tony Hawk is likely the world's most famous skateboarder. He has his own world record by being the first to do a 900—spin two-and-a-half times in midair—in a competition.

Professional skateboarder Danny Way broke two world records in a single run by jumping 79 feet (24 m) without the help of a motor vehicle. He used that speed to do a 35.5-foot (10.8 m) air off a large quarterpipe attached to the same structure. Long and high airs are Danny Way's specialty—though he is exceptionally talented in many types of skateboarding. For his large jumps, Way uses a skateboard tuned in a way he keeps secret.

Land-speed records also require special skateboarding equipment. When Gary Hardwick set the world record for speed, he wore a special aerodynamic suit. Naturally, his skateboard was finely tuned for going fast. He reached 63 miles per hour (101 km/h).

Skateboarding and skateboard technology are getting better every day. People will spin more, go faster and higher, and jump farther as things progress. This type of skateboarding may appeal to you. It is bolder and more extreme, and it can be both thrilling and dangerous. If you would like to explore the outer limits of skateboarding, there are a few things you should know about safety before you jump in.

VERT

Vert skating is the pinnacle of extreme skating. Although there is no shortage of gnarly street tricks, jaw-dropping gaps, and huge drops, vert has the biggest airs and provides the kind of riding that appeals most to nonskaters. The history of vert skating goes back decades. Its pioneers are names you may recognize: Jay Adams, Tony Alva, Steve Caballero, Christian Hosoi, and Tony Hawk, among others.

With changing attitudes toward lawsuits and injuries during the late '70s and '80s, many skateparks were closed and demolished. Skateboarding took to the streets because that was where the terrain was. Skaters interested in the flowing snake runs and deep bowls of the skateparks had nowhere to ride. The easiest structure to build that came close to mimicking that kind of terrain was the halfpipe. Halfpipes were popular before, but during this time they were being built in backyards across the country. Although most skaters were doing ollies around town, the others were skating vert on backyard ramps.

The biggest challenge with learning tricks on vert is actually finding a full-size halfpipe or deep bowl. The most dramatic vert tricks require vertical terrain, and that can be hard to find.

What is vertical terrain? In the simplest terms it is any transition that smoothly reaches a straight up and down incline. True vert has long, smooth transition, so if you find a little bank or wall that has a kicker poured into the bottom, it's not really vert. Although many people can ollie or slam their boards into a wall ride, and the wall is a vertical surface, it also isn't vert. Vert is—in the strictest sense—a deep bowl or tall halfpipe that has at least an inch (2.5 cm) of vertical face. Most vert ramps have 6 inches (15 cm) or more of truly vertical face. Some people struggle with this definition and consider any kind of transition to be "vert."

Not all vert tricks require vertical terrain. You can learn the techniques of many vert tricks on smaller terrain; for the aerials that require a lot of hang time, you'll want to launch up into the air. If the ramp isn't vert, you will launch out over the deck.

Most of the tricks are very technical, take months of practice, and require a mastery of other skills in this book. For this reason, we provide a brief description of each trick rather than step-by-step instructions.

Combining Gnarly With Safety

It's impossible to remove all the risk from airs that can take you 15 feet (4.6 m) off the ground, but there are many things you can do to make routine falls from this height no more inconvenient than having to pump back up to the deck.

Wearing pads while skating vert is an absolute necessity. Wearing a helmet and thick knee pads in a bowl or halfpipe is completely acceptable from a cultural standpoint. Although it can be difficult to face wearing a helmet while everyone else in the skatepark is going without—particularly for people who would rather be brain damaged than risk being unpopular—on the ramp a helmet and knee pads are totally normal.

Knee pads present some unique opportunities when it comes to skating vert. Falling while trying to ollie or while doing a 50-50 on a miniramp usually means jumping off and trying to land on your feet. When you fall doing a faster street trick, such as ollieing off stairs, you can roll out of it and avoid landing on any of the hard points of your body. With vert you use your knee pads whenever you can. This takes agility and practice.

Dedicated vert skaters get a lot of use out of their knee pads, and if this type of skating appeals to you, investing in a good helmet and knee pads can save you thousands of dollars in hospital bills. Imagine your knee pads as if they were stuffed with five-dollar bills. How many five-dollar bills do you want to put between your knees and the flat-bottom of the ramp while you drop 8 feet (2.4 m)? The answer is, of course, as many as you can afford.

You won't find knee pads suitable for vert skating in your local sporting goods store. Even the mall stores that carry skateboards will usually have just the thin, cheap kind that provides only marginal protection from small falls. Head to one of your better skate shops for the best knee pads and look for ones that are thick and comfortable and that grip your knee without cutting off the blood to the rest of your leg. Most designs feature a neoprene sleeve that your leg slips into, with elastic Velcro straps to adjust the grip.

The plastic cap on better knee pads can be replaced. Some people glue a replacement cap over the original to help protect it. That allows the replacement cap to get beaten up and ultimately replaced without damaging the base cap.

Knee pads can be worn over pants, but unless the pads have exceptional straps wrapping around your leg, you'll probably want to wear them with shorts. Your shorts should not be so baggy and low that they fall below the cap of the knee pad. If the fabric from your shorts comes between the surface of the ramp or bowl and the pad when you fall and need to knee-slide down the transition, you may end up slamming into the ground. At the very least you'll shred the front of your shorts, and the problem will have solved itself.

Skills for Vert

The first useful skill in vert skating is learning how to fall. Doing tricks on a 9-foot (2.7 m) ramp raises the stakes for failure, so you need to do everything you can to prepare yourself for the worst. When skating vert you *will* fall. It's absolutely inevitable. If you fall by getting hung up on the coping on a 9-foot ramp, you have a 9-foot fall to deal with. Being prepared and having the skills to handle this contingency can be the difference between wondering what you did wrong and wondering where you are.

KNEE SLIDE

Wearing a helmet is the most important thing. The second most important thing is learning how to knee-slide out of a bail. Put on your knee pads and make sure they're comfortable but tight. You should be able to knock them around with your hands and jump hard up and down without them jiggling around.

This is the basic technique for knee slides:

1. Find a smooth chunk of concrete at the skatepark (or even your garage).
2. Drop heavily to your knees. The impact should be comfortable.
3. Stand up, run a few steps, and drop to your knees again. You should slide forward a foot (30 cm) or so. Again, the impact should be comfortable. You'll notice that you also slid on the top of your feet. Unless you're wearing thin slip-ons, you shouldn't feel the slide in your feet.
4. Repeat the slide a few times. You'll feel the pads tug at the ground over imperfections and rough patches in the concrete. Lean back and distribute your weight between your knees and your shoes.
5. Now take it to the bowl. Pump back and forth until you're about halfway up the transition. When you roll up fakie and are looking down the bowl, drop off the board and land on your knees, with your feet tucked under you.
6. Lean back slightly and slide down the transition.

You should also try a few practice bails while facing the wall and sliding backward. It's more challenging but is a great thing to know.

Some people complain that after skating in knee pads for a while, they forget how to run out of unsuccessful tricks. They instinctively want to fall to their protected knees any time they are bailing. When they take off their pads, they find themselves wanting to land hard on their unprotected knees. This is a better conversation piece than an actual risk. Any skaters who have gotten hurt by thinking they were wearing pads when they weren't may want to reevaluate their skateboarding hobby.

PUMPING

Pumping on vert is similar to pumping on smaller transition. The biggest difference is the sensation of weightlessness that occurs at the apex of each wall. Because your weight is moving straight up, you will find the wheels lose their traction. The best way to keep yourself on the board and the board against the ramp or bowl is to compress your legs and apply very gentle pressure against the deck. As you become comfortable going high on vert ramps and deep bowls, this action will be second nature.

Learning how to pump in vert terrain is more a matter of practice than taught technique. Just like pumping in smaller transition, on vert it's best to start at the bottom of the ramp or bowl and start fakies back and forth. As you dial in your timing, you will feel yourself picking up speed and going higher on the wall. If you can build more and more momentum, you should be able to go as high as you are comfortable. With practice you should be able to go very high on the wall after just a few times back and forth.

The challenge of pumping on vert is psychological. For most people, it's scary to go so high on a wall. Skating on vert will take you higher off the ground than any other type of skateboarding, and your inner voice of self-preservation may tell you to stop now before it's too late. The practical view on vert skating is that if you are wearing a helmet and knee pads, skating high poses very little risk.

One reason skating vert tends to be less risky than street skating is that falls typically result in the skater sliding down the slope of the ramp or bowl. Without the corners and drops of ledges and rails, vert skaters don't have to worry as much about rolled ankles.

Pumping high on vert requires that you compress as you reach the apex of your ascent. You may find that putting your hand against the wall at the apex helps you stabilize your body over your board.

KICKTURNS

After you've become comfortable pumping high onto vertical walls in a bowl or half-pipe, it's good to try some kickturns and carves. This is the next level of progression in becoming a halfpipe killer. Even if skating vert isn't one of your goals, being able to cruise a deep bowl is one of the greatest joys of skateboarding. For many people, this is the only reason to skate. The feeling that comes with going fast through a bowl—pumping and carving every pocket and hip—is as good as it gets. Some people can skate for years without ever doing a technical trick on or over coping. Even if you don't see yourself being one of these "soul skaters," being comfortable working deep transition is a valuable skill to have.

Learning to carve on vert starts with the kickturn. Once you are able to pump fakies up to a reasonable height on transition, do some backside kickturns. You'll notice that the feeling is different from doing them on a miniramp or on flat. Your body isn't putting as much pressure on your legs, and the board should feel nimble and light. Doing kickturns on vert is more about board control and finesse than it is about upper-body rotation and balance.

Once you can do a backside kickturn up on vert—or even near it—you can experiment with pushing the board around a little more. For example, try kicking the tail of the board *up* the transition while you bring the nose downward. This is basically splitting your 180-degree backside kickturn into two halves—the nose does a 90-degree kickturn downward while your tail does a 90-degree slide upward. This is an easy and stylish way to dress up a simple maneuver.

Opening up kickturns so that you roll up the wall at an angle, kickturn just a bit, and then roll down at an angle will let you traverse the wall and use the whole bowl. Without these long kickturns, you will be confined to using a bowl like a halfpipe. Going back and forth is fun, but you're missing out on the high-speed whirlpool that you can get going when you're comfortable arcing the kickturns into long carves.

Eventually you should be able to traverse whole walls without lifting your front wheels. This is a true carve, although if you watch carefully, most people who are carving around a bowl are sliding or lifting their front wheels just a bit.

The pumping motion you use to build speed up and down the transition can be applied to the pockets of a bowl. If the bowl has a rounded corner that you can reach high on the wall, you should be able to press into it as you roll across laterally. Conversely, you can "suck up" extra speed in these pockets by compressing as you enter the corner. There are lots of places to build or lose speed in a bowl. By carving high on the walls and going fast, you will gain great speed control.

DROP IN TO VERT

You must know how to drop in on a quarterpipe or miniramp before trying it on vert. The technique is identical but amplified because you aren't slamming your front wheels onto the diagonal surface of the ramp. Instead you will be putting your wheels onto a surface that is literally straight down. Dropping in on vert requires confidence and a willingness to go fast.

Even if you've been riding miniramps for a long time, you'll probably feel flutters of fear when you stand on the deck of the vert ramp. It doesn't look very high from the flat-bottom, but once you're standing on the deck with your board hanging out into space, it's easy to start having second thoughts about doing it. However, just like dropping in on the miniramp, once you do it once or twice, you'll be surprised at how easy it actually is. Your initial fear will seem insignificant compared with the excitement of riding the vert ramp like a champ. As with learning to drop in to the miniramp, you may find it helpful to hold the end of the board with your hand as you shift your weight out over the edge.

A few tricks may help you when you're ready to try this. There's a good chance you'll have a few other skaters, probably your friends, urging you on. They'll tell you the same things you already know, such as "Lean forward," "It's easy," and "Don't think about it, just do it!" Although all these things may be true, the only person you should be listening to is you. If you want to drop in on vert, you know what to do. If you're not ready, then tackle it another day. Listen to your inner voice. It knows you better than the people you skate with.

If you want to drop in on vert but simply cannot build up the courage, you can try pumping fakies in the ramp to see how high you can get. If you can get high enough that your rear wheels almost touch the coping, you are basically dropping in without the "leaning in" part. If you're comfortable doing these high fakie pumps, you have all the skills you need. If you're feeling bold, you might even try a tail stall to get a better sense of what it might take.

OLLIE ON VERT

The ollie plays a huge role in vert tricks. However, ollies on vert aren't quite the same as they are on flat. For example, to ollie onto a ledge or over a curb, you compress your body, pop the tail, and scoop the nose with your lead foot. As the board comes up, you compress your body again to let the board rise up. On vert, you and the board are traveling quickly on terrain that is literally straight up. If you were to compress and pop your tail against the ground, you would fly away from the side of the bowl or ramp. A big ollie on vert would have you landing somewhere near the bottom of the transition.

Dial down your ollie when you are on vert. A very small ollie will produce plenty of air. Lots of vert skaters don't ollie at all and instead use the bonk of the coping to pop the board away from the wall.

As you might imagine, all of your ollie variations can be done on vert. You can do kickflips and bigspins and all the rest, but the two that will help you most with your aerial tricks are the frontside and backside ollies. If you can get these over coping, you're in business for learning some incredible airs.

Early Grabs

Early grabs are aerial maneuvers, or airs, where the board is lifted with the hand. They are easy to learn and present little risk.

There are two great places to learn early grabs: fly ramps and deep transition. Both of these types of structures will provide the vertical lift you need to propel your body mass upward. You can do an early grab on flat or a flat-bank, but your height will be limited by how high you can jump off the board while holding it against your feet with your hand. Ramps and transition will give you the "jump" needed to really get airborne.

Most airs cannot be learned with an early grab technique. Early grabs are useful for the boneless tricks, for handplants (or inverts), and for getting used to the feeling of being airborne on larger ramps and deeper bowls.

When you can pull airs over the coping using an early grab technique, you should be trying very small frontside ollies. When you can get frontside ollies high on the transition, you are ready for the aerials.

There are four main styles of aerial grabs you can experiment with: Two involve grabbing the board with your lead hand and the other two with your rear hand. Each of these can be combined with the toe side of the board or the heel side.

Each type of grab has its own name, and most have variations that are also named.

EARLY GRAB BACKSIDE AERIAL ON TRANSITION.

Some of these grabs are easier than others. Grabbing your toe-side rail with your lead hand is easy, whereas grabbing the heel-side rail with your rear hand is difficult. Because everyone skates a little differently, some people find a certain trick comes naturally while others may struggle to get their bodies to cooperate. Try all the tricks, and see what works for you.

Sometimes there is a different name for the frontside and backside versions of the same grab. And things can get even more complicated. Reaching between your legs with your lead hand to grab the heel side of the board has a name (Grosman), but if you reach through with your rear hand it's called something else (roast beef). All these variations can get very confusing.

INDY AIR

If you can do backside ollies on transition, then you're very close to learning indy airs. Get enough speed so that you can go up the transition enough to do a big backside ollie. Right after you pop the ollie, reach down with your rear hand, and grab the board between your toes (i.e., grab the toe-side rail between your feet). Hold it for just a second, and then release and open your body to land the ollie. You'll notice that you really need to compress your body to get the board close enough to grab.

LIEN AIR

The lien air is an uncomplicated frontside air where you grab the nose or heel side of the front of the board with your lead hand. If you are skating a ramp that doesn't go completely to vert, you can learn this trick in the same way you learn indy airs.

Roll up the transition quickly at a slight frontside angle and prepare a big ollie. Pop the ollie and when your legs are compressed reach down with your lead hand and grab the board somewhere near the nose. At first you will probably just be able to put your fingers on the board before you have to let go, but with practice you should be able to hold it long enough to have your friend snap a great picture.

BODY JAR

The body jar is more of a flourish than a standalone trick. As you are landing an air, instead of planting the wheels against the side of the ramp or bowl, slam the tail of the board against the coping while holding on to the board's nose with your lead hand. Your body weight should come right down onto the board so that you drop in immediately. The body jar looks a lot like a backside ollie to tail except there is no tail stall. The tail hits the coping with a crack, and then you drop in immediately.

METHOD AIR

The method is a variation of the indy where the skater's hips are thrust downward toward the ramp. This pushes the board up and behind the skater. The bottom of the board is straight up like a small table, while the skater's belly is facing straight down into the ramp. The method is a flashy trick that has been a vert contest staple for years.

MUTE AIR

The mute air is always backside. There is no frontside mute. The grab is with your lead hand on the toe-side rail. The best way to warm up to this trick is to work on backside ollies high on the transition. You may have a tendency to lean back on the board during the ollie, which can make grabbing the toe side of the board very difficult. So, while you're practicing your backside ollies on transition, try to compress deeply while the board is airborne. The more you can compress, the easier it will be to reach down and try to grab the board.

JAPAN AIR

If you get mutes down and you are getting some good time in the air, you can start tweaking the mute into different variations. The Japan air is a popular one. As for the mute, you'll pop off the coping or backside ollie. Grab the toe-side rail with your lead hand and pull the board back toward your butt. You'll have to push your hips out, and your knees will be pointing straight down. It's a stylish tweak that has been showing up in vert competitions since the '80s.

SLOB AIR

The slob is essentially a frontside mute. There is no backside slob, just as there is no frontside mute. You can learn slobs the same way you learn indys: Roll up the transition and pop a frontside ollie. When the ollie is at its highest and you are most compressed, grab the board's toe-side rail with your lead hand. Hold it for as long as you can and then release the board and straighten your legs.

STALEFISH

The stalefish is identical to the indy except you grab your heel-side rail with your rear hand. Your rear arm wraps behind your rear knee. This takes a lot of compression and flexibility. You'll need some serious time in the air for this to come together, so bone up on those big frontside airs and indys before you start trying the stalefish.

JUDO AIR

To do a judo on vert, you will need to have your lien airs on lock. The judo is a backside air where you use your lead hand to grab the heel side of the nose while you kick downward with your lead foot.

MADONNA

The Madonna is similar to the judo in that you kick your lead foot downward toward the ramp. However, the Madonna kick is to the heel side of the board. (The judo kicks out toward the toe side.)

As for the judo, you should grab the board as if you were doing a lien air (lead hand on the nose or near the heel side of the nose). Where you grab the board isn't as important as nailing the style of the Madonna by extending your lead leg all the way.

BENIHANA

The Benihana is one of the few airs where you grab the tail and kick your rear leg out behind the board as if you were doing the splits. It is difficult to do a Benihana without looking kind of silly, particularly at first when the height and kick motion aren't at their potential.

The Benihana is a great fly ramp trick. You can let the rear wheels bonk on the coping and bounce the tail right into your rear hand. However, the technique for learning the Benihana on a fly ramp is not likely to convert quickly to a vert environment.

AIRWALK

Like the Benihana, the airwalk is a fun trick for fly ramps. In the airwalk you essentially grab the nose with your lead hand to keep the board near you while you scissor-kick your legs in midair.

Inverts (Handplants)

Inverts are lip tricks on vert in which the skater supports his weight with his arm. There are lots of invert variations based on which hand you are planting and whether you are doing the trick frontside or backside or approaching the trick in switch or fakie stance. The basic handplant is where all the inverts start.

To do a basic handplant, grab the toe-side rail of your board with your front hand. As you near the coping, place your rear hand squarely on the coping, with your fingers on the ramp and your thumb on the deck. If the ramp is vert, you shouldn't feel any weight on your hand, but you'll need a good grip on the coping so that you don't slip off. (Slipping off or missing the coping in a handplant is bad.)

Just as the board is bonking over the coping, throw your shoulders back as if you were doing a backward somersault. This motion will help roll your body mass up as you pivot for a second on your planted arm. You will probably find it very difficult to get your full weight up into a completely inverted position. Take it slow and easy by first just planting your hand and rolling your shoulders back to lift the board away from the coping. As this becomes more comfortable, with time your handplants will start getting higher.

There are only two good ways to get out of a handplant. One is to come back in the way you came (landing fakie), and the other is to keep going in a big arc over your planted hand (landing normal).

A popular handplant variation is the eggplant. In the eggplant, you grab the toe-side rail with your rear hand between your legs. This causes your knees to splay out. You'll be planting your lead hand on the coping. There are lots of other invert variations that you can explore after you have mastered the handplant.

DOWNHILL AND SLALOM

Downhill skateboarding is all about going fast, preferably on a long hill in a secluded area. Downhilling is the most thrilling and most dangerous form of skateboarding. It requires very little skill to go down a hill fast. It requires a great deal of skill, however, to go down a hill fast without crashing. Nearly all skateboarding deaths in the United States are the result of being hit by a motor vehicle or losing control because of speed. On average, one person dies a week due to one of these two causes. Be careful, be safe, and make good decisions. You can easily tell who is an experienced downhiller because he or she is wearing a helmet. "Bombing hills," as it's sometimes known, without a helmet is a sure way to look like an idiot with a death wish.

Slalom is similar to downhill, but it is much more structured. In slalom, skaters weave the board through a series of cones as quickly as possible. Slalom is a format common in skateboard racing because the courses are reasonably short, the rules are easy to administer, and the risk (compared with high-speed longboarding) is relatively acceptable.

Downhill, or longboarding, and slalom are considered skateboarding, but the skills used in the respective types are very different. Many people devote their lives to learning street tricks, lip tricks, vert tricks, slalom, or longboarding and racing techniques without ever touching any of the other types. Because longboarding and slalom require different types of boards than street and transition skating, they are considered more closely related to each other than they are to other distant cousin forms of skateboarding.

Go Fast Without Dying

The faster you go on a skateboard, the more dangerous it becomes. The danger can be reduced to a reasonable level with a few simple precautions. It is dumb to take risks you are not prepared to handle. When you are ready to challenge yourself with the most dangerous kinds of skateboarding, keep yourself from ending up in a coma (or worse) and putting your friends and family through the grief by protecting yourself as well as you can.

The most important thing you can do is wear a helmet. When you fall while going fast, your head will have about the strength of a watermelon. It's possible to hit your head with enough force to kill you on the spot while traveling as fast as you can run. It will literally snap into the ground. Without a helmet, your skull can easily shatter, and you will die right there while your friends scramble to call 911. It happens approximately once a week in the United States, and if you think it won't happen to you because you are too good, you should know that many former skateboarders once thought the same thing.

Of course, there's also a chance you won't suffer a head injury. You might just break your neck or back. At least you won't be dead or in a coma, but you might be on a respirator for the rest of your life, lying in bed with a body that doesn't work.

For every person who dies in the United States while skating, there are many more who suffer "only" a debilitating head injury, paralysis, or some other life-changing injury. If you think we're being dramatic and think you would feel stupid wearing safety gear, there are hundreds of people who will never leave their beds or wheelchairs who would *love* to swap places with you.

Professional skateboarders understand the risks, and if they wear full leather suits and motorcycle helmets, what makes you think you will be okay in a T-shirt and shorts? Are you more skilled and practiced than those who skate for a living? There's one consistent truth in skateboarding: Everyone falls. The trick is to keep it so that when you fall, you can get up and keep skating instead of lying in the street bleeding while your friends stand around wondering what to do.

Accidents that change lives don't happen in slow motion. Nobody sees them coming. They happen in the blink of an eye, often because of something small and dumb—a rock, or a manhole cover, or a dog. Whatever the cause, falls will happen quickly, and they will hurt. If you take a few easy precautions, the pain will be limited to a few scrapes and maybe a chipped tooth or broken bone instead of your parents crying next to your hospital bed.

There is always the chance that each time you go out skating, it could be your last time, so manage that risk like someone who wants to skate today *and* tomorrow. Wear a helmet.

Bombing Hills

So you want to go fast? Let's go fast.

First, you need a hill. The longer and smoother it is, the better. There's a strong possibility that skating in a roadway like this is illegal in your area. Even if it isn't, most police officers give out citations if they see skaters doing it. You must be prepared to accept this risk.

Your course should have limited access. Driveways, cross streets, and intersections are all places where cars can suddenly be an issue. Parking garages can be a good place to practice, particularly on days when there is no traffic. New housing developments frequently have fresh roads put in before the homes are built. These can be good places to practice, too, before people start moving in. Wherever you choose to practice, remember that the first priority is your safety and the safety of those around you. No skateboarding trick is worth an injury.

The end of the course should flatten out or even go uphill slightly. This will help you slow down at the end of your run. Seek out hills with smooth pavement or asphalt. A smooth surface means greater speed and fewer obstacles.

For very long hills (a mile [1.6 km] or more), have a friend drive a "pace car" to keep other motorists from running you down from behind and also to provide a ride back up the hill after each run. The pace car follows you down the hill while staying about 100 yards (90 m) back with its hazard lights on.

You'll need a specialty board for this type of skateboarding. Downhill skateboards are a subset of the longboard category of products. As you get more comfortable with this type of skating, you may go as fast as 40 miles per hour (64 km/h). At high speeds, an ordinary skateboard will begin to wobble and be unstable. Downhill boards are longer and more stable. Many types of downhill boards are bent in a way so that the middle of the board—the space between the two trucks—drops down so the skater stands about an inch (2.5 cm) off the ground. These are known as drop-through boards and are designed to provide lots of stability at high speeds because of the low center of gravity.

Downhill wheels are larger and softer than ordinary skateboard wheels. The size allows them to spin faster, and the softness provides traction at high speeds even while cornering. Downhill skateboard trucks are designed for stability. They are wide and become more maneuverable as they go faster.

Plus, bombing hills on an ordinary skateboard cannot compare with the excitement of doing it on a board designed for this purpose.

The first time down the hill should be leisurely and slow. Use the first run to identify serious hazards. Large board-stopping cracks, gravel patches, and rough patches on corners are best to avoid, so knowing where they are before you are really flying is important.

Speeding Up

Going faster is not generally a problem on steeper hills, although sometimes you will require the maximum amount of speed to clear a gentle spot or coast up a small rise in the course. The speed in downhill skating is achieved through the reduction of factors that slow you down. You reduce, or tuck in, everything that gets between you and gravity. Air will be the thing that slows you down the most. This can be used to your advantage when you need to slow down a little, but if you don't want to slow down, you can use an aerodynamic posture to minimize air resistance. This is known as going into a tuck.

Slowing Down

Downhill skaters develop special skills for dealing with the high speeds. Techniques for slowing are most important. It's easy to get too much speed, and because skateboards aren't equipped with brakes, special moves are employed to moderate speed.

Downhill skaters use air resistance to brake or lose speed by standing up and holding their arms out to create an "air dam" with the body. This is useful when approaching tighter corners and nearing the end of the course. It will not slow you down quickly enough to avoid a collision or any other critical situation. Air resistance is an ally only for general speed management.

The traditional way to slow or stop a downhill board is by dragging your tail foot on the ground next to the board. Naturally, you don't want to step heavily on that foot or it will grip the ground and you will lose your balance. Gently slide the sole of the shoe against the ground, and increase the pressure while maintaining your balance over the board with your lead foot.

For more drastic speed reductions, many downhill skaters slide their boards. This is a sophisticated technique that requires lots of practice. When sliding, the back end of the skateboard will drift out to the side so that the board is traveling sideways. Small slides will lose a little bit of speed, while wide, fully sideways slides will lose a lot of speed. Most downhill experts can slide their boards completely around so that they come out of the slide rolling backward (or switch).

To practice slides on a downhill board, you will need gloves. Most downhill skaters use gloves with plastic palms that allow the hand to slide heavily on the ground without yanking the skater off the board. These are sometimes called pucks, and these special gloves can be found in better skate shops, although many skaters simply make their own using less expensive materials.

It will also save you a lot of grief to wear protective clothing. When you are learning slides, you will often fall off the board and slide yourself. Cover your arms with a sturdy jacket and your legs with denim. And wear a helmet, of course.

Learning slides is easiest if you try them while going fast. It's very difficult to slide a board that is going slow. Find a broad, open downhill space without traffic or other hazards. The bottom of the hill should flatten out to give you plenty of space to stop the board.

For many people, slides are easiest to learn when the ground is slightly moist. This decreases the friction and traction of the wheels. Because downhill wheels are so large, a slightly sandy surface will also help reduce the wheels' grip without stopping the board. You might even try practicing your slides on a smooth, hard-packed dirt path. The most important thing is that you have plenty of room and can get enough speed.

Getting the board to start sliding is the most difficult part of a perfectly executed slide. Once the board is sliding, it is relatively easy to control how lateral the slide will be. Sliding frontside is much easier than backside. In other words, sliding the board sideways while facing the direction of travel makes it easier to retain your balance and manage the drift of the board. Let's start with a frontside slide, sometimes referred to as a drifter.

Push off and get a comfortable amount of speed. When you're ready to start your slide, crouch slightly and start a gentle frontside turn by leaning slightly on your heels. As the board begins to respond, push the board forward—in front of you—by extending your legs swiftly. The amount of pressure required to break the traction of the wheels will depend largely on the type of surface you're skating on, your speed, and the softness of your wheels.

There's another technique for sliding that you may find easier and more comfortable. Grip the toe side of the board with your rear hand while crouching over the board. As you lean back and begin turning frontside—toward the direction your back is facing—reach out with your lead hand behind you, and let it slide on the ground. Your compressed weight on the board should allow you to turn it hard enough for the wheels to break their grip

without the risk of losing your balance. Your center of gravity is very low, and you have an extra point of contact on the ground, which makes this technique good for getting the feel of sliding without requiring the degree of balance needed for stand-up slides.

Although slides require a lot of practice and balance, the real secret to them is in the speed. A board that isn't moving won't slide at all. A board that is moving slowly is very difficult to slide. The faster the board is going, the easier it is to slide. The drawback is that the faster you are going, the less control you have over the board. Finding that perfect balance between speed and control is what slides are all about.

Slalom

A slalom course can be quickly created on any smooth hill where there is no traffic. You will need a number of small, light cones. (Do not use traditional traffic cones because they are too heavy and will cause you to wipe out if you hit them.) The number of cones you need will depend on the type of format you feel like setting up. Your cones should be 140 mm in diameter at the base and made of bright, lightweight plastic. For sanctioned competition, there are specific rules governing the exact specifications of the cones, but for practicing, any small and light cone without a base flange should be fine.

Unlike downhill, in slalom skaters are not allowed to touch the ground with their feet or hands during a race.

Slalom boards are different from longboards and ordinary trick boards. They tend to be shorter, with narrow wheelbases that permit the board to turn quickly. The boards are equipped with narrow trucks and big, fast wheels. Few groups within skateboarding are as focused on performance as slalom racers. Every piece of equipment on a serious slalom racer's board is carefully considered.

If you are interested in timing yourself, you will need a stopwatch and a piece of chalk. All cone positions should be traced with chalk so you can return hit cones to their proper places. (Placing spilled cones in even slightly different places effectively changes the course and makes your recorded times meaningless.)

During sanctioned races, the penalties for hitting a cone hard enough that it leaves the chalk circle is generally .1 second added to your finish time, although the exact penalty may vary from contest to contest. Passing a cone on the wrong side (the inside) is a disqualification. Some interesting opportunities may emerge in a course where intentionally hitting a cone may end up saving you more time than going around it properly, particularly if it's in a difficult place to get to. The rules on this kind of behavior are complicated and often debated.

The starting gate for slalom events is a platform with a curved ramp contour for rolling in. The ramp is usually about 4 or 5 feet (1.2 or 1.5 m) tall and features two vertical poles that the racer uses to grip and pull himself down the ramp. This pull at the beginning of the race is the only human propulsion allowed throughout the race.

There are several types of slalom formats.

The most traditional slalom format is the straight parallel. In this course, approximately 50 cones are spaced between 1 and 3 meters apart. Shorter

courses may use only 25 cones, while longer ones may be as large as 100. The straight parallel slalom tests the skater's ability to consistently turn sharply in alternating directions. Straight parallel courses can be on flat or slightly sloping terrain.

A more challenging version of slalom is the tight slalom. Similar to straight parallel, tight slalom cones are placed about 2 to 3 meters apart, but there will occasionally be groups of cones that veer off the fall line of the hill, making the navigation of the course more dynamic. Tight slalom is like straight parallel except for these sections that veer off course.

The most dynamic slalom courses are known as hybrid slalom. In these courses, the cones may vary a great deal in terms of distance and proximity to each other. The cones may be between 1.5 and 4.5 meters apart. Hybrid slalom is typically held on steeper hills.

Giant slalom is an even faster format. Although the courses tend to feature fewer cones, they are typically set up on steeper terrain. The courses will have some sections where the cones are placed more tightly and other sections where the cones are spaced far apart. The intervals tend to be irregular to test the skater's ability to navigate tight corners at high speeds.

Super giant slalom is the fastest slalom format. From 20 to 100 cones are used on a steep hill, spaced between 3 and 20 meters apart. In super giant slalom, skaters are often tucked (i.e., slightly crouched to reduce air resistance) throughout the whole course.

A full set of rules for slalom skateboarding can be found at the International Slalom Skateboarding Association's website: www.slalomskateboarder. com.

Slalom racers have their own unique and supportive community that has little relationship to "ordinary" skateboarding's subculture. Slalom racers are friendly and eager to introduce new people to the sport, so if this sounds like something you might be interested in, head over to www.slalomskateboarder.com and see if there are any events being planned near you.

TAKING SKATEBOARDING FURTHER

You may think that after big airs on vert, downhill, and slalom, there would be nowhere else to take skateboarding. But new tricks are being developed every day, and classic tricks are being tweaked or taken to new levels. Reverts and adding another 180 to any of the aerials are just a few ways that skateboarding is more technical now than it's ever been. Structures are changing, too. New styles of skateparks and event structures such as the megaramp are having a huge impact on how people skate. The thing you need to remember while trying tricks that are just outside of your abilities is to skate safe and have fun.

PART III

The Skateboarding Life

Your bag of tricks will grow and shrink as you learn new tricks or retire old ones. Eventually you may find that you want just a little bit more out of skateboarding. At some point in your life as a skateboarder you might want to expand your involvement and do something beyond working on your trick-skating skills. This section offers ideas for ways you can take your commitment to skateboarding a little further.

CHAPTER 9

CHALLENGING YOUR ENVIRONMENT

Lots of people are happy grabbing a skateboard and doing a few tricks in the driveway or meeting their friends down at the skatepark. For them, skating is something they do. Some skaters might be really into it and spend much of their free time getting their tricks on lock or learning something new.

For other people, skateboarding is a way of life. They've devoted thousands of hours to riding a skateboard and feel ready to take it to the next level. If this sounds like you, then exploring the opportunities laid out in this chapter is a good way to start.

There are many activities and careers related to skateboarding. Options include performing tricks for audiences (see chapter 10, Skating Competitively), engaging in friendly competition with friends, attending camps with other skaters, finding or creating places to skate, supporting competitive athletes, and working for skateboarding publications and organizations.

SKATING GAMES

Skating games can be a fun way of improving your skills and learning new tricks. By its nature, skateboarding is an individual activity and doesn't lend itself easily to competition. Skating is creative and diverse; all skaters bring a little something special to their way of skating regardless of how many tricks they know. As a result, skateboarding games tend to be very loose and interpretive. Who wins and who loses isn't as important as having fun.

SKATE

Most people are familiar with the basketball game of HORSE. SKATE is the skateboarding version. It can be played with any number of people, although with more than five skaters things can get confusing and progress slowly.

Pick someone to go first. That person names a trick and then tries to do it. If he doesn't land the trick, then the next person names a trick and tries to do it. Once a skater lands a trick that he named, everyone else must do the same trick. Those who don't get an *S*. Once everyone has landed the trick or gotten a letter, the person who called and landed the last trick then calls out a new trick and tries to land it. If he makes it, everyone else must then try the new trick; if not, the next person calls another trick, and so on. Whenever someone misses, he gets a letter in the word *SKATE* (so if he had an *S* from the first trick, when he misses his second trick, he will get a *K*, and so on).

When a person gets his last letter, *E*, he is eliminated. Some people require the person who named the last trick to then land it again to "prove it."

Addatrick

Addatrick ("add a trick") is a fast game usually played on a miniramp or some other structure that provides for a continuous flow. It can be played with any number of people, but more than six will slow it down and make things confusing.

The first player drops in, does a trick on the opposite side of the ramp, and then returns to where she dropped in. The second player then drops in, does the same trick the first player did, and then does a trick on the other side of the ramp. The next player then must do both of those tricks and add her own onto the end. A player is eliminated if she messes up or skips a trick. For most people, addatrick is over within just a few runs, but true miniramp champs can have epic addatrick battles.

Park Slalom

You'll need a few small orange cones (but chalk will work in a pinch), some duct tape, and a skatepark to play this game. If you want to turn it into a competitive game, you'll also need a stopwatch. Basically, set up a race course around the park, and use the cones to mark the route. Tape the cones down so that if they're nudged they won't go flying. You can tape cones to the sides of bowls so that the skater needs to go over the cone. The course can be a few simple turns, or it can be complicated and use parts of the park that require rolling in or a high ollie. It's up to you!

SKATE CAMPS

Schools, churches, and parks departments all over the country hold skateboarding classes. There are relatively few skate camps, however. These are extended workshops where the skaters skate, eat, and sleep at the facility. Some skate camps are a few intense days, while others can go for weeks.

There are several well-known skate camps in operation right now, and they offer similar services. More community groups are getting into the skate camp business every year. Campers get to skate on world-class ramps and learn tricks from a dedicated staff of experienced skaters. Sometimes professional skaters are the actual trainers. Most of these camps you can easily research on the Internet. Whenever possible, you should talk to people who have gone to the camp you are interested in. They will give you the best insight into what kind of experience it is.

Although the overnight camps aren't cheap, you'll stay plenty busy there, and it will be impossible to get bored. That said, if you're looking for a major boost to your skateboarding skill, it's questionable whether the money and time spent at a camp is automatically going to turn into incredible skateboard control. Just like visiting a local skatepark or experimenting with a new trick in your garage, what you get out of your time at a skate camp is in direct proportion to what you put into it. If you go and play video games and hang out with professional skaters, you'll have a great time. And if you focus on skating and pick up as much advice and coaching as you possibly can while you're there, you'll certainly leave a better skateboarder.

If you're unsure about camps, most of them offer one- and two-day programs that you can go to. These are a great way to find out if skate camps are your thing at a more economical price.

SKATEPARKS

Skateparks have been a part of skateboarding since the 1970s. Although there was a period during the 1980s where most were closed and demolished, today there are new public skateparks opening every week. Every major American city has some kind of skateboarding terrain, and most are planning to add more to their list of facilities.

One of the greatest things about skateboarding is that you can take it to all kinds of different terrain. Naturally, you can skate in your driveway or on the sidewalk near your house. There are hundreds of tricks you can learn, perfect, and build on without leaving your block. All you need is a small space that is smooth. Eventually, though, you will want to test your skills on more challenging terrain. Few of the photos you see in magazines and videos show skaters doing their tricks on flat. They're usually doing the trick on something: a picnic table, jersey barrier, stair set, and so on. This is one of the greatest things about skateboarding. It's flexible. You don't need a special place to do it, and you don't need to round up a team of people to do it with. However, if you want to skate with people and are looking for more advanced terrain, there's no better place than your local skatepark.

All the skills and tricks described in this book can be done in a skatepark, but there are some additional things you should know when you visit.

Park Rules

Different skateparks have different rules. Some parks might just be paved areas in the corner of a parking lot with a few ramps and boxes that you can use whenever you feel like it. Others might require that you wear a helmet. Some others might require a helmet and elbow, wrist, and knee pads. (Yes, even if it's just a few boxes and rails!)

There are indoor skateparks where you can pay to skate. This is nice in lousy weather. They might charge you up to $10 for a session—generally a few hours—or maybe they let you skate all day for one price. Any skatepark that charges you will require you to sign an insurance waiver. If you're not over 18 years old, you will need a parent or guardian to sign for you. They won't make any exceptions, so be prepared. The better indoor skateparks will have waivers available online that you can print and have your parents sign before you go. Don't leave it at home!

Skatepark Materials

Skateparks come in all sizes and shapes. There are big ones and small ones, tall ones and fat ones. There are skateparks that look like prison exercise yards and skateparks that you can't even tell were built for skateboarders. Sometimes they are made of concrete, sometimes metal, and sometimes wood.

There is no "right" kind of skatepark. There is only what is right for you. If you are just beginning and want some peace and quiet so you can concentrate on your skills, the best skatepark is one that isn't crowded. Most people consider the skatepark nearest their house as the best one because it's closest. That's a valid point of view. Who wants to get a ride, drive, or catch a bus every time they want to skate?

Concrete skateparks are the most durable and allow for the coolest terrain. At better concrete skateparks, you will see structures that you could never find "in the wild." Many of these modern parks use dyed concrete and imprints on the surfaces to make parts of the park look like brick, rock, and so on. This is nice because it doesn't feel as much like a sterile place for skating rather just an ordinary public space.

When you talk about concrete skateparks, realize that there's a difference between concrete and cement. Cement is what holds all the rock and gravel together in concrete. In other words, cement is a part of concrete. If you're talking to people who are really into skateparks, don't refer to them as cement skateparks.

Asphalt is also not concrete. Asphalt is the black, tarry material that parking lots are often made of. It gets lighter as it ages, and after a few years it can look like concrete from a distance. Asphalt cannot be easily shaped into the forms you see at skateparks. Sometimes, however, you'll see an asphalt bank next to a parking lot somewhere. In general, asphalt is not a great skating surface.

Some skateparks contain prefabricated ramps, boxes, and pyramids. These are built somewhere else and brought out on the back of a truck. Then they're installed onto an old tennis court, parking lot, or concrete slab. Although most communities that get these kinds of skateparks are excited at first, before too long the structures fall apart and become unsafe. Serious skaters tend to stay away from these types of parks because they are uninspiring and often worn out. These are the most popular kinds of skateparks because they are cheap, but they're not built to last, and they lack the design flexibility of concrete. These parks are almost always steel, wood, or covered with some kind of tough paperlike material known as Skatelite. When you visit this type of skatepark, inspect the area you will be skating for screws and places where the ramp surfaces don't line up. Lots of people hurt themselves because of problems such as these, and if you know what to avoid it will help you a lot.

There's a new kind of skatepark that uses prefabricated concrete. These are called *precast* and often look like the prefabricated steel ramps except they're made of concrete. This is great for keeping the ramps durable even after a few years of use. If the precast structures use metal plates at the bottom of the quarterpipes, it's an area you will want to look out for. These transition plates often come loose. The better precast skateparks are concrete all the way to the bottom and don't feature any steel plates anywhere. Precast skateparks are relative newcomers to the skatepark world, and chances are if you have a concrete skatepark near you, it is the traditional kind.

Skatepark Terrain

Just as skateparks come in different materials, they also come in different flavors. Some skateparks are characterized by round, flowing shapes, while others feature blocky forms and flat-banks. Sometimes these flavors are mixed together like a peanut butter cup.

Skateparks that feature a lot of transition (i.e., rounded forms) are known as flow parks. Flow parks have many smaller designations as well. A flow park might feature nothing but a few bowls or maybe even one big complicated one. It might have a snake run—a serpentine channel with pockets and hips. (More on pockets and hips in a minute.) Maybe it has a snake run that leads to a bowl with a channel that leads out to some twinkies (concrete moguls). Skaters can flow through this kind of park effortlessly without having to push. All your speed is found by pumping the different rounded walls.

At the opposite extreme is the street plaza (sometimes called street courses). A plaza is mostly square forms and structures that you might find in a typical city. Rails, ledges, planters, benches, and ramps are all typical in a plaza. These types of skateparks are favored by street skaters because they mimic the natural city environment.

There are many smaller designations within these categories of skateparks. Each form within a park also has a name, and although it's not important to remember what everything is called, it can help when you want to describe what's in the park to someone who hasn't been there.

Skatepark Elements

In flow parks there are some distinctive forms that show up again and again.

Bowls come in several flavors. The character of a bowl is largely determined by the radius of the curved walls. A smaller radius makes a tighter transition, and it is more difficult to ride. A larger radius slopes upward more gradually and is easier. Bowls with fast transition (i.e., a tight radius) are sometimes known as pools or backyard bowls because they closely replicate an actual empty swimming pool. To reinforce this, many skatepark builders use pool coping along the lip and even include stairs in the shallow end. Sometimes they include a fake filter box just under the coping somewhere in the deep end. This is known as a "death box" because if you catch your wheels in it you will almost certainly fall. (There is a well-known skateboard company called Deathbox. This is where they got their name.)

Pools tend to have traditional pool-like shapes. The most common shape is a kidney. Kidney bowls are popular because they offer lots of terrain options within a modest footprint. A kidney bowl can be "left hand" or "right hand," meaning it is a pinched oval that curves left or right, respectively. A kidney will have a shallow end—if there are stairs this is where they will be—and a deep end. Most bowls like this are 4 feet (1 m) or so in the shallow end and between 7 and 11 feet (2 to 3 m) in the deep end.

There are other popular shapes—such as clovers and combis—that you can learn about in your own time. The main thing to remember is that pools are self-enclosed shapes that don't connect to other parts of the skatepark.

Bowls are a little bit different. A bowl is any contained area that is transitioned on all the walls. Unlike pools, bowls can have crazy, complicated shapes. They may have portions that use pool coping, but usually it's steel. Many skaters won't differentiate between a pool and a bowl, but if you are a stickler for details, bowls tend to have more flat in the bottom than pools. (Pools sometimes don't have any; they just curve all the way across the bottom and back up the other side.)

Unlike pools, there aren't any names for the different kinds of bowls because they often incorporate lots of different types of features along their walls. Bowls can be shallow or deep, but they usually have a mellower transition than pools. They tend to be more complicated and offer different kinds of attractions around their sides.

In some bowls there may be sections that curve completely up to vertical and continue until they hang into the bowl. These areas are called oververt because they go beyond vertical. Getting into these areas requires a lot of speed. Oververt sections can be found in full pipes (complete tubes that can be skated inside), capsules (a full pipe that ends in a cradle), cradles (a perfectly round pocket like a mixing bowl on its side), and clamshells (pockets that rise up and go only slightly oververt).

There are other common bowl features that you may find fun to try your skills on. Tombstones—or extensions—are vertical faces that rise up higher than the top of the bowl and are useful for getting extra speed. Pockets are small, whippy corners that you can use to pump through sideways (instead of the traditional pumping while you're going up or down the transition). Hips are convex-shaped transition walls. Spillways are places where the flat-bottom of the bowl changes elevation. Spillways are another great place to pick up speed.

You will not find tombstones, pockets, hips, or spillways in prefabricated parks. This creative terrain is found only in concrete skateparks. That is why most experienced skaters prefer concrete; there's simply more fun terrain to experiment on.

Bowls and miniramps will sometimes connect to other parts of the skate-park with a single piece of coping. In these areas, one transition wall rises up to meet another wall on the other side. This is known as a spine. Any lip trick you can do in a miniramp you can do on a spine. However, spines are also great places to amp up your lip tricks because you can come down the other side instead of landing up on the deck. When you do a trick on a spine—or even just roll over it—it's known as a spine transfer because you are transferring from one part of the bowl to another. In other areas, bowls and miniramps will use channels, or a narrow break in the transition to facilitate rolling in. A line is a path through a skatepark that provides an appropriate speed and direction for several different parts of the structure or elements.

Street terrains, or plazas, also have their own nomenclature. Street areas are mostly flat with different structures standing alone. Skating these areas is a little different because speed is controlled through pushing rather than pumping, although there may be banks and small quarterpipes in a street area that provide for some pumping.

The most basic form found in plazas is the ledge. These are usually concrete or granite and about 10 to 18 inches (25 to 46 cm) tall. Most plazas will have ledges of different sizes to suit different tastes and skill levels. When a ledge slopes, usually next to stairs or a bank, it's generally known as a hubba.

Manual pads are short boxes that are good for ollieing up onto. They also serve as ledges; there is a ledge on each side. Sometimes two different-sized manual pads are connected in some creative way.

A space between two structures is a gap. A parking strip might be a gap if you were trying to ollie from the sidewalk into the street. In a skatepark, a gap might be the space between two manual pads or the space created by a channel going into a bowl. Some skateparks have gaps built right into the flat ground, and sometimes they have ledges next to them. The gap provides an extra degree of drama and gnarliness to the trick done over it.

Rails are also common in plazas. There are round rails, named such because they are round. (It's nice to have something in skateboarding named for what it looks like.) You might think that flat-rails would therefore be square, but no. Flat-rails are rails that are parallel to the ground. Yes, flat-rails are usually square, but you will occasionally see a round rail that is also a flat-rail. Confused yet? Rainbow rails arc in a curved fashion like a rainbow.

 **Amoeba bowl**—A bowl with four or more nonuniform pockets.

 **Bank wall**—A very steep bank, usually with a small amount of transition at the bottom.

 **China bank**—A bank with a ledge midway up its side.

 **Clover bowl**—A three- or four-pocket bowl of semiuniform shape. The pockets are generally different depths.

 **Concrete**—"Liquid stone" that is composed of gravel, cement, and other additives. Not to be confused with cement, which is merely a component of concrete.

 **Coping**—The protruding lip at the top of a transition. Coping is usually steel pipe, but concrete blocks are also used. (The latter is called pool coping.)

 **Cradle**—An overhang in a transition pocket.

 **Death box**—The small hollow space found in swimming pools just under the coping. Although not needed for skatepark bowls, the obstacle is sometimes included to give the bowl a "backyard pool" feeling.

◀ **Deck**—The platforms adjacent to the transition on miniramps and halfpipes.

◀ **Dragon or kinked rail**—A rail with a curved or angular elevation change, respectively.

◀ **Extension**—A raised portion of wall that extends past the coping. A narrow extension within a bowl is often called a tombstone.

◀ **Flat-bank**—An inclined plane.

◀ **Flat-rail**—A simple structure that is a small interpretation of a full-size handrail sometimes found next to walkways. Most flat-rails are less than 2 feet (.6 m) tall.

◀ **Gap**—Any space between the launch and the landing.

◀ **Halfpipe**—A large miniramp. The transition will go to vert sometimes. Although a halfpipe can be considered half of a full pipe, the halfpipe has a flat-bottom whereas full pipes do not.

◀ **Hip**—The round projection within a bowl or snake run.

◀ **Hubba**—A ledge that is set at an angle. The hubba is usually next to a bank or small set of stairs. Hubbas are almost always unidirectional structures. In other words, nearly everyone grinds or slides down them—few people will ever go up.

◀ **Jersey barrier**—Traffic barrier with a flared bottom. Most jersey barriers in skateparks are designed and built specifically for skateboarding.

◀ **Kidney bowl**—A bowl that is shaped like a bent oval, usually with a shallow and a deep end.

◀ **Ledge**—Blocky form used for sliding or grinding along its edge.

◀ **Loveseat**—A projecting platform midway up a transition or bank wall.

◀ **Manual pad**—A short, wide ledge.

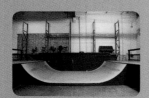

◀ **Miniramp**—Two opposing quarterpipes with a flat space between.

◀ **Pocket**—A tight corner in transition.

◀ **Pole jam**—A short pole jutting from the ground at a low angle.

◀ **Pool**—A bowl, although usually a closer swimming pool replica with tighter transition in the shallow end.

◀ **Prefab**—Ramps and other skatepark structures that arrive at the skatepark location to be assembled and installed rather than built from scratch on site.

◀ **Pump bump**—A round protrusion used for pumping over. Oblong pump bumps are sometimes referred to as twinkies, while circular pump bumps are occasionally called nipples.

◀ **Pyramid**—Two or more converging flat-banks. The top is almost always flat.

◀ **Quarterpipe**—A small curved ramp.

◀ **Slab**—The flat concrete surface that prefabricated ramps sit on.

◀ **Snake run**—A curving channel of transition.

◀ **Speed wall**—A quarterpipe with a tall vertical extension.

◀ **Spine**—The highest point where two transition walls meet, usually with a single or double coping.

◀ **Street (and street plaza)**—A skatepark designed to mimic the kinds of structures found in an urban landscape.

◀ **Volcano**—Free-standing transitioned cone with a flat top.

Dragon rails are rainbow rails that have an extra upward stroke at the end like a ski jump. Rails that slope downward don't have a name, although sometimes they're called handrails. Handrails are usually positioned over a bank or small stair set. It gets weird when handrails are very low to the ground. When a handrail has a portion that is flat, it's typically known as a kinked rail. A double-kinked rail would have two kinks. (A kink in a rail is acceptable and gnarly. A kink in a transition means the transition is flawed and is not desirable.)

Flat-banks are also a common sight in skateparks of all types. Flat-banks are usually gentle slopes ending in a flat top or ledge. When two flat-banks meet at an outward angle, it creates a bank hip, just like an outward-curving transition wall. Flat-bank hips are sometimes called pyramid hips. They are great for ollies because they provide more lift and airtime than the same ollie on flat ground. When a flat-bank has a notch taken out of the top just below the deck, it's called a eurogap. Sometimes quarterpipes will feature a eurogap at the top as well.

There are many other terms unique to skateparks. Different regions even have local terms for particular structures, and some specific structures have become so famous that their names are now used to describe all the forms that look like them. China banks and hubba ledges are both names for famous skate spots that are now used to describe common elements in a skatepark.

Navigating Skatepark Traffic

For beginning skaters, a crowded skatepark can seem chaotic. There's no question that collisions occur, but it is the exception. There is an order and rhythm to skatepark traffic that inexperienced skatepark skaters don't usually understand at first.

Skateparks have invisible lanes of traffic. These are sometimes called "lines" through the park. A line is the most common direction of travel across the park. Skateparks, particularly the larger ones, may have different areas to them—almost like neighborhoods or rooms of a house. These rooms allow skaters to use the different areas at the same time because they are separate and there's little risk of a collision. For example, there may be an area with a few flat-banks and ledges on one side, a miniramp next to it, and a bowl off to the side. This skatepark has three rooms; the street area, the mini, and the bowl.

Before you start rolling around a crowded skatepark, take a look at where people are standing on the tails of their boards and looking. These skaters are probably waiting to take their turn, called a run, and you will want to watch what area they are going into. It's very poor manners to get in someone's way at the skatepark. Sure, accidents happen and people get in each other's way all the time, but it's usually a misunderstanding, and there is no harm. When it happens a second time, people begin to get irritated. If it happens a third time, people will probably let their feelings be known. In other words, you don't want to be the person that is constantly in everyone's way. The people that share the skatepark all the time and understand the traffic will let it be known that they don't want you there if you continually disrupt everyone's good time. Don't worry; it's not that hard to figure out. You just need to pay attention to a few things.

First, look at the different "rooms" of the skatepark. You'll see areas that are out of the way, and nobody seems to go into them. Before you go off to that area to skate on your own, make sure it's not clear of skaters because someone is using it for some kind of big, crazy trick that he has to start clear across the park to get enough speed for. If you go over there and you are in someone's way, he'll usually holler at you to move—sometimes politely, sometimes not—so pay attention to anyone wanting to share your area. A great rule of thumb is that you do not go out into the middle of the park and scoot around in circles. The middle of the park is almost always a very important area for getting to other parts of the park. It would be like playing hopscotch in the middle lane of a freeway. People will get bummed out, and they'll ask you to move it.

After you've spent some time at the skatepark, you will begin to see where people stand and wait their turn for different areas of the park. Bowls are easy because only one person will be using it at a time. Larger, flowing areas can be confusing because there may be three or four people skating through the area at once. Just because they are using the area at the same time doesn't necessarily mean they're just going wherever they want. Experienced skaters know where everyone else is at all times, even you. They'll be looking out for you, especially if you're inexperienced (and they can tell), but it's still great manners to try not to get in anyone's way. After you understand the traffic pattern of the park, you can begin taking your runs through the more congested parts of the park.

WHERE TO SKATE IF YOU DON'T HAVE A SKATEPARK

If your town doesn't have a skatepark and there isn't one nearby, finding interesting places to skate can be difficult. There are a few important things to keep in mind when you are hunting for a good place.

First, and most important, you need to be away from traffic. Approximately 50 skaters die every year in the United States. Most of these deaths involve a motor vehicle. Sure, being hit by a car doesn't always kill someone, but it might just make it so you never skate again, or play video games, or get out of a chair. It takes only one bad decision to change your life and the lives around you forever, so don't be an idiot. Don't skate in traffic.

Second, you'll need to know the law. Obviously you can't just skate wherever and whenever you like. Skating in the mall, for example, is a pretty good way to get snagged by security. In some towns, even skating downtown on the sidewalk is enough to get you a ticket. Find out before you head out. It sucks having to pay a fine just for rolling down the sidewalk. Skate where it's legal.

Finally, you need to skate where it's appropriate. This means not skating where your tiny, hard wheels are making a racket in front of an apartment building in the middle of the night. It means taking it easy when skating down a sidewalk where there are people walking their dogs. It means letting people pass without feeling as if they're about to get hit by a flying skateboard. Ultimately it means just being respectful and not reinforcing the "skate punk" stereotype skaters have had to live with for so many years. Be a good neighbor and a good citizen and represent skateboarding well—and if you can't help yourself and you need to be bad, put the skateboard away first.

STARTING A SKATEPARK

Unfortunately, there isn't a skatepark in every town and city. Sure, some have several, but most small towns don't have one at all. There are a few reasons for this.

First, skateparks don't build themselves. They require land, money, and willpower. Because even large skateparks are small by ordinary park standards, land is not usually an issue. Skateparks can go anywhere.

Money for skateparks is a different story. Parks budgets are always tight, and finding the money to build new parks is usually complicated and requires a lot of dedication. Getting the money to create new skateparks starts with people—usually skaters—making a case to the city leadership that a new skatepark is needed. This isn't usually just a meeting or two but many months of regular pressure and coordination. There are also people who have other desires; maybe they don't like skaters and don't want a skatepark in town, or maybe they have other kinds of interests and don't want to see money and resources going to a new facility that they won't use. (Maybe both!)

That's where the third ingredient comes in. Willpower is the tenacity and dedication it takes to not stop until it's done. It's like learning to ollie. If you don't ollie the first time you try, you don't just stop there, you try again. (At least we *hope* you try again!) It's the same with skateparks. At first it will seem as if nobody in town wants a skatepark except for a handful of skaters. With time and dedication, that handful of skaters can turn the whole place around so that nearly everyone in town is excited about the new park. We've seen it happen dozens, maybe even hundreds of times. Nearly every public skatepark is the result of this kind of process.

There are new skateparks being built every week across the nation. Every single one of them had a group of skaters who worked closely with the city to make that skatepark happen. As you read this, somewhere there is a group of people who are planning the next step in making their skatepark vision a reality.

This process usually takes a year or more. For many people that is simply too much time. For a few, skatepark advocacy presents a special kind of challenge that is irresistible. Although skateboarders sometimes find themselves on the wrong side of public opinion, the skatepark advocate embraces public opinion and works to depict skateboarders as important members of the community.

The process of creating a new skatepark is similar regardless of where you are. There are some great resources online that can provide all the details and support you need, but here is a brief overview of the stages in skatepark development.

1. **Find out what's going on.** It's possible that there's already a group of people working with the city in your area to get a new skatepark. You may be able to ask other skaters or your local shops if they know anyone who is currently pushing for a new skatepark. If you can get involved with an existing effort, it will save a lot of time, and they could certainly use your help.

2. **Develop a vision.** Gather a few of your friends, parents, or anyone else who might be interested in this effort. The first real step toward

a new skatepark is figuring out what it is you want to accomplish. Your group's vision might be a large regional skatepark that everyone in the area will use, a single skatepark in a particular neighborhood, or even a number of small skate spots strategically placed around the city. Developing your vision will help you explain to people who don't understand skateboarding what you're trying to do.

3. **Advocate!** Take your skatepark vision to anyone who will listen. The idea of a skatepark will make perfect sense to skaters, but everyone else may need to be told about the greater benefits to the community. The more you talk about the new skatepark, the better you'll get at explaining all the reasons why it's a good thing. For some great tips on how to advocate for skateparks, visit Skaters for Public Skateparks at www.skatepark.org.

4. **Raise the funds.** The most challenging part of building new skateparks is getting them paid for. Fund-raising events, T-shirt sales, change jars, and car washes will all help, but a large skatepark can cost upwards of $400,000. If you expect to actually skate in the new skatepark before you are receiving Social Security benefits, you will need to find larger funding sources. You'll need to work closely with the city government and parks department to find grant opportunities. Many foundations will be interested in supporting your new skatepark, but first you need to find them.

5. **Design.** The nation's most successful skateparks are designed by professional skatepark designers. The skatepark designer will work directly with you and your local skaters to find out what kinds of things you like to skate. Maybe you want a street plaza, some crazy bowls, or a little of everything. The designer will then work up some ideas. Over time those ideas will be talked about, changed, refined, and eventually transformed into a finished design: This is your skatepark on paper.

6. **Construction.** The designer takes the design that everyone is happy with and creates a collection of diagrams and instructions for the builder. The builder is usually from a different company than the designer, but sometimes the skatepark designer will be from a company that also builds skateparks. The builder then gets to work moving the ground around, putting in rebar, pouring and shaping concrete, then adding the finishing touches.

7. **Opening day!** After more than a year of planning and hard work, the skatepark opens. It wouldn't exist if it weren't for you. Congratulations!

The job doesn't end there. The skatepark will certainly be a popular spot for people, especially at first, but you will need to stay involved with what goes on there to make sure the facility stays as successful as you expected. There are a few things you will want to consider doing after the skatepark is open.

Cleanup Days

Organizing a skatepark cleanup will demonstrate to the community that the skaters are committed to keeping the skatepark attractive and comfortable for everyone. Even without a regularly scheduled event, picking up around the park each time you visit will help send a message that you want people to see skateboarders and skateparks in the best possible way.

Learn-to-Skate Days

Teaching less experienced and beginning skaters some fundamental skills during times when the skatepark isn't usually crowded, such as midday on the weekend, will help new skaters understand how the skatepark works and what kinds of stuff you can do there. This will help steer slower, beginning skaters in the right areas of the park so they can visit when it's crowded without feeling as if the environment is too intense. The skatepark is for everybody, but it's still important that beginning skaters know what is expected and how experienced skaters will be sharing the space. Learn-to-skate days can help new skaters get up to speed at the skatepark.

Contests and Demos

Demonstrations and competitions are both fun ways to bring a larger audience to the skatepark. The details of putting together a successful contest are beyond the scope of this book, but they are not difficult to figure out when you start small. Demos are much easier because they don't require as much scheduling and coordination. Demos can be kept small by using your local rippers, or they can be more ambitious by working with any traveling teams that might be coming through the area. The more ambitious the event, the more planning and work it will require, so think carefully before you launch a monster event. They're worth doing though! The attention these types of events get from the broader community, news organizations, and city agencies can bring a lot of positivity to the skatepark.

BUILDING YOUR OWN SKATING STRUCTURES

Skateparks are large, complicated, and artistic structures that require construction knowledge and experience to build properly. It's unrealistic to start off with bold plans to build a full-size concrete skatepark without any previous experience. So, where do you get experience? That's easy. You build smaller things to skate!

Some terrific ramp plans are available online. The better plans explain all the tools and materials you'll need to make these structures right the first time. There is not enough room in this book to cover all the information, but here are a few places you can start.

One of the first things most people build is a grinding box. This is essentially a manual padlike box with steel on the edge. You can grind it, tail-slide it, manual across it, or do any number of tricks. It is not only versatile but also easy to build.

After the grinding box, the next structure you should consider is a fly ramp or quarterpipe. This is a bit more complicated because you will be building a curved surface.

Once you have some experience building quarterpipes and fly ramps, you can put it all together to make a miniramp or halfpipe.

Grinding Box

This is a simple rectangular frame made from 2 by 4s (5 by 10 cm boards). On top is a sheet of plywood. One or more of the leading edges are covered in angle iron to make a smooth surface for sliding or grinding.

Start by committing to the overall dimensions you'd like to build. You might want something shorter for doing manuals across or something taller for tail and nose slides. For a shorter manual pad, a block 10 inches (25 cm) tall by 8 feet (2.4 m) long and 4 feet (1.2 m) wide is pretty good.

Ledges for tail slides should be between 12 and 24 inches (30 to 60 cm) tall. They can be narrower to make them lighter and more portable, but they shouldn't be so narrow that they move or tip when you jam your board into them—2 or 3 feet (.6 to .9 m) wide is usually adequate.

Fix your 2 by 4 framework and top sheet with screws whenever possible. Nails will vibrate loose, and you'll end up spending more time adding nails to keep the thing from wiggling around than actually skating it.

The final touch on either type of block is the angle iron lip. You might be able to find precut angle iron in your local hardware or home supply store. If not, any iron shop should have plenty on hand. It's very common. You can fix the angle iron to the ledge with any industrial-strength epoxy, such as Liquid Nails.

Fly Ramp

Fly ramps are easy to build and will provide you with experience on cutting transition forms.

You'll need some different types of lumber for a good fly ramp. You'll want 1/2-inch (13 mm) (or thicker) plywood for the sides, then 1/4 or 3/8 inch (6 mm or 10 mm) for the substrate (the sheet of plywood on the skating side of the ramp). On top of your surface sheet, you'll want something smooth and fast such as Masonite.

Your side sheets will determine the height and curve of the transition. If you want to make a 2-foot (.6 m) tall fly ramp, mark off 2 feet from the corner up one side of your thick plywood. The corner that you measure from will become the bottom back corner of the ramp.

Fly ramps don't typically have decks. (If you add a deck, then you've made a quarterpipe.) Now you'll take a thick pencil and draw in the curved line that establishes the curve of the ramp.

You could draw the transition by hand, but unless you're great at drawing perfect circles, we don't recommend it. Instead, think about how whippy you want the transition. If you want a very quick, high jump, a smaller radius transition will work better—maybe 6 feet (1.8 m) or so. For a longer, mellower fly ramp, 7- or 7 1/2-foot (2 m) transitions will work better. You can draw either one out and see if you like the looks of it. If not, make your adjustment and draw a new line. When you're happy with the character of the transition, you can cut it.

To draw a perfect transition, grab a long piece of string, a pencil, and a tape measure. Lay your plywood down on the ground. Make sure you understand which corner is going to be the bottom back corner of the ramp and that the desired height of the fly ramp is clearly marked.

Tape or tie the pencil onto the end of the string and measure out a length that is the size of the transition you'd like to try. For example, if you wanted a 7-foot transition, you would have a 7-foot piece of string with a pencil on the end of it.

Here comes the fun part. You're going to want to draw an arc from the mark that shows the height of the ramp to the side of the piece of plywood. You'll need to move the end of the string around until it's exactly the same distance between the height mark and the side of the wood.

Once your pencil is hitting the height of the ramp and the side of the plywood, draw in your line. It should be a perfect curve. You should now be able to see what your ramp is going to look like. Maybe it's not what you had in mind. Now would be the perfect time to make adjustments.

When you're happy with the character of the transition, cut that piece out. If you've designed a very whippy, tight ramp, you may need a narrow handsaw that will bend along the line. For most transitions, a circular saw can usually be forced through the corner.

When you have one side cut, you can simply lay that piece down on another part of your plywood for the second side. Trace the curve and cut. If your ramp is wider than 4 feet (1.2 m), you will probably want a third piece for the middle of the ramp to add strength. Most fly ramps aren't more than 4 feet wide, however.

With two side pieces cut and ready to go, you can place the joists. You'll want to place one every 6 or 8 inches (15 or 20 cm), so estimate how many you'll need and cut a heap of them beforehand. You'll need one or two for the back and bottom of the ramp to keep the whole thing stable. Don't drive your screws all the way in until you're sure that everything is coming together perfectly. Having a little wiggle room will help you fit the joists between the two side sheets. (If you tighten everything down and then try to add another joist, you may find it all too tight to fit the new piece in.)

Laying the top sheet is the hardest part. Cut your top sheet down to the width of the ramp, but leave it a little longer than you need so it will stick up into the air. Bending the sheet will increase the amount of material you'll need. It's better to have too much that needs to be cut down than not enough.

Put the ramp framework on the ground normally and lay the bottom of the substrate sheet directly where the ramp starts. The sheet will be stiff, but the ramp is curved. You need to push the sheet into the curve of the ramp's frame and screw it into place. You may need to have your friend stand on the sheet so that it flexes. Once the sheet is making solid contact with the joists, you can drive a screw to hold it down. Start at the bottom and move up. Keep moving along like this, and your plywood should bend into place just right. The first few screws are usually the most difficult.

Your Masonite sheet should bend easily. You won't need more than a few screws to hold it in place. You might want to use smaller screws for the Masonite since it doesn't provide any structural strength. It's only there to make your ramp smooth.

Cut down the top of your substrate and top sheets, clean up, and go skate!

To build a quarterpipe, follow the same process as for the fly ramp, but leave distance on your side sheets for a deck. You'll cover this area with plywood. Most quarterpipes tend to be wider, so you may want to include a third identical side piece down the middle of the ramp to serve as a rib.

Miniramp

Miniramps and halfpipes combine things you learned by making ledges and fly ramps. You will need quite a bit of lumber, and it can become expensive, so be prepared to spend a few hundred dollars on wood before you start plugging in your tools.

You'll need a place that is level to build your ramp. A firm surface such as a driveway or garage works best. If you are going to build your ramp on grass or dirt, level off the area first and make sure the ground is hard. If it seems a little soft, you can place a few heavy paver stones down around the perimeter of your ramp. This will keep the ramp from sinking into the ground, where it may get wet and start to rot.

Cut your side sheets like normal using the string method. You will want a rib for every 4 feet (1.2 m) of width, if not more. (The more ribs and joists you use, the stronger and more stable your ramp will be.)

You'll need to include a frame for the flat-bottom of your ramp. You won't need to cut plywood for the sides of the flat-bottom; you can use 2 by 4s.

People who have built excellent miniramps claim you should use two sheets of substrate under your top sheet. They recommend one thick piece of plywood with a thin 1/4-inch (6 mm) sheet on top of it. This helps smooth any of the seams and subtle bumps in the ramp that you won't be able to see (but you will absolutely feel the first time you ride it).

The trickiest part of building a miniramp is setting your coping properly. There are lots of methods for doing this. The most common is to build a small L-shaped "pocket" from 2 by 4s and lay your steel tube into it. Your deck and substrate sheets should overlap the coping slightly to hold it in place. If you want to make your coping very sturdy, drill a hole into the side of the steel tube near the ends and bolt the coping to a 2 by 4. With the two pieces firmly attached, you can fix the wooden part to the ramp's sides wherever you want it.

Unlike ledges and fly ramps, miniramps can't easily be hauled inside when you're not using them. Unless you don't mind replacing Masonite every few weeks, you should throw a tarp over your ramp when you expect it to rain. Be sure to pull the tarp off when the weather clears to let the ramp dry out; the tarp can trap condensation and keep your ramp wet even when it's not raining.

WORKING IN A FIELD RELATED TO SKATING

Many people find other ways of getting involved with skateboarding apart from or in addition to learning all the coolest tricks. Whatever your interests, there is probably a way to apply them to skateboarding on a professional level. Here are some options.

Skate Photography

Photos and video are a great fit with skateboarding. It's common to see skaters being photographed or videotaped at the skatepark or popular street spot. The skater is only part of the story; the person behind the camera needs to know how to make that trick look as good as possible.

Photography is an art and a craft. The craftsmanship comes from knowing how to use the tools, understanding lighting and composition, and having the insight to know where to be and when. The art of photography comes from personal interpretations—seeing something in the background or a particular way of framing the shot that nobody else sees. A creative light placement, the camera angle, or even a postproduction or editing effect can become your signature style.

It's difficult to get rich doing skate photography. It's a crowded market, and because most skate photographers love skateboarding, they are often willing to do it for less than most other commercial photography projects. Companies and magazines are well aware of this and understand that they can adjust their rates to whatever meets their budget. There are few other publishing opportunities for the prolific photographer, although many websites are starting to have real capital to spend on professional photography.

There are two types of commercial photography. Unsolicited photography is when you go out and take a bunch of photos and try to sell them to a magazine. Commissioned photography is when you are hired to take photos by a company of an event or particular skater. Commissions are almost always for a specific photo or purpose; it's out of the ordinary to have someone commissioned to simply take pictures of whatever they like, even if it is skateboarding related. To be popular enough for magazines to hire you to take photographs, you will need a strong portfolio that demonstrates your abilities.

The pinnacle of still photography is landing your photo on a magazine cover. These are the exceptional photos—that "one in a million" shot that works with the editorial theme, is timely, is unique, and has superior technical merit. Even this "best of the best" photo will usually pay only a few hundred dollars to the photographer, but the pride and bragging rights that come with a cover shot are priceless. The more your photos appear in

BAD PHOTO

GOOD PHOTO

magazines and on websites, the more notoriety you will earn. With notoriety come larger projects and, hopefully, bigger budgets.

Shooting video is different from still photography, but the tools, techniques, and skills are similar. If you are skilled with a still camera, picking up video shouldn't be too challenging.

If you are truly serious about a career in photography, it is a good idea to take photography or video classes. These will give you the fundamentals that would otherwise take you months or even years to learn on your own.

Writing About Skateboarding

There are many opportunities within the world of writing to employ your interest in skateboarding. What you are holding in your hands right now is the product of two people who want to share their love of and experience in skateboarding with you through writing. Of course there is also a handful of excellent print magazines that are dedicated solely to the activity. Every article has a writer (and editor) behind it.

When you are starting out as a writer, you probably won't land a big feature in a skateboarding magazine right away. Like everything, it takes time—not only to develop your skills and personal style but also to build a reputation as someone who really knows how to write. A great place to do this is through the thousands of websites devoted to skateboarding. Sure, they probably don't pay very much, if at all. That will be okay with you if you write about skateboarding because you love to write about skateboarding. The money will come eventually.

After writing for a blog or website for a while, you should consider pitching a concept to the editor of one of the magazines you would most like to write for. Your pitch should be short and to the point. The concept should naturally be something that skaters would want to read about, but it should also be unique and fresh. "Tips & Tricks" simply isn't going to excite anyone, but maybe you have a short piece about the skate scene in Egypt. A good idea, along with a sample or two of pieces you wrote previously, could be enough to get your name into the pages of one of the big magazines.

Working in a Skate Shop

For many skaters, this is a dream job. Employees not only get paid to be around skateboards all day but also probably get a discount on product. They get to kill two birds with one stone. They save money that they would normally spend, and they make money at the same time. Cool! Unfortunately, working in a skate shop is a job, and it's not all just sitting around talking about skateboarding all day. In the end you will need to make your presence worth it to the owner; the value you provide must be greater than the expense of your being there. If you're interested in working in a shop, you shouldn't approach the idea in terms of what it can offer you rather what you can offer the shop.

Having a reasonable sense of how retail business works, interacting positively with customers (especially the troublesome ones), and being meticulous in your appearance and work habits are all characteristics that a skate shop owner or manager will be looking for. You probably won't want to flaunt your knowledge of skateboarding because that will be apparent when you talk about it.

It may help to have been a regular customer in the shop for some time before you begin asking for a job. As a regular, you can get to know the personalities of the people that currently work there and the person who would be in charge of hiring. If you are on comfortable speaking terms with the owner or manager, you might consider just asking him how he's doing for staff and if he needs any help. Chances are he'll say that they don't need anyone right now. That's okay. You've taken an important step by letting that person know you're interested and available. If he does find himself with an opening, you may already be on his list of candidates. Check in every few weeks by saying hi, and keep it professional by not lingering too long or using up a lot of his time.

Teaching Skateboarding

Some people are natural teachers. If you find yourself frequently sharing tips with less experienced skaters on various techniques to improve skating, you might consider teaching skateboarding in a more official way. Of all the ways to go about this, the best approach is to talk to your local parks and recreation department. There are a few reasons this is the best agency to help you teach skateboarding. First, and most important, it is structured for recreation classes and has the insurance and staff support for organizing skate classes.

Putting together the actual class will take preparation. There are some excellent resources available, including Ben Wixon's 2009 book *Skateboarding* (Human Kinetics). The lessons you intend to cover in your classes should be tailored to very beginning skaters and have an emphasis on safety and basic skills. This will allow you to build experience and develop some effective teaching techniques. You should never attempt to teach more than six students by yourself, and it's a great idea to always teach any size group with two instructors so that while one of you is helping an individual student, the other can keep an eye on everyone else to make sure they are doing well.

If you like the idea of teaching skateboarding, it is a great idea to take a class on CPR and first aid. These are often free at local fire stations.

Event Management

What would skateboarding be today if it wasn't for the demos and contests? Hosting a skate jam, contest, or demo is a great way to get more involved in your local skate scene. An event can be any number of things, and how you organize it is dependent on a few important factors such as the desired size of the event, if you will allow random people to show up and skate, if you intend to have prizes, if there will be spectators, and so on. When it comes down to it, organizing a skateboarding event is not much different from any other kind of event. The main thing is that skateboarding is inherently risky, and if you are encouraging the participants to take risks by offering prizes, as in a contest, there are likely going to be a few spills. You will need a clear plan on how to deal with injuries both for your participants' sake and for your own legal protection. Don't fake it and think that things will just work out. Do your homework before you put yourself and everyone else at risk.

As with all the other activities outlined in this section, it's a good idea to start small to build up some experience before launching your more ambitious event plans.

CHAPTER 10

SKATING COMPETITIVELY

Competing is one of the strange places in the world of skateboarding where the skater's individual drive and passion meet judges, routines, and trick lists. For many people, skateboarding is a deeply private and individualistic activity where it's just them, their board, and gravity. Other people enjoy their competitive side and want to compare their skills to those of their peers. Neither approach is better than the other; it's simply a matter of personal opinion.

It's great to challenge yourself whenever you get the chance. If you find out about a contest near you, it can't hurt to enter. You might discover that you really like the environment and structure; the worst that can happen is that you find out you really don't. Whatever the result, you won't find out anything if you don't give it a shot. To get through the intimidating aspect of entering a contest, it can help to enter with a friend who also skates. You might even find yourself entering your first contest as a "wing man" to a friend who wants to try it out.

Some people aren't interested in contests because they're afraid of losing. That's a common fear, and many people have it. Nobody really likes to lose, and that's essentially what makes winning fun. If you are competitive by nature, then you probably understand this completely.

CONTESTS AND COMPETITIONS

Skate contests are arranged so that people with similar skill levels are competing against each other. Smaller contests usually have age divisions, while bigger ones are divided into pro and amateur categories. Most amateurs can wrangle their way into the pro division, but it's strongly discouraged for pros to compete in the amateur division.

You'll be required to sign an insurance waiver and usually pay a small entrance fee. If you are under 18, you cannot sign the waiver yourself; you'll need your legal guardian to do it. You'll need your helmet as well, of course.

In judged contests each rider usually takes two or three runs, each one a few minutes long. The runs are scored by each of the judges separately. Each judge then removes the lowest scored run. This allows someone to blow it on one run but skate exceptionally well on the others and still do okay. Contests can be scored in a variety of ways, so you should ask about the scoring system when you register.

Although it depends largely on what kind of contest it is, most judges will score your runs based on the technical skill of the tricks you're doing along with your grace, smoothness, style, originality, and maybe even sheer gnarliness. Judging skateboarding is difficult and highly subjective, so it's not uncommon for your score to be influenced by the crowd reaction. Skate to impress the spectators and your fellow competitors, and the judges will probably fall right in line. If you really need to know what the judges are looking for, you might want to ask when you register. If the contest organizers can't (or won't) tell you, just skate as well as you can and have a great time.

If you happen to skate well enough to earn a prize, congratulations! Smaller contests will often give away products—decks, bearings, wheels, shoes, and clothes. At bigger contests there might be some money for the top winners. No matter how well you do, it seems as if everyone who goes to contests walks away with a handful of stickers and some good stories to tell.

SPONSORSHIPS

There is more bad information than good advice circling around about how to get sponsored. No aspect of professional skateboarding is steeped in more misinformation than what it means to be sponsored.

Some people think that being sponsored means the skater has finally achieved the pinnacle of success. Nothing could be further from the truth. The fact is that getting sponsored means you'll be working harder and doing more, but now you will have people there to help you. When someone helps you, there is an expectation that you will provide something in return beyond skating at your best. If you are a ripper, a company may want you to wear a shirt with its logo on it. When people see you skate, they'll see the logo and associate that company with your high level of skill. The company naturally hopes that people will run out and buy that company's gear because that's what the pros wear or use. Being sponsored is a lot like being a spokesperson or even a moving advertisement.

If you think you'd like to get a sponsor, the process is easy to understand but difficult to accomplish. The requirements are simple:

1. **You must skate at a level that is clearly higher than the regional average.** This basically means that people who know you or have seen you skate unanimously consider you a ripper. There's no doubt in your mind or in the minds of your local skateboarding community that you are one of the best in the area.

2. **You should carry yourself like a professional.** People who are considering putting you on a team or getting you on a flow program are going to have serious concerns if they believe you are going to get into trouble, could have a drug or drinking problem, would consider lying

IS BEING SPONSORED COOL?

The perks of being sponsored come in all shapes and sizes. If asked if they would like to be sponsored by a major skateboarding company, many skaters would say yes before they even knew what the specific offer was. Experienced professional skateboarders know these deals can be good or bad depending on the details.

Getting sponsored might include any or all of the following:

- Free boards, wheels, bearings, and trucks (known as hard goods)
- Shirts, shoes, and other clothes (known as soft goods)
- Parts in videos or features on websites and magazines
- Opportunity to meet and skate with some of the world's most famous skaters
- Signature board or shoe
- Royalties on sales of those boards or shoes
- Opportunity to skate all over the nation or even the world
- Thrill of being famous and having people want your autograph
- Expectation to keep skating at a higher and higher level
- Competing against other skaters in high-pressure events
- Constant risk of career-ending injury

or stealing, or would do anything else that might put them in a tough situation. Sponsors want someone who is going to take the sponsorship seriously.

3. **You have that "something special."** Most sponsors are looking for more than just a high level of skateboarding. It can be hard to describe what mixture of qualities and personality seems like a good fit for a company's team. Think about your favorite skaters and how some of them might be clean cut while others are kind of ratty. Some are smooth while others are gnarly. A company may have a reputation for having a technical team, and you like to go big and go fast. Although the company may respect your skills and style, you simply may not be a good fit for them. There's little you can do about this except to just keep skating and stay focused on what makes you happy.

Handling these requirements is sometimes easier said than done. Challenging yourself all the time to consistently learn new tricks and to progress in your style and abilities requires a lot of dedication, hard work, and bravery. The more advanced your skating gets, the more dangerous it can become. It's not a career for the weak of heart or the pain averse. If you are a timid skateboarder—and many of us are—it doesn't mean you are any less skilled than someone who has a sponsor, although being sponsored may require you at times to push yourself into situations that are truly sketchy. You should never do something you aren't prepared to do just for the sake of impressing a photographer. Always skate within your limits and according to what your conscience dictates is sane and reasonable.

The first step in getting sponsored—provided you meet the requirements—is talking to the owner or team manager at your local shop. The franchise skate shops you find in malls don't typically have teams or sponsor skaters. You'll need an independently owned shop. If it's your local shop, you probably already know the people who run it, and they may even know you. Simply ask what it would take to get sponsored.

If there's a contest coming up that you plan on competing in, it's a great opportunity to bring up the topic. You might tell the owners that you plan on competing in the contest and maybe even that you plan on winning it in your division. Provided that your division isn't an unsponsored one, ask the shop owners if they would like to have you wear their shirt. It might be as easy as that at first.

When you do what you said you were going to do by winning the contest, the shop will understand that you are as good as your word. You could then tell them you would like to continue to ride for them. If they agree, you can work out the details. If they have a team already, they probably have a discount or flow program in place. The discounts will usually be on hard goods: 30 percent off boards, wheels, bearings, and so on. If this works out well for you and the shop, they may start providing those goods for free. This is the flow program. The flow won't be so generous that you can start selling the stuff you don't need, but it should keep you from having to buy a new board when one breaks.

The shop may produce a team video. It's important that you get lots of time on camera. Many people will see it: Most important (for you), professional skaters and team managers from bigger companies may notice you.

Shop sponsors are the first step in a career as a professional skater. The next level is getting a manufacturer sponsor. If your video appearances interest a manufacturer, company representatives will probably contact your shop sponsor and ask about you. They'll want to know what kind of person you are, if you've been a valuable rider for the team, and if the shop would recommend you. There are some well-known shops in the nation that have a reputation for "incubating" top-level pros. You may be lucky enough to live near one of these.

If you have been skating hard for the shop and been professional in handling your responsibilities, the shop will have little reason to not recommend you to a larger company. The company will then contact you or find you at an event and talk to you about skating on its team. This will probably be a similar situation as the shop sponsor. At first you'll just get some gear and maybe some help getting to different contests and events. If you prove yourself, there might be talk of a pro-model board. By this time other companies might be taking an interest in you as well. While you are competing against other skaters in contests, companies are competing against other companies to have the best riders. It can be easy to get caught up in that like a pawn in a game of chess.

What too many skaters do is send "sponsor me" videos to every company they can think of. These people are lucky if anyone even watches the clip; most get put into a box with other unsolicited recordings. Sending unsolicited demos of your skating to a company is a long shot with about the same odds of success as winning the lottery. (If you win the lottery, you can start your own company and sponsor yourself!) The reason this doesn't work is that it's not enough to be good. You have to be *better* than people who are already on the team. In other words, if you send in your demo to big companies, you must be confident that you are skating at the same level as their current team —if not better—or why should they make room in their crowded van for you? If there is any doubt in your mind whether you are skating at this level, it's probably wise to focus your attention on your local shop and smaller regional companies.

A final word of advice about being sponsored: Sponsorships are a partnership between you and the shop or company. It's a lot like having a job. If you accept a sponsorship and another offer comes your way shortly after, you'll want to think hard about your obligation to your first sponsor. These people have made an investment in you and may be disappointed to see you take those benefits on to their competitor just when you were on the rise. Other companies will look at your record as well when they consider you as a potential team rider, much as a company will look at your resume to see how long you tend to work in the same place. People will pay attention to your allegiance and loyalty.

NEVER THE END

Through practice and patience, you can master all the tricks in this book and more. It may take you a year to truly learn everything here, or it could take a lifetime. There's nothing wrong with either pace. Similarly, whether or not you compete with others, strive to improve your own skills or develop a repertoire and stick with it is a matter of personal choice. Most lifelong skaters have reached a level of skating ability that is fun for them and simply maintain their skills by skating regularly. Some maintenance skaters are rippers, while others have humble skills. What they have in common is that they've been skating their entire lives.

This could be you if skating fits your personality and you keep yourself safe.

See you at the skatepark!

A

ABEC (Annular Bearing Engineer's Committee) factor 21
Addatrick 220-221
advocacy, for new skateparks 234
airs (aerial maneuvers)
  airwalk 207
  Benihana 206
  early grabs 194-195
  indy air 196
  inverts (handplants) 208
  Japan air 201
  judo air 204
  lien air 197
  Madonna 205
  method air 199
  mute air 200
  safety guidelines 187-188
  slob air 202
  stalefish 203
airwalk 207
alley-oop 121
all-terrain vehicles (ATVs) 106
Alva, Tony 16
amoeba bowls 226
asphalt 223
attitude
  in learning tricks 104, 165
  others' opinions and 46, 73
  as skateboarding rule 6
ATVs (all-terrain vehicles) 106
axis rotation 33

B

backside
  defined 32
  versus frontside 164
  understanding term 108
back side, defined 32
backside bluntslide 178
backside boardslide 180, 181
backside drifter 40
backside feeble grind 173

backside 5-0 grind 121, 162-163
backside 50-50 grind 166-167, 170-171
backside kickturn 120-121
backside lipslide 180
backside 180 ollie 68-69
backside pop shuvit 88-89
backside rock (and roll) 130-131
backside 50-50 170-171
backside 50-50 stall 140-141
backside 360 shuvit 90-91
backyard bowls 224
bailing technique 37
balance 6, 30
bank hips 231
bank walls 226
baseplates 18, 19
basic maneuvers
  kickturns 47
  manual 50-51
  need to learn 46
  no comply 57
  no comply 180 58
  nose manual 53
  180s 55
  progression from 59
  spacewalk 52
  360 56
  tic tac 48
  up the curb 49
beanplant 154
bearing press 21, 24
bearings
  described 19
  inserting and removing 21, 24
  ratings 21
  worn or dirty 25
beginners
  benchmark trick 62
  falls 8
  first board 17-18, 27
  longboarding 15
  pushing technique 36
  stance 34

Benihana 206
bigspin 94-95
blunt (to fakie) 150-151
bluntslide 178-179
blunt to backside 5-0 151
board rotations 33
boards
    building 22-24
    buying 26-27
    decks 16-18
    inspecting 25
    landing on 63
    size guidelines 17
    trucks 17, 18-19
    tuning 25
    types 14-16, 210-211
    wheel assembly 19-21
boardslides 180-182
body jar 198
bombing hills 209-213
boneless 152-153
bonk 110
bowls 106, 224-225
bragging 6
braking techniques 36-40
bullying 6
bushings 19

C
camaraderie 5
camps 221
capsules 224
cardiovascular benefits 6
careers, in skateboarding 239-242
Carrasco, Richy 16
cars, and skateboarding 10, 209, 232
carves 191
cement 222-223, 226
center of gravity 30
channels 225
chicken foot 91
China banks 226, 231
clamshells 107, 224
cleanup days, in skateparks 234-235
clockwise direction 34
clothing 188, 212
clover bowls 226
collectible boards 27
community support 4
complete boards 26

concave 17
concrete structures
    versus cement 222-223, 226
    ledges and rails 160
    transition 108
confidence, as benefit 7
contests
    competing in 244-245
    organizing 235, 242
coping (lip). *See also* lip tricks
    defined 107-108, 226
    grinds and slides on 161
    ramps without 110
cost, of boards 27
counterclockwise direction 34
counterpumping 112
cradles
    defined 224, 226
    structure type 106, 107
creativity 4
criticism, of skate culture 7
crooked grinds (crooks) 176-177
curbs, crossing 49

D
death box 224, 226
deaths, from skateboarding 10, 209, 232
decks (boards) 16-18, 25
decks (miniramps) 107-108, 227
demos 235, 242
disaster (trick) 148-149
discount programs (sponsorships) 247
diversity, in skaters 4, 5
double-kinked rails 231
downhill boards 15, 210-211
downhill techniques 209-213
drag foot technique 37, 212
dragon rails 227, 231
drifters 39-40, 212
drop in
    miniramp 114-116
    vert terrain 192
drop in switch 116
drop-through boards 15, 210

E
early grabs 194-195
easy tranny 108-110
elbow pads 9
equipment. *See also* boards

helmets 10-11, 15, 41, 160, 187, 209-210
  pads 8-9
  shoes 8
eurogaps 231
event management 235, 242
extensions 225, 227

F
failures 6
fakie 35, 49
fakie ollie 136-137
fakie rock 129
falls
  injury prevention 40-41
  safety equipment and 9
  vert skating techniques 188
  wrist injuries 8
fastplant 154
fast tranny 108-110
feeble grind 172-173
50-50 grind
  backside 166-167, 170-171
  frontside 168-169
50-50 stall
  backside 140-141
  frontside 142-143
540s, defined 54
5-0 grind
  backside 121, 162-163
  frontside 164-165
5-0 stall 144-145
flat-banks 227, 231
flat-bottom 107-108
flat-rails 225, 227
flick, defined 33
flow parks 224
flow programs (sponsorships) 247
fly ramps 235, 236-238
fly ramp tricks 206
footplants 152-156
freestyle 16
frontside
  versus backside 164
  defined 32
  understanding term 108
front side, defined 32
frontside bluntslide 179
frontside boardslide 180, 182
frontside flip 78-79
frontside 5-0 grind 164-165

frontside kickturn 122-123
frontside lipslide 180
frontside ollie, on transition 138-139
frontside 180 ollie 66-67
frontside pop shuvit 86-87
frontside rock (and roll) 132-133
frontside 50-50 168-169
frontside 50-50 stall 142-143
frustration 6
full pipes 107, 224
fun and enjoyment 6, 46, 73, 165
fundraising, for new skateparks 234

G
games 220-221
gaps 225, 227
gear bags 26
giant slalom 214
gloves 9, 15, 212
goofy-footers (right-footers) 31, 34
granite ledges 160
grinding boxes 235, 236
grinds and slides
  backside 5-0 grind 121, 162-163
  backside 50-50 166-167, 170-171
  bluntslide 178-179
  boardslides 180-182
  crooked grind (crooks) 176-177
  feeble grind 172-173
  frontside 5-0 grind 164-165
  frontside 50-50 168-169
  lipslides 180
  overcrook 176
  progression of 183
  safety guidelines 160
  Smith grind 174-175
  structures for 160-161
grip-tape 22-23
Grosman (grab) 195

H
halfpipes
  building 238
  defined 227
  structure type 106, 107
handplants (inverts) 208
handrails 231
hangers 18
hardflip 102-103
Hardwick, Gary 186

Harris, Kevin 16
Hawk, Tony 186
heelflip 80-81
heel side, defined 31
helmet use
  airs 187
  downhill and slalom 15, 209-210
  fit of helmet 11
  grinds and slides 160
  need for 10, 41
  speed and 209-210
hips, in structures 225, 227
hubba ledges
  defined 225, 228
  term 231
hybrid slalom 214

I
impossible 100-101
indoor skateparks 222
indy air 196
injury prevention
  airs 187-188
  downhill and slalom 209-210
  falls 40-41
  grinds and slides 160
  safety equipment 7-11
inspecting boards 25
insurance waivers 222, 245
International Slalom Skateboarding Association
    215
inverts (handplants) 208
inward heelflip 98-99

J
Japan air 201
Jersey barriers 228
judo air 204

K
kickflip
  basic 76-77
  old-school (M-80) 82-83
  360 (tre flip) 92-93
  varial 96-97
kickturn
  backside 120-121
  basic 47
  frontside 122-123
  on vert 191

kidney bowls 224, 228
kingpins 18, 25
kinked, defined 110
kinked rails 227, 231
knee pads 9, 187-188
knee slide 189

L
landing 63
lateral rotation 33
lead foot, defined 33
learning tricks 104
learn-to-skate days, in skateparks 235
ledges
  appropriate for practice 160-161
  building your own 236
  defined 228
  versus rails 168
  in skateparks 225
left-footers (regular footers) 31, 34
legal issues 160, 232
lien air 197
lines, in skateparks 225, 231
lip (coping). *See also* lip tricks
  defined 107-108, 226
  grinds and slides on 161
  ramps without 110
lipslides 180
lip tricks
  backside kickturn 120-121
  backside rock (and roll) 130-131
  backside 50-50 stall 140-141
  blunt (to fakie) 150-151
  blunt to backside 5-0 151
  defined 106
  disaster 148-149
  drop in 114-116
  fakie ollie 136-137
  fakie rock 129
  5-0 stall 144-145
  footplant 152-156
  frontside kickturn 122-123
  frontside ollie 138-139
  frontside rock (and roll) 132-133
  frontside 50-50 stall 142-143
  nose stall 125
  ollie in 118-119
  ollie to fakie 134-135
  pivot 146-147
  progression of 157

reverts 126-127
rock to fakie 128-129
roll in 116-117
on spine 225
tail stall 124-125
on vert 198, 208
longboarding techniques 209-213
longboards 15, 210-211
loveseats 228
Lucero, John 16

M
M-80 (old-school kickflip) 82-83
Madonna 205
manual pads 225, 228
manual 50-51
manufacturer sponsorships 248
marble ledges 160
method air 199
miniramps
building 238-239
defined 228
etiquette 111
finding right one 110
parts 107-108
qualities 108-110
structure type 106, 107
mongo 36
motor vehicles, and skateboards 10, 209, 232
Mullen, Rodney 16
mute air 200

N
NBS rating, of shoes 8
900s, defined 54
90s, defined 54
no comply 57
no comply 180 58
nollie 74-75
noping 110
nose
defined 31
marking on board 19
nose blunt 151
nose manual 53
nose stall 125

O
old-school kickflip (M-80) 82-83
ollie in 118-119

ollie north 72-73
ollie. *See also* kickflip
backside 180 ollie 68-69
basic 64-65
fakie 136-137
as foundation move 62, 75
frontside 180 ollie 66-67
learning 62, 64
ollie north 72-73
progression of 104
shifty 70-71
versus shuvit 62
switch 69
360 ollie 62
on transition 134-139
on vert 193
ollie to fakie 134-135
Olson, Steve 16
180 drifter 40
180s
defined 54
technique 55
opinions of others 46, 73
overcrook 176
oververt structures 107, 224

P
pace cars 210
pads 8-9, 187-188
park slalom (game) 221
paying your tax 160
personal expression 4
photography careers 239-240
physical benefits 6-7
physical risk 7, 9, 15
pivot cups 18
pivot 146-147
places to skate 160, 232. *See also* skateparks
plazas 223-224, 225, 230
pockets, in structures 225, 229
pole jams 229
pools 224, 229
pop shuvit
backside 88-89
frontside 86-87
versus ollie 62
power slides 39-40
precast structures 223
prefab structures 223, 229
pressure flip 84-85

price, of boards 27
private property 160
pro skaters quiz 16
pucks 212
pumping
     on miniramp 112-113, 114
     on vert 190
pushing mongo 36
pushing stance 34
pushing technique 35-36
pyramid hips 231
pyramids 229

Q
quarterpipes
     building 235, 238
     defined 229
     structure type 106, 107
quiz, on pro skaters 16

R
racing. *See* longboarding techniques; longboards
rails
     appropriate for practice 161
     versus ledges 168
     types 225, 231
rail tricks. *See* grinds and slides
rainbow rails 225
ramps, building 235
razor tail 25
rear foot, defined 33
rebates 111
regular-footers (left-footers) 31, 34
respect for property 160, 232
reverse camber boards 15
revert 126-127
right-footers (goofy-footers) 31, 34
risers 21
risk 7, 9, 15
roast beef (grab) 195
rock to fakie 128-129
roll in 116-117
rolling backwards 113, 128
rotations, by degrees 54
round rails 225
roundwall 107
rules, of skate culture 6
Russian boneless 156

S
safety equipment
     coolness and 7-8, 9
     helmets 10-11, 15, 41, 160, 187, 209-210
     pads 8-9, 187-188
safety guidelines
     injury prevention 10, 40-41, 160, 187-188
     skateboarding deaths and 10, 209, 232
     skate culture rules 6
scoop, defined 33
720s, defined 54
shifty 70-71
shoes 8
shoulder movement
     backside rock 130
     frontside kickturn 122
     frontside rock 133
     ollies and shuvits 104
     tic tacs and kickturns 48
shuvit
     backside 360 shuvit 90-91
     versus ollie 62
     progression of 104
     360 shuvit 62
SKATE (game) 220
Skateboarding (Wixon) 242
skateboards. *See* boards
skate camps 221
skate culture 5-7
Skatelite 223
skateparks
     cleanup days 234-235
     contests and demos 235
     etiquette 111
     learn-to-skate days 235
     materials 222-223
     rules 222
     starting new parks 233-235
     terrain and elements 223-231
     traffic in 231-232
skate shops
     buying from 26-27, 187
     sponsorships 247
     working in 241
skate tools 20
skating competitively
     contests 244-245
     sponsorships 245-248

skating games 220-221
skating styles 14-16
slabs 229
slalom boards 15, 213
slalom game 221
slalom skating 209, 213-215
slides, on downhill board 212-213. *See also*
    grinds and slides
slob air 202
slowing techniques 36-40, 211-212
slow tranny 108-110
Smith grind 174-175
snake runs
    defined 223, 230
    structure type 106
snake session 111
snaking 111
social deviance 7
spacewalk 52
speed, in downhill skating 209-211
speed check technique 38
speed walls 230
spillways, in bowls 225
spine, in structures 225, 230
spine transfer 225
sponsorships 245-258
stalefish 203
stance 30, 34
standing stance 34
steel transition 108
stereotypes 5, 7, 232
stink bag 26
stopping techniques 36-40, 212-213
street terrain (street plaza) 223-224, 225, 230
structures. *See also* miniramps
    building 235-239
    for grinds and slides 160-161, 168
    in skateparks 223-231
    transition terrain 106-107
    vert terrain 107, 186-187
super giant slalom 214-215
sweep, defined 33
sweeper 155
switch 35, 49
switch ollie 69

T
tacos 106

tail
    defined 31
    marking on board 19
tail stall 124-125
teaching
    as career 241-242
    as skatepark offering 235
1080s, defined 54
terminology 31-34, 226-231
terrain. *See* structures
360 kickflip (tre flip) 92-93
360 ollie 62
360s
    defined 54
    technique 56
360 shuvit 62
tic tac 48
toe side, defined 31
tombstones 225
tools
    for building boards 22-24
    list for gear bag 26
traffic
    motor vehicle 10, 209, 232
    in skateparks 231-232
tranny skaters 106-107
transition, on miniramp 107-110
transition terrain (tranny) 106-107
tre flip 92-93
trucks
    described 18-19
    downhill 211
    mounting 23-24
    tuning boards and 25
    turning radius and 17
tucked stance 211
tuning boards 25
turns, degrees of 54

U
up the curb technique 49

V
varial kickflip 96-97
vert (vertical) skating. *See also* airs
    carves 191
    described 186
    drop in 192

vert (vertical) skating. *See also* airs *(continued)*
   early grabs 194-195
   kickturns 191
   knee slide 189
   lip tricks 198, 208
   ollie 193
   pumping 190
   safety guidelines 187-188
   skills 188
vert (vertical) terrain 107, 186-187
volcanoes 106, 230

W
waivers 222, 245
Way, Danny 16, 186

wheel assembly, defined 19
wheelbase. *See* trucks
wheelies. *See* manuals; nose manuals
wheels
   downhill 211
   drifters effect on 39
   hardness 19-21
   mounting 24
   size 19
whining 6
Wixon, Ben 242
wood transition 108
wrist guards 8-9
writing careers 240-241

Google **Per Welinder** and your search will reveal the history of a pro skater—a legend who performed all the skateboarding stunt scenes for Michael J. Fox in the famous film *Back to the Future*, a two-time world champion freestyle skateboarder, and an iconic pioneer in the second generation of skateboarding. Today he is an entrepreneur who earned his MBA from the Anderson School of Business at UCLA. Welinder is the president and cofounder of Blitz Distribution, a major player in today's skateboarding world thanks to brands like Baker Skateboards, Hook-Ups, Sk8Mafia, Fury Trucks, and JSLV clothing.

The accomplished lifelong skater brings a unique perspective to the brands he works with and believes that skateboarding serves a vital role in youth culture. Welinder has promoted the growth of skateboarding worldwide through his roles as the former chair and current board member for the International Association of Skateboard Companies.

Peter Whitley is a lifelong skateboarder, artist, and advocate for skateparks. He is the former executive director of Skaters for Public Skateparks, a nonprofit organization dedicated to skatepark awareness, advancement, and advocacy. Currently he serves as the programs director for the Tony Hawk Foundation. He is also the author of the *Public Skatepark Development Guide*. When not working with communities on skatepark matters, Whitley is a graphic designer and illustrator.